C000259929

# I'm celibate...
# Get me out of here!

## The Memoirs of an Internet Dater

# Jo Elliott

# I'm celibate...
## Get me out of here!
### The Memoirs of an Internet Dater

# Jo Elliott

www.knowthescorebooks.com

Although the events described in this book did occur, all the names and many of the places have been changed, so that people cannot be identified. Therefore any similarity to real persons, living or dead, is entirely coincidental. Equally Digital-Cupid does not exist as an internet dating site. You can, however, tell us your real life dating horror stories by logging onto www.digital-cupid.com.

First published in the United Kingdom
by Know The Score Books Limited, 2006.

Know The Score Books Limited
The College Business Centre
Uttoxeter New Road
Derby
DE22 3WZ

Copyright © Jo Elliott, 2006.

The right of Jo Elliott to be identified as the author of this work has been asserted by her in accordance with sections 77 and 78 of the Copyright, Designs and Patents Act, 1988.

This book is copyright under the Berne convention. No part of this book may be reproduced, sold or utilised in any form or transmitted in any form or by any means, electronic or mechanical, including photocopying, recording or by any information storage and retrieval system, without prior permission in writing from the Publisher.

© and ® Know The Score Books Limited. All rights reserved.

A CIP catalogue record is available for this book from the British Library.

ISBN 1-905449-48-8

Typesetting and design by Jo Elliott.

Printed and bound in Great Britain By Cromwell Press, Trowbridge, Wiltshire.

www.knowthescorebooks.com

# Thank you...

... to Sophie Darbyshire, without whom this may never have seen the light, and to Simon Lowe for believing in it and making it happen. To Liz Rowlinson for your help and guidance. To Paul *'what you thanking me for'* Keenan, Ian Alwis, Billy Thomas, Colin Barker and Tequila\London. To Cal, Lucy and the Elms Crescent Massive for keeping me in Sunday roasts, red wine and basic social skills. To Claire – what can I say? You are good! Big, big thanks to Pat Comer and Pip Crook for all your time and invaluable help and advice. And lastly to Mum and Dad for your never-ending support (and not asking too many questions).

# Contents

For Chas and Joan.
Cheers!

*It's hard to believe…*

…but the content, grammar, spelling and sentiment of all the random emails in this book are as I received them. However – names, locations and some personal details have been changed to protect the innocent.

As for the dates – all the events documented happened, although not necessarily in the same order. This is my account, the way I see it. Again – names, locations, and some personal details have been changed to protect the guilty.

# One

*Introduction*

*Women are like apples on trees.*
*The best ones are at the top of the tree.*
*Men don't want to reach for the good ones,*
*because they're afraid of falling and getting hurt.*
*Instead, they get rotten ones from the ground.*
*They're not the best, but they're easy.*
*The apples at the top think they're no good,*
*when in reality, they're amazing.*
*They just have to wait for the right man.*
*The one brave enough to climb to the top of the tree.*

My best friend Claire emailed me the above anecdote one day. My latest three-week relationship had just come to an end and I was devastated. I liked the sentiment. Plus I didn't have to forward it to ten people or risk bad luck for the rest of my life. Or worse still, certain death. I kept it in my inbox and read it whenever my horoscope didn't tell me what I wanted to hear.

I'm great at relationships. Just not romantic ones. My first love was John Taylor (yes, the one from Duran Duran). It was a one-sided love, but one that ran so deep I'd cry myself to sleep, staring at his picture. Tortured by the fact that he'd never be mine. It wasn't a phase. I felt the same when I saw Duran Duran last year. Admittedly I'd got over the crying.

There were other, more realistic encounters, but none of them matched up to John. Gary Church asked me out in the school playground. We held hands for a few months before he chucked me for Theresa Collins.

Kevin Johnson was the school heart-throb. I wasn't sure if I fancied him just because everyone else did, but I had his name etched on my pencil case. He spoke to me once and I went mute. A few years later in a nightclub, someone touched my bottom at the bar. I turned round and it was Kevin. He was about 5ft tall and still looked 12.

Darren Sutherland was a friend of a friend. He was older than me and went out in town. Town was Northampton. I grew up in a small village just outside. Knowing people from town gave one great kudos. Darren even had a car. We went out a few times before he went to find himself on a kibbutz.

I learned to drive as soon as possible. That way I could get out of the village and into the bright lights of Northampton. All dressed up and nowhere to go. And god did I look good. Tight perm, high-waisted stonewashed jeans, pastel accessories and white pixie boots. Not a good look when your legs are like matchsticks.

"Are you really going out like that Josephine?" my Mum would say. "You look ridiculous." What did she know about fashion? She wore comfy shoes and drove a Hillman Imp.

I would have liked to have studied fashion, but instead I did graphic design. A miracle really seeing as my art teacher told me I'd never get anywhere. Hardly surprising given that I had to draw a lawnmower in the medium of my choice for O level art.

I got a job at the local paper designing ads. Estate agents, hairdressers, car-boot sales, Dave's Mobile Disco... challenging it wasn't, mind-numbingly boring it was. As was drinking Cinzano and lemonade and smoking

Superkings for kicks. The highlight of the week was the erection-section at Cinderella's on a Saturday night.

I was 21. There had to be more to life than this. I didn't want to end up in a Barratt home in the Nene Valley. So I sold my car and bought a ticket to Australia. I had a one-year working visa, a backpack and no friends.

Australia was everything I dreamed it would be and more. I met the best people and did the worst jobs. Picked fruit, cleaned the MCG, handed out leaflets, answered phones, trod wool, worked in a fairground, punched numbers, stuffed handbags, and loved every minute of it.

I got a camper van with my new friends and we pointed it west, vaguely heading for Perth. Didn't care when we got there. I got drunk in the Barossa valley, broke down on the Nullabor, swam with dolphins, kayaked down rapids, fell in love, fell out of love, camped with crocodiles, climbed Ayres Rock, dived on the Barrier Reef, partied down the east coast and pretended to be a hippy in Byron Bay. I ended up in Sydney with 50 dollars to my name, but I wasn't going home. I got another rubbish job and a flat with friends. Six months later I was devastated when my visa expired. Instead of Sydney Harbour Bridge and Sydney Opera House every morning, it was back to the M1 bridge and Northants Crematorium. Did I really have to go? Being a law abiding citizen I left the country like a good girl, but a different girl. I brought back some confidence, and I left my perm behind.

Northampton hadn't changed. I got my old job back and Dave was still flogging his mobile disco. Friends were co-habiting and having babies. I was 22, claustrophobic and intent on getting back to Australia as soon as possible, so I applied for permanent residency. I was astonished when they turned me down, but Sydney's loss was London's gain. I packed my bags and headed south to where the streets were paved with gold. I got a design job and moved in with Jane, my Sydney flatmate. A blur of parties and good times ensued.

Life happened. There were ups and downs. Friends got married, divorced, came out of the closet...

———————— ❤ ————————

I'm 31 now. Got a one-bed flat in Wandsworth, a P-reg Renault Clio, 25 pairs of jeans and a Topshop store card. I work in advertising and I'm a statistic in a magazine. Thirty-something, solvent and single. Apparently there's lots of us. Were we so busy having a good time in our twenties that we missed the love boat? Do we want too much? Are we too fussy? Well I am. I'm a Virgo. I've been put off men for wearing the wrong shoes before, and they have to be taller than me.

I'm no supermodel myself, but I scrub up OK. Put it this way: if I was in a beauty contest with Kate Moss and Waynetta Slob, I'm confident I'd come second. I'm 5ft 7 and everything seems to be in the right place. Average size (10 in M&S, 12 in Topshop, 18 in H&M), and I can hold my own in a conversation. Meeting someone suitable shouldn't be a problem in theory. But in practice? Nigh on impossible. He doesn't have to be Brad Pitt, although I would overlook the shoes for him it has to be said.

"The trouble is, there's too much choice these days," my Mum said. "Look at bread. In my day, there was one white loaf and one brown loaf on the shelf. Simple. Now there's granary, pumpkin, wholemeal, baguette, soda, pitta, naan... all this fancy stuff. There might not be time to try them all. You might have to settle for second best before its too late."

Settle for second best? How can I? I'm a Virgo.

# two

## *Delete if you have a loving partner*

| From | Timothy Horne | To: | Jo Elliott |
|---|---|---|---|
| Subject: Delete if you have a loving partner | | Date: | 27.01.00 |

Hiya!

I hope you don't mind me writing to you like this. I got your email address from an online directory. Having had no luck at the dating game for yonks, I thought I'd give the internet a try – it is the new millennium after all!

I'm Timothy and I'm 37 years old. I live in Edgware and in my spare time like watching old movies, experimenting in the kitchen and pottering around at home. I drive a cute little hatchback and enjoy trips out of town every now and then, or just pootling around locally at the weekend.

I don't smoke or drink, but I enjoy a glass of wine on special occasions. I'm 5ft 8 inches tall, caucasian and of slim build. I'm very romantic and sincere and am looking for a partner to snuggle up on the sofa with, watch old movies and enjoy happy times.

Are you looking for a happy, fulfilling relationship with a lovely guy? Then look no further. Email me back and let's hook up. If you have a loving partner already, sorry to have bothered you and please delete this message.

Smiles!

Tim :)

The email landed in my hotmail inbox totally out of the blue. I'd never heard of an online directory, let alone knew that I was in one. I re-read it. And I read it again. It wasn't until the third time that I scrolled down far enough to notice there was a picture attached. A bald, grinning man who looked like Reggie Perrin's younger brother. Surely this was a wind-up. I showed it to a couple of colleagues, who after their initial hysteria, decided it must be a joke. I wondered if it was a clever marketing ploy. One of those emails that gets you curious and when you respond you're unwittingly bombarded with spam, or subscribed to porn.

I'd heard of internet dating, but it wasn't something I'd considered. I associated it with freaks and weirdos. But this was something different if it was to be believed. This brought a whole new meaning to direct marketing. Timothy was marketing himself directly into people's inboxes. And the target audience was presumably anyone with a female sounding name in their email address. I couldn't decide whether it was cheeky, clever or downright crazy. Either way, curiosity got the better of me and I had to reply.

| From: Jo Elliott | To: Timothy Horne |
|---|---|
| Subject: Re: Delete if you have a loving partner | Date: 28.01.00 |

Are you for real?

| From: Timothy Horne | To: Jo Elliott |
|---|---|
| Subject: Re: Delete if you have a loving partner | Date: 29.01.00 |

Yes. Of course. Why? I am very serious about finding a loving partner. Do forward me your details if you're keen, which I hope you are.

Tim :)

He didn't know anything about me. I could have been a

pensioner for all he knew. Or a bloke, with a name like Jo.
I felt a pang of guilt. It seemed he was for real and I didn't
want to ridicule the poor man. At least he was being
innovative in his search for love. I was single. Of course I
was looking out for a 'lovely guy' to have a 'happy, fulfilling
relationship' with. Who wasn't? It just wasn't going to be a
random stranger from the internet. The man of my dreams
would just fall into my lap at some point in the near future.
Probably riding a white horse and carrying diamonds. All I
had to do was carry on as normal, keep smiling and all
my dreams would come true. I knew that. It said so in my
year ahead forecast.

———— ❤ ————

So much for horoscopes. One year after Timothy's random
email and still no sign of Mr Right. The odd Mr Wrong, but
the elusive Mr Right was nowhere to be seen. I was still
everyone's mate and no-one's date.

"You should try Digital-Cupid," said Jane.

We were quiet at work and I'd had enough of Pacman so
I phoned her for a chat. She'd left me a year earlier for a
man and they'd recently got engaged. Their eyes had met
across a crowded pub some years before. It's amazing what
you can see whilst dancing on a table to Fat Bottomed Girls
with a can of lager in your hand. Not the most romantic
setting, but it just goes to show – love moves in mysterious
ways. It can strike at any time. There was hope for me yet.

"What on earth is Digital-Cupid?" I replied.

"It's a dating website, but you..."

"Internet dating! You must be joking. Forget it."

"Listen! A girl at work met a really nice guy on there.
OK, so she met a few losers first, but the point is, she met
him and they're moving in together. It can work."

"Look, I'm not that desperate. Internet dating's sad."
I protested.

"You don't have to go on any dates. You can just chat

to people, have pen-pals, whatever. There's no harm in looking is there? You never know, you might meet the man of your dreams!"

"Yeah right!" I said scathingly.

I'd read about people that met on the internet. Trudie from Basingstoke, unhappily married with five kids. But after exchanging emails with BigTrucker_Bob in Indiana for six weeks, ups sticks to America declaring undying love. Not a second thought for her kids, just a few packets of crisps and an open window.

I went back to Pacman and forgot all about it. For a while at least. But Digital-Cupid was lurking in the back of my mind. What if there was someone on there for me? Then it started jumping out at me all over the internet. Banner ads and annoying pop-ups. Pictures of gorgeous people with white teeth and perfect skin. *'Meet new friends and maybe more...' 'love is just a click away...' 'join now for free...'*

Free? Hmmm. Nobody would know if I just logged on and had a quick look would they? And if the members all looked like the models they used to advertise it, I'd misjudged it completely.

I'd been in a chat room once. Despite having to field the constant 'A.S.L?' messages (Age, Sex, Location?), four hours later I was still there. It seemed like four minutes at the time. I chatted to someone in Tasmania about the royal family, a woman in Leeds about the state of her marriage, and some bloke in Watford who wanted to meet that night, despite never having seen me or vice versa. I had been vaguely tempted when I was lost in conversation with him, but the minute I logged off I forgot all about it. People tell you their innermost secrets in chat rooms, and you can say things you'd never dream of saying in real life. I could certainly see how it might get addictive.

Without another thought, I clicked on the link to Digital-Cupid, hiding the window behind some work. I couldn't stand the embarrassment of somebody seeing. Even though I was merely curious...

---

Welcome to *Digital-Cupid* ♥

Meet new friends, make a date and maybe more!
Sign up now! It's free!

( Click here to join )

---

A few mugshots popped up under the heading *'This week's gallery'*. ShyGuy_Andy looked quite nice actually. But it soon became clear I couldn't do much without entering my details and creating a profile. Shouldn't take long, and I guess it beat Pacman.

( Enter your username )

Username? That could be anything right? I could be as anonymous as I wanted to be (and that was *very*). What was I going to call myself? Jo-from-London? I had no inspiration. What did other people call themselves on these things. I had a quick browse of *this week's gallery*. In the girls' section I found Sweetbunnie, Sugarlips, Tallulah_babe, BicuriousDoll, Gypsyrose, LuLu4U, Minxy, Saucy_Pot, Lovelymuff, and Snugglybuggly. Oh dear. How could I possibly compete with such discerning aliases? Looking at the boys, there was nice_guy_dave, CuteSmile, pimpdaddy, EssexBoy69 and Bite_Me_Now. I lost interest. It looked like I was right. Internet dating was for freaks, weirdos and sex pests.

I went to get some lunch but found myself in the fantastic Topshop at Oxford Circus. I convinced myself I needed the skirt and two tops, and by the time I'd paid for them it was quarter past two. I hurried back to work and nipped next door to get a sandwich. The girl wrote down my order.

"Mediterranean wrap for Jo. Take-away."

I was always running late, especially when Topshop was

involved. There's so much choice, you need to take your time. That top would look good with those jeans though. And I think I'll probably need to go back tomorrow and get those boots. They were a bargain reduced from £95 to...

"Jo to go!" shouted Mario from behind the counter.

He winked and looked at his watch as he gave me my lunch. He knew me well. Late or hungover, he always got it right. Mario's hangover cures were second to none. Overdone bacon sandwich and the perfect coffee. None of your fancy skinny latte or mocha chocha focha here. It was like tar and it did the trick.

"Thanks Mario."

I ran back to my desk, trying to hide the Topshop bags. Not sure who from. Did hiding them relieve the guilt of being late, or spending the money? Or both? As I filled my keyboard with new crumbs, my screen came to life. I'd forgotten all about Digital-Cupid and my quest for a username, but with Mario's help it suddenly came to me. I shall call myself jo-to-go!

---

### Digital-Cupid ♥

Welcome jo-to-go!

Please take your time to complete your profile fully. Your answers are important and will significantly affect the number of members who contact you!

( Continue )

---

Take my time? How long could it take? Surely they just wanted a few vital statistics and off we go. I clicked the link and soon realised there was far more to this than simply sign-in and start chatting. I was about to find out that they wanted more details than a tax return. Could I be bothered?

Did I want anyone to contact me anyway? Consciously, no. but subconsciously? Maybe.

I'd come this far. I was jo-to-go now, so I may as well carry on. Although I had no intention of meeting anyone, at least if I submitted a profile, I could converse with people. Right then. Here goes...

---

### The basics

Gender: [ Female ]

Sexuality: [ Straight ]

Nationality: [ British ]

Location: [ London, UK ]

Year you were born: [ 1969 ]

Star sign: [ Virgo ]

Ethnicity: [ Caucasian ]

Religion: [ Agnostic ]

Relationship status: [ Single ]
In relationship
Engaged
Married
Unhappily married
Married but we swing
Separated/divorced
Rather not say

Why are you here: [ Pen-pals ]
Friendship
Romance/relationship
Fun!
Sex
Marriage
Not really sure
Research

---

## *More about me*

Have children:     | No |

Want children:
Not sure
| Yes, one day |
Don't want children
I hate kids

Education:     | College diploma |

Occupation:     | Advertising/Media |

Annual income:     | Rather not say |

Height:     | 5ft 6in – 5ft 8in |

Build:
Petite
Slim
Athletic/toned
| Average |
Curvy
Muscular
A few extra pounds
Overweight
Obese
Rather not say

Hair colour:     | Blonde |

Hair style:     | Medium straight |

Eye colour:     | Blue |

Body piercings:     | Ears |

Tattoos/body art:     | None |

Facial hair:
None/clean shaven
Goatee
Stubble
Moustache
Short beard
| Long haired beard |
Beard & moustache

Ask a stupid question...

## Languages

| | | | |
|---|---|---|---|
| English ☒ | French ☐ | German | ☐ |
| Italian ☐ | Spanish ☐ | Portuguese | ☐ |
| Dutch ☐ | Finnish ☐ | Norwegian | ☐ |
| Swedish ☐ | Japanese ☐ | Chinese/Mandarin | ☐ |
| Arabic ☐ | Greek ☐ | Turkish | ☐ |
| Korean ☐ | Urdu ☐ | Chinese/Cantonese | ☐ |
| Russian ☐ | Afrikaans ☐ | Others | ☐ |

## Personality traits

Are you independent?    ( Very independent )

Are you faithful?    ( Very faithful )

Are you spiritual?    ( No, but I read my stars )

Sense of humour?
> I don't have one
> Quite amusing
> Good sense of humour
> ( Dry )
> Slapstick
> I'm hilarious

Are you sexy?    ( Me! – sexy? )

Do you like cooking:    ( Enjoy it )

Do you like shopping?    ( I'm a shopoholic )

Do you like gardening?    ( Not really )

Do you like DIY?    ( Don't mind it )

Does it make me a bad person if I don't like gardening? I was going to extraordinary lengths here to find a pen-pal. Surely we could cover all this once we got chatting? We'd have nothing more to talk about at this rate.

13

---

*Social scene*

---

Smoking habits:               Gave up years ago

Drinking habits:              I enjoy a drink

What about drugs?             I don't do drugs
                              I'm trying to give up
                              I take drugs on occasion
                              I love drugs
                              Rather not say

Nights out per week?          3 to 4 times a week

Do you like dining out?       Love it

Do you like fast food?        No

Do you like bars/pubs?        Yes

Do you like clubs?            Not over keen

Do you like raves?            Can't think of anything worse

Do you enjoy live music?      I enjoy it

Do you like the theatre?      I enjoy it

Do you enjoy the arts?        I enjoy it

Do you like museums?          I enjoy it

Do you like reading?          I can't read
                              I hate reading
                              It's ok
                              I enjoy it
                              I'm a bookworm

Preferred newspapers?         I don't read newspapers
                              Broadsheets
                              Tabloids
                              Local newspapers

How do you keep fit?          Running for the last train

Submit

---

Thank god for that! OK, so I lied about the broadsheets. I don't like broadsheets. If I want to know what's going on in the news I either consult Trevor McDonald or check out page 3 to see if Vikki from Romford thinks we should join the EU.

---

### Digital-Cupid ♥

Nearly there! Now explain a bit about you and what you're looking for, in your own words. Think carefully about what you say as this will affect your success!

( Continue )

---

Blimey. What more was there to say? I hadn't undertaken such an extensive personality test since I almost inadvertently joined the Church of Scientology in Australia.

My mind went blank. I'm not very good at selling myself and I wasn't sure I wanted to. Could I just leave this bit empty? Nice try. It wouldn't let me. I had to type at least 100 characters before I could get through to the next page. Sod this, I thought. Who was I trying to impress anyway? Perhaps I could copy the 'hobbies & interests' section from my CV. *'In my spare time I enjoy skiing, gymnastics and horse riding.'* I hadn't been on skis since I was 14 and the last time I did gymnastics was in PE. As for horse riding, I once came third in *best turned out pony* at a gymkhana. (That's a well groomed small horse by the way – not cockney rhyming slang.)

This was terrible. I was alarmed to realise I had no hobbies, and no particular interests anymore. Life had been swallowed up by work, paying the mortgage, having a good time, and well... just time. Where had it gone? How depressing. I managed to string a few words together and vowed to join a night class.

---

### In my own words

---

I'm not really sure what I'm doing here. I was just curious and now I find myself writing an essay about myself and answering questions about the state of my facial hair.

I enjoy the world, socialising and singing into my hairbrush. I have a dry sense of humour and laugh at my own jokes. My job is creative but I don't wear jeans that hang off my bottom or ride a silver micro scooter.

I'm not interested in indulging anyone's fantasy. Just a bit of banter and amusing conversation with like-minded people who suffer from spells of downtime. If you feel the same, drop me a line!

( Continue )

---

Hooray. That should be it. Now I can check out the site. Start chatting to people. Get some electronic pen-pals.

---

### Digital-Cupid ♥

Well done! You have successfully completed your profile. All you need to do now is upload a photo. This is optional, but members with photos enjoy an 80% higher response rate than those without!

( Click here to upload your photo )

---

A photo! No way. From what I'd seen in that chat room, they were all so obviously fake. The women all looked like Pamela Anderson and the men looked like Glenn Medeiros. There was no way I was putting a picture of myself on the world wide web. What if someone I knew saw it? I doubted they would somehow. Who did I know that did internet dating? I reassured myself that I wasn't here to meet anyone, but Jane's friend and her new live-in lover were lurking in the back of my mind. It still felt odd, but maybe a picture wasn't such a big deal after all. I could always take it off again. I could delete the whole profile and forget jo-to-go ever existed. Oh god. In for a penny, in for a pound. I found a half decent shot I'd had taken for work recently, airbrushed out the spot on my chin and uploaded it. Was I mad?

---

### Digital-Cupid ♥

Congratulations! You have successfully uploaded your photo*. You can now start browsing Digital-Cupid♥ and exchanging messages with other members.
Good luck!

( Click here to start using the site )

*Please note: it may take 24 hours for your photo to be approved and appear on the site. We do not accept offensive or pornographic material.

---

At last, I was up and running. Considering I'd only logged on to the site to feed my curiosity, I'd come a long way. Now what? My phone rang. It was Claire.

"You gonna be ready for six?" she asked.

I'd known Claire since we were two years old. She'd split up with her husband last year, come to see me in London a few months later and never left. She'd just got a new job and a flatshare and we were going out to celebrate. It was great to have my best mate with me, and single too for once. Somehow I doubted it would be for very long. I'd just bet her a pair of Kurt Geiger wedges she'd have a new bloke within three months. Claire always had a bloke. How *do* people do that?

I looked at the clock on my computer. It was gone five.

I'd been on Digital-Cupid all afternoon. What was it with time on the internet? It seemed to go quicker than real time. I almost wished I'd been busy at work. It felt like I'd wasted the day really.

"Yep. Reckon I should be. I've been stacked out with work today," I lied. "Just about done now though. See you in reception at six."

# three

*jo-to-go you have new messages*

I woke up late the following day to find chips all over the lounge and a chilli in the bathroom. Why was it that whenever I went out with Claire, there was no such thing as a couple of drinks? All good intentions went straight out the window. We were excited at the prospect of being in London together and had gone somewhat over the top with the celebrations. Jane had joined us later, as had Lucy, my partner in crime since Jane's demise on the singles scene. We'd ended up in a dodgy club in Covent Garden sinking two-for-one cocktails and getting chatted up by tourists. Not the best idea on a school night, but it seemed like it at the time.

The Northern Line was its usual welcoming self. Ten people deep on the platform, first train in seven minutes and someone announcing there was a good service running in both directions. I might have been hungover but they couldn't fool me! I managed to squeeze on eventually to a chorus of tuts at my sheer audacity. £80 a month for this pleasure. I felt nauseous. I needed a Mario special ASAP.

It was almost like he was expecting me.

"Late night was it Jo?" Mario always looked like he'd had a late night. I don't think he ever left the cafe.

"Uuuuuugh don't remind me," I mumbled, without even placing my order. I didn't need to. It tended to be a foregone conclusion on Fridays.

19

I felt slightly more human after my breakfast, and sat down at my desk, hoping for a quiet day again. Please don't let me have to do anything complicated – like work. I switched on my computer and read my emails. Apparently my visa payment at WorldPay had been securely processed, Dictionary.com's word of the day was serendipity and my picture had been accepted at Digital-Cupid. And further to that – I had new messages! Yippee! How exciting!

---

### Digital-Cupid ♥
Welcome back jo-to-go!
It's always good to see you. Great news – you have
7 new messages waiting in your inbox.

( Continue )

---

Seven new messages – wow. From complete strangers. This was odd. I wondered who'd contact me. What sort of person, and why? I felt half embarrassed and half excited as I navigated my way to the mail page. But excitement turned to amusement rather quickly...

---

| From:   Ali-G | To:   jo-to-go |
|---|---|
| Subject:  Jo babe | Date:  19.01.01 |

don't worry coz I am here for u now. Get in touch. I will rock you so u r lonely no more, get me into your life and you will not regret it. I need you babe. Thanks.
Ali G inda house.

---

Oh dear. The picture complemented the words perfectly. A darkish man posing next to a Fiat Uno, grinning proudly as if it were a Ferrari. And what's more, he was 33 and should have known better.

| From: | RomfordGuy | To: | jo-to-go |
|---|---|---|---|
| Subject: hi | | Date: 19.01.01 | |

My name is Brian & i am 39 i live in Romford in essex i work in asda. I like listening to music & watching allsorts of sports especially football and snooker. I have a good sense of humour & i am caring & honest & down to earth i am 5ft 7 brown hair & eyes & slim. :)

Brian

Hmmm. Not sure the vocab was there for the kind of conversational banter I was hoping for. I clicked on his profile and had a look at his picture anyway. He was wearing a pair of red pants and flexing his arms. Euggghh! No thanks, Brian.

| From: | Turkey-man | To: | jo-to-go |
|---|---|---|---|
| Subject: Hi from Turkey!!!!!! | | Date: 19.01.01 | |

Ohh my god! :-)

I can not believe that U r single! UK men must be bloddy stupit! :-) U r wonderfool! Would u marry me? :-) I promise I will be perfect husbant for u! :-) Everyday Massage! :-)

But I must warn you jo-to-go – I am a very, very sexual boy, no holes bard, and nothing taboo for me. I love sex and I love pleasing my partner. Yes I love to f*ck!!!! Once I get going, I can't stop. It's bloddy fantastik!!! :-)

kisses and hugs!

Turkey Ali xxxxxxxx :)

Right back at ya with the 'oh my god'. Did he realise the hilarity of the words 'no holes bard' in the context in which he said them? Either way, it only fuelled my growing suspicions as to what I'd let myself in for. Roll up, roll up... the freak show is in town.

| From: | woman_lover | To: | jo-to-go |
|---|---|---|---|
| Subject: | <none> | Date: | 19.01.01 |

wile i was loggin in i saw u beautiful and fought i wod say how sexi i think u look!! Better than Zeta Jones.

I live in Wembley and am lookin for someone to share Gr8 Gr8 sex with this italian stallion. u wont be disapointed i can tell u. Hope you don't mind that i messaged u. message me back soon and we can talk some bizniss.

Frankie

---

I nearly gave the game away by laughing too loud. I pretended I was reading an email from a friend. Better than Zeta Jones! I've heard it all now. This was brilliant. Nothing like a good laugh of a morning to clear away the cobwebs. However, call me old fashioned, but Gr8, Gr8 sex with a self proclaimed Italian stallion from the internet wasn't quite what I was after.

---

| From: | gordy | To: | jo-to-go |
|---|---|---|---|
| Subject: | Happy Friday | Date: | 19.01.01 |

Hi there Jo,

I don't know if I am your ideal man. I hope so. My name is Gordy – thats short for Gordon. I wern't named after the gin, at least I don't think so. Silly name anyway, but I am stuck with it. So how are you this Friday morning?

Gordy x

---

I'm glad he cleared that up. There was me thinking 'Gordon – probably named after the gin'. Somehow he looked like a Gordon (whatever they look like). His picture was a staged self portrait. Posing in front of a yellow sponge-effect wall, he was trying desperately to look natural, arm outstretched, taking his own photo.

---

| From: Silky_Steel | To: jo-to-go |
|---|---|
| Subject: Hey you! | Date: 19.01.01 |

---

Well i must say Jo, you look good enough to eat. What's a gorgeous girl like you doing here? I'm sure you have no problem meeting members of the opposite sex.

My name's Roger, I'm 39 and from Illinois, U.S.A (I know, don't shoot me!), but I've been working in New Zealand for 3 years. I enjoy films, nature, and watching ice hockey.

I'm hoping to meet a wife who will enjoy some adventures with me and then bear my children. I'm not outgoing, and still finding my feet in terms of inter-personal relationships. I plan my spontaneity very carefully. Please reply.

Kind regards,
Roger.

---

Roger had a mass of brown curly hair and a matching beard, topped of with a baseball cap and thick double-lensed glasses. I thought about responding just to ask how one plans spontaneity very carefully, but I didn't want to give him the wrong idea. He was still finding his feet.

---

| From: Gaz_69er | To: jo-to-go |
|---|---|
| Subject: want miss rite | Date: 19.01.01 |

---

My names Gaz, 32, from Croydon. Don't get out much coz I work 2 hard. I never got no qualificatons but its done me no harm. I earn over 100 grand a year.

Lookin 4 miss rite. She would have 2 have a nice smile, good body and be a good cook. I'm trendy and like clothes – casual or smart. Write back soon and we can get going. Dont like time wasters so if you aint interested just say.

Gaz.

---

Let me have a think about that, Gaz...

Were these people real? Where did they come from? Judging by their well-crafted masterpieces they were all verging on illiterate. Seven messages and only one of them knew how to string a sentence together (but he was a social retard). I was shocked and very amused. Perhaps it would have been more beneficial for Digital-Cupid to set a grammar test rather than an in-depth questionnaire about social preferences. If they had the thousands of members they claimed to have, there must be some higher calibre options than this. Despite quietly protesting my reasons for being here to myself, I did a search to check it out.

| | |
|---|---|
| I am a | Woman |
| looking for a | Man |
| Aged | 30 to 40 |
| Who lives | Anywhere |

I wasn't averse to talking to women. It just seemed a bit wrong searching for them on a dating website. Hundreds of profiles came up and I was happy to confirm that the majority could indeed string a cohesive sentence together. It's just that none of them had contacted me. Yet.

"Hi there girls! I'm fresh off the boat and I'm looking for a London tour guide..." said Brendan from Adelaide.

"I love the sun, sea, sand and s... angria! You can't beat a moonlit walk along the beach..." gushed Mark from Bournemouth.

"I'm just as comfortable in a tux as I am in a pair of jeans..." stressed Darren from Milton Keynes.

"I take much pride in my appearance..." said Fabien from Stockholm. I begged to differ when I saw the picture. He looked like a member of eighties rock group *Europe* with his cut-off denim hotpants and long black hair.

Every morning an eclectic array of messages greeted me. Some funny, some ridiculous and some downright disgusting, but nothing really to write home about. Even so, it was becoming addictive and part of my morning routine. In the two weeks since I'd joined Digital-Cupid, I'd managed to strike up a couple of interesting conversations with people who appeared to be on my wavelength.

Steve lived with his girlfriend and two cats in Tufnell Park. He worked in IT in the city and seemed to have an unusual amount of down time. His user name was willow-the-wisp and he made me laugh. We liked the same things and I was impressed and slightly envious when he told me he'd been on Cheggers Plays Pop once. I asked him what his girlfriend thought about him talking to girls on the internet. He said what she didn't know wouldn't hurt her and that he wasn't really doing anything wrong.

Then there was Ian. He came from Northampton too. He'd taken a similar path to me, going travelling and ending up in London, before being transferred to New York. We decided our paths must have crossed and spent ages trying to work out where and when. He seemed like a decent bloke who was just there for curiosity and to pass the time.

On top of these affable exchanges with my new pen-pals, the bizarre messages were still keeping me amused. It was interesting to hear how many men thought I was their perfect match. If only it was so simple in real life. Married men, divorced men, short men, fat men, women-men, and even couples were all on the lookout for something. Sex, marriage, a bit on the side, a passport...

| From: | Handsome_Gentleman | To: | jo-to-go |
|---|---|---|---|
| Subject: | My soul mate | Date: | 23.01.01 |

Dearest Love,

It will be a nice surprise for you to hear from me today I am sure, but we must be thankful to Digital-Cupid, who arranged this opportunity.

Your performance for introducing yourself was brilliant. You speak with deep conviction, sincerity, purpose and passion. A wise man once said "the good women is distinguished by something big and large". It doesn't mean that she is big in measurements or that she is fat, it means that she has a large, generous heart and soul. After all, the more the girl is developed, the better.

Every successful man has a successful women behind him. You look very beautiful and I am sure you are most successful. Can you please send me one large, nice photograph of yourself, dressed up in your preferred style and colour?

I am allowed in my religion to marry the girl of my own choice and selection. That is why I have selected and accepted you as my future partner. In my own family my priority is to create an atmosphere of happiness and peace. Life is full of unexpected turns and the constant flow of events of everyday life. How pleasant it will be for me to escape from this hustle and bustle, to come home and be hugged by the dearest woman, for you to make a delicious dinner for me and to spend a quiet evening at the family table. To hear the laugh of our children and to smell the kind breath of the shaggy dog.

Our weekends would be spent with parties, interesting games, fun and adventures in the countryside. The only noise will be the birds singing, and the loud voice of the cookoo beside the stagnant pond in the high mountains.

I would be interested to know how you imagine your future family and am hoping your vision is similar. I will be impatiently waiting for your reply.

With affection,
Your tender HANDSOME_GENTLEMAN
P.S - I wish to PROPOSE to U. xxx

---

Handsome_Gentleman was from Cairo. He looked at least 50 in his picture and I think he meant business. It was a soft-focus studio shot, in which he was wearing a smart suit and tie, with slicked back hair, a serious face and a comedy tash. It was nice to know he thought I was beautiful and that he wanted to propose to me. Me and every other female UK citizen on the site who wasn't already married. My first ever marriage proposal. After much deliberation and with heavy heart, I decided against it.

| From: | nicey_nicey | To: | jo-to-go |
|---|---|---|---|
| Subject: Hey Jo | | Date: 24.01.01 | |

What kind of freakish life are you living? You look well attractive, educated and seem to know what you like, but you can't meet a bloke? Well look no further. I'm Pete, 27 live and work in Basildon, 5'9, dead sexy and HUGE. Drop me a line and I'll sort you out.

Pete xxx

Thanks for the kind offer Pete, but I think I'll continue to sort myself out for the time being.

| From: | menage-a-trois | To: | jo-to-go |
|---|---|---|---|
| Subject: Jo | | Date: 24.01.01 | |

Hi there Jo,

We are a couple looking for someone like you for fun and games in the bedroom. You sound like good company. Please let us know if you're interested.

O&T

There was a picture of two backsides. One male, one female (I think). I was flattered they'd considered me, but I'm far too square to be indulging in a ménage à trois with a couple of strangers from the internet. Call me dull, but I'd sooner find a single man in the real world.

| From: | Guy-in-London | | To: | jo-to-go |
|---|---|---|---|---|
| Subject: Hi | | | Date: | 29.01.01 |

How are you. Where abouts in London are you from?

Not the most interesting message but I was scraping the barrel so I had a look at 'Guy-in-London's' profile. There was no photo and he'd just copy and pasted the words *'I'll fill this in later'* about 100 times in the last section. Why didn't I think of that? Although I had nothing to go on, for some reason an image of a geeky fat bloke sitting in his pants in a grotty basement with no job and nothing better to do entered my head.

I could understand why people were reluctant to put up a photo. I had been myself. But what was the point of joining a site like this and saying nothing on your profile? It hardly invites conversation. I came to the conclusion that if someone couldn't be arsed to at least write a bit about themselves, then I couldn't be arsed to reply.

| From: | Andrew_Harris | | To: | jo-to-go |
|---|---|---|---|---|
| Subject: Hello | | | Date: | 29.01.01 |

My name is Andrew. I'm 29, about 5ft 9in have brown hair & brown eyes. Sometimes I wear glasses but mainly contacts. I'm medium build. I have a good sense of humour & I like watching TV, reading & going out. I also like watching Football & sometimes go to live matches.

I'm single, don't smoke or have any children. I drink occasionally & go out with friends to pubs or the cinema. I live in Essex and friends consider me to be very loyal and honest, sometimes too honest for my own good. I work as a Case Officer to do with Third Party Motor Claims.

Andrew :)

And your point is?

| From: Moscow_Man | To: jo-to-go |
|---|---|
| Subject: From Russia with love... | Date: 30.01.01 |

Good evening Jo. I have seen your picture and I think you are so beautiful sweet and sexy. It is a shame I am not in London, but in Moscow now for my businesses.

I have a construction company in Russia and I also own TV studios, an advertising company, and a print house. I have shares in an oil field and several interests in Istanbul.

I want to communicate with you constantly. Please accept.

I am also an established cartoonist and an amateur pilot, having recently got my licence. I play tennis almost to professional level. I enjoy astrology and philosophy and am an excellent violin player.

Kisses,
Vladimir

And I can suck an orange through a hosepipe...

| From: Guy-in-London | To: jo-to-go |
|---|---|
| Subject: Hi again | Date: 05.02.01 |

How are you. Where abouts in London are you from?

It was him again. The geek in the grotty basement with no photo and no details. What did he want? Didn't he get the message with my lack of response last time? He'd just re-sent the same message. Did this Guy-in-London have anything to say? I decided to put him out of his misery and reply with as much enthusiasm and thought as him.

| From: jo-to-go | To: Guy-in-London |
|---|---|
| Subject: Re: Hi again | Date: 05.02.01 |

Live in south London work in west end.

Surprisingly, he came straight back.

| From: | Guy-in-London | To: | jo-to-go |
|---|---|---|---|
| Subject: Re: Hi again | | Date: 05.02.01 | |

Cool – I work in the west end too. Maybe we should meet up for a drink! LOL!

Meet up for a drink! On what basis? I used to think LOL meant 'lots of love', but I'd come to learn that in this arena it meant 'laugh out loud', which is pretty much what I was doing at his suggestion. There was a lot more annoying internet speak too. ILMAO (I'm laughing my arse off) and BTW (by the way). I have an aversion to all of it. It's almost worse than those wonky smiley faces that people insist on signing off with : )

At least Guy-in-London had a job though. That meant he probably wasn't sitting in his pants in a grotty basement. My mental image changed to a 40-something desperado at the last chance saloon. I didn't bother replying again.

| From: | Guy-in-London | To: | jo-to-go |
|---|---|---|---|
| Subject: Re: Hi again | | Date: 12.02.01 | |

I'll take that as a no then.

He was perceptive, I'll give him that.

| From: | jo-to-go | To: | Guy-in-London |
|---|---|---|---|
| Subject: Re: Hi again | | Date: 12.02.01 | |

Well done! I'm not meeting you or anyone else from the internet. You could be a complete weirdo for all I know. And you're not exactly fuelling my interest with your one line messages and lazy profile. Why would I want to meet you?

| From: Guy-in-London | To: jo-to-go |
|---|---|
| Subject: Re: Hi again | Date: 12.02.01 |

Point taken. You could be a complete weirdo too!
I was joking about the drink by the way. I'm only here to
pass the time. But I saw your profile and it made me
laugh. It's different from the others. So chill out! I don't
want to meet you either!

| From: jo-to-go | To: Guy-in-London |
|---|---|
| Subject: Re: Hi again | Date: 12.02.01 |

Oh right. Well thats OK then Guy. I'm glad we've
established that. You don't say much on your profile, and
your opening line was rubbish. If you want people to
reply, you need to try a bit harder.

| From: Guy-in-London | To: jo-to-go |
|---|---|
| Subject: Re: Hi again | Date: 12.02.01 |

Guy? Who the hell is Guy?

| From: jo-to-go | To: Guy-in-London |
|---|---|
| Subject: Re: Hi again | Date: 12.02.01 |

You are aren't you? Guy in London?

| From: Guy-in-London | To: jo-to-go |
|---|---|
| Subject: Re: Hi again | Date: 12.02.01 |

Ha ha!

Yeah! I am a guy in London, but my name's not guy.
It's Tom. Thomas Evans to be precise.

Why – is your name Jo Togo?

| From: | jo-to-go | To: | Guy-in-London |
|-------|----------|-----|---------------|
| Subject: Re: Hi again | | Date: 12.02.01 | |

No! My name's not Jo Togo! It's Jo. Josephine Elliott to be precise, but everyone calls me Jo.
So which part of Wales are you from?

| From: | Guy-in-London | To: | jo-to-go |
|-------|---------------|-----|----------|
| Subject: Re: Hi again | | Date: 12.02.01 | |

Wales? What are you on? I'm from LA. I'm living and working in London at the moment.

My ears (or eyes) pricked up all of a sudden. LA – this could be interesting, but I wasn't going to let him know that.

| From: | jo-to-go | To: | Guy-in-London |
|-------|----------|-----|---------------|
| Subject: Re: Hi again | | Date: 12.02.01 | |

So you call this working do you?

| From: | Guy-in-London | To: | jo-to-go |
|-------|---------------|-----|----------|
| Subject: Re: Hi again | | Date: 12.02.01 | |

Work is slow this week. Just browsing to pass the time.

| From: | jo-to-go | To: | Guy-in-London |
|-------|----------|-----|---------------|
| Subject: Re: Hi again | | Date: 12.02.01 | |

Glad to be of service!

| From: | Guy-in-London | To: | jo-to-go |
|-------|---------------|-----|----------|
| Subject: Re: Hi again | | Date: 12.02.01 | |

OK. Well I'm off to find someone more interesting. Bye!

How dare he! The image in my head had changed again. Now he was a corporate 40-year old wearing a suit, polished loafers and too much hair gel. And he'd eaten too many burgers. But at least he could construct a sentence. I was strangely intrigued. From the few words we'd exchanged, I could tell there was more to Tom than the average Throbman_69 from Staines (no pun intended).

I wasn't sure I wanted him to find someone more interesting to chat to. I could do interesting. My dry wit was obviously not coming across very well in cyber space. Or was there an American/British humour divide taking place? Either way, I decided a dignified silence would be best. Something I wasn't very familiar with.

However miffed I was, I'd forgotten all about Tom Evans when he contacted me again a week later. I was secretly pleased to hear from him and I didn't know why.

| From: Guy-in-London | To: jo-to-go |
|---|---|
| Subject: Hi | Date: 19.02.01 |

And how is the boring English girl today?

| From: jo-to-go | To: Guy-in-London |
|---|---|
| Subject: Re: Hi | Date: 19.02.01 |

If you're referring to me, I'm fine thank you. How's the personality-free yank today?

| From: Guy-in-London | To: jo-to-go |
|---|---|
| Subject: Re: Hi again | Date: 19.02.01 |

Ahhhh. Thats better isn't it? Exchanging pleasantries like this. I'm also fine thank you for asking. A little quiet at work today, but otherwise fine.

Have you changed your mind about that drink yet?

---

From:   jo-to-go                        To:   Guy-in-London
Subject:  Re: Hi                         Date:  19.02.01

No I bloody haven't! I told you. I'm not meeting you.
You're off the internet. And not only that – you're
American. But I'm glad you're fine.

---

From:   Guy-in-London                   To:   jo-to-go
Subject:  Re: Hi                         Date:  19.02.01

Relax Jo Togo!
Damn you Brit girls are so easy to wind up!

---

From:   jo-to-go                        To:   Guy-in-London
Subject:  Re: Hi                         Date:  19.02.01

Us Brit girls!? How many girls are you chatting up on
here (if that's what you can call it)?

---

From:   Guy-in-London                   To:   jo-to-go
Subject:  Re: Hi                         Date:  19.02.01

I'm not chatting anyone up. Well I might be chatting you
up, but only because you're playing hard to get. You're a
challenge. I like a challenge.

---

From:   jo-to-go                        To:   Guy-in-London
Subject:  Re: Hi                         Date:  19.02.01

Easy on the compliments Mr Evans.

So it's like a game is it? I get it now. Well we seem to
have passed go, so why don't you take the opportunity
to tell me all about yourself?

---

| From: | Guy-in-London | To: | jo-to-go |
|---|---|---|---|
| Subject: Re: Hi | | Date: 19.02.01 | |

Why not indeed? Are you sitting comfortably?

I live in Maida Vale and I work in Soho for a film company. We produce documentaries mainly. I've been over here almost 2 years, prior to that I worked at head office LA.

I'm single as of a year ago, 34, 6ft, slim, blonde hair, green eyes and... well, not sure what else I can tell you really. I hate all this self promotion crap – hence the lack of info on my profile. But you have a rough idea of who you're talking to at least.

I'm not sure why I'm on this site. It just happened one day in a moment of boredom, not with the intention of dating anyone. That seems kinda weird.

Tom

P.S - I thought your picture was cute. That's why I wrote to you really.

He'd just described my ideal man – 34, single, solvent, tall, slim and fair. And he said my picture was 'cute'. I was beginning to think he might not have eaten too many burgers after all. And he probably didn't use hair gel.

| From: | jo-to-go | To: | Guy-in-London |
|---|---|---|---|
| Subject: Re: Hi | | Date: 19.02.01 | |

Well thanks. I'm flattered (I think). And apologies if my initial impression of you was somewhat inaccurate, but I didn't have much to go on. It would be nice to see what you look like. Why don't you post a picture on here?
Go on  – I dare you!

Jo

Tom didn't want to put his photo on Digital-Cupid, but it

35

wasn't because he was hiding something. He directed me to his work website where he said there was a picture of him. I couldn't log on quick enough. I waited in anticipation for the page to load, hoping he'd fit the image I now had in my head. Tall, blonde messy hair, quite good looking but not in a head-turning way, and dressed in Gap.

I wasn't disappointed. In fact I was pretty spot on. '*Tom Evans, Managing Director*' said the caption. Wow. He had a proper job too. I felt a surge of excitement as I logged back on to Digital-Cupid to break the good news. I could continue corresponding with him because he'd passed the acceptability test. With flying colours too.

---

### Digital-Cupid ❤

Hi jo-to-go, your special offer FREE month's
trial period has expired.

( Click here to subscribe )

---

Free month's trial period? I didn't even realise I was on a free trial period. I thought it was free, full-stop.

On closer inspection I found out that joining was free, creating a profile was free, but corresponding wasn't. I'd been lured in with a cleverly worded banner ad, and now I'd met Tom. Why had it expired at this precise moment when I urgently needed to to let him know that I was in receipt of his rather nice face. I panicked, realising I had a funny feeling about him that I couldn't explain. A *virtual* attraction. How could that happen? I'd never met him. But something was making me interested in finding out more.

I clicked the subscribe link. You could join for one month, three months, six months, a year. It was £18 for a month. Was I really going to pay to join an internet dating site? If I ever wanted to communicate with Tom again I was. While I was sitting here procrastinating about whether to pay up or not, he'd be at the other end of the computer wondering why I hadn't answered his last message. What if he thought I was so repulsed by his picture I'd quit on him? I guess he'd live. Why did this free trial period have to end now? And what's more – why did I care?

They had me by the proverbial balls. I was going to have to become a fully paid up member of Digital-Cupid.

# four

## *I'm in the Crown & Anchor quaking in my boots*

There were definitely advantages to being a proper member of Digital-Cupid, I just didn't know what they were yet. And it didn't really matter. As soon as I'd paid my £18 I swapped email addresses with Tom and we continued our 'relationship' on MSN messenger (once he'd explained what it was). So much better than email, but also very addictive. Tom was already online most mornings and saying 'hi' before I'd even had a chance to stir my tea. I could keep the little panel at the side of my screen and whenever I wasn't busy, we'd chat. Sometimes all day long. If I was busy, I'd go in early and have a chat with him first.

It wasn't long before I felt like I knew everything about him, and he about me. He was an only child and grew up in Philadelphia. His mum was a teacher and his dad worked in telecoms. He'd left home at the earliest opportunity and moved to LA. He'd worked his way up for several years before landing the job in London two years ago. He'd had a girlfriend in the UK but they'd split up a year ago. He had lots of friends, was happy with his life, but said he felt that something was missing. I could relate to that. He wasn't into casual flings. Said he was sick of drifting and wanted to meet someone and settle down. We named our virtual children.

Weeks passed and I couldn't wait to get to work every morning. We exchanged more pictures, then Tom had to go to LA for a week on business. I missed him like I'd miss my right arm. How did that work? I'd never even met the man. It wasn't normal. In fact it was verging on the ridiculous.

I began to realise around this time that I may have taken the unthinkable step of falling in love with a computer. I could now relate to the likes of Trudie from Basingstoke and the open-window scenario. Well, perhaps not the open window. But life without Tom online seemed like a distant memory. I couldn't wait for him to get back and log on. When he did, things quickly moved up a gear.

| | |
|---|---|
| Tom says: | Hi! How are you? |
| Jo says: | I'm fine. How are you – how was your trip? |
| Tom says: | Oh you know. Pretty boring really. Work mainly. Caught up with a couple of friends. It was odd. I don't know how to say this... |
| Jo says: | What's wrong? |
| Tom says: | Nothing's wrong! On the contrary. Just weird. |
| Jo says: | Go on... what!? |
| Tom says: | OK. I thought about you a lot. I missed you. There. I've said it. Pathetic! |

Oh my god. He felt the same. I was ecstatic. Obviously I wasn't the only one experiencing the strange phenomenon of virtual feelings. I couldn't play it cool anymore.

| | |
|---|---|
| Jo says: | I know the feeling. So did I. Miss you I mean. It's stupid. You're not real. |
| Tom says: | I know. Well, I am real. Oh no! – We're weird internet freaks! |
| Jo says: | Bloody hell! I know! Don't tell anyone! |
| Tom says: | You do realise we're gonna have to meet... |

Jo says:     *I know. Can't carry on like this forever.*
             *But you're off the internet! You might really*
             *be an axe wielding murderer!!!*

Tom says:    *So might you! But I'll take the risk.*

I knew he was right. We couldn't carry on like this. It was now inevitable that we should meet. But I was scared. What if the illusion was shattered? I almost wanted to keep him where he was, in the corner of my screen. But even I knew I couldn't have a computer for a boyfriend.

We swapped phone numbers. The next logical step was to chat on the phone. Talk about proceeding with caution. It was a warm night in May and I was sitting in the garden reading a book but taking nothing in. Tom said he'd call at seven and I checked the clock every five seconds. It had never crossed my mind what his voice might be like. What if he sounded like he was on helium or something?

Just after seven the phone rang, and although I was expecting it, I nearly jumped out of my skin. 'Virtual Tom' said the screen. My heart was pounding. I cleared my throat, drank some water and answered in my best matter-of-fact voice as if I wasn't expecting anyone.

"Hello."

"Hi. How are you?" he replied with a nervous laugh. He spoke slowly and in the right octave thank god. His American accent wasn't strong and his voice was quiet.

"Oh hi. I'm fine thanks. How are you?"

"Yeah. Good thanks. Where are you?"

"I'm at home. Sitting in the garden. Where are you?"

"I'm only just leaving work. D'you fancy meeting for that drink?"

"What. Now?" I almost shrieked.

"Yeah. Why not? No time like the present."

Panic stations. "Errm. Well – I've got a friend coming round for dinner now. I just got off the phone to her before you called. Split up with her boyfriend. She's distraught."

Where that came from I had no idea. What I really meant was I'm not quite ready to meet yet as I need a haircut. I also had a few spots that needed dealing with and a couple of days' clearance.

"Oh, really. That's not good. Another time then."

"Yes definitely," I assured him.

"It's strange talking after all this time, hey?"

"Yeah. Really strange. Not as strange as meeting will be, no doubt." I said, trying to sound relaxed.

"Strange but good," he added. "OK. Well I better go. I haven't got much battery. Good to talk to you at last. Chat tomorrow."

"Yep. Good to talk to you too. Have a good night."

I put the phone down and congratulated myself. He'd sounded as nervous as me which was good. We were in the same boat and I couldn't wait to meet him now. Nothing could possibly go wrong. Everything was so right, and it was slowly becoming real. Finally, a week after the first phone call, we had a date.

*Tom says:* Looking forward to tonight?

*Jo says:* Course. Although somewhat nervous.
You looking forward to it?

*Tom says:* Yeah. Same. Perhaps we should have a get-out clause.

*Jo says:* A get-out clause? Are you that worried?

*Tom says:* No! Might be an idea – just in case...!

*Jo says:* In case what? Stop! You're making me even more nervous!!

*Tom says:* I don't know – in case anything goes wrong I guess.

*Jo says:* You've been going on about meeting since your very first message (which seems like a lifetime ago). 5 hours before said meeting and now you want a get-out clause!???

| | |
|---|---|
| *Tom says:* | *It works both ways you know. You might think I'm a total loser and want to get out!* |
| *Jo says:* | *I probably will, but lets not worry about that now eh!* |
| *Tom says:* | *Thanks! Anyway... I'm in meetings all day so won't be online. Where shall we meet? I'll probably be done about 6. I can head towards you if you like.* |
| *Jo says:* | *Yeah OK. How about the Crown & Anchor on Neal Street?* |
| *Tom says:* | *Sounds good. I'll text you when I get there. Sometime after 6.* |

It was really happening. I was going on an internet date, although it didn't feel like that. It felt like I'd known Tom years. We just had the small matter of actually meeting each other to clear up.

I hadn't told anyone about my virtual boyfriend. How can you explain that you have feelings for someone you've never met without sounding like a complete muppet? I'd mentioned to Jane that I joined Digital-Cupid after she suggested it. I'd forwarded some of the messages I'd received to Claire. She laughed hysterically and said "you'd never get me on the bloody internet". Lucy was a bit more curious. She said she might have a look herself if she got really desperate.

The day dragged and I just wished it would hurry up so we could get this over and done with. Five o'clock came. To say I was nervous was an understatement. But I was excited at the same time. It played havoc with my stomach. All sorts of thoughts crossed my mind. There was still the possibility that Tom wasn't who he said he was. After all, you can be anyone you like when you're hiding behind a computer. Tom was genuine though. I knew it.

Ten to six. Oh god. Ten to six. My phone was at the ready and my hair was shiny. I'd had it cut at lunchtime in a bid to look like I'd just stepped out of a salon. I went in the toilet to freshen up and made a real effort to make it look like I'd made absolutely no effort at all.

Just as I was about to leave work, the heavens opened. Was it an omen? I didn't have an umbrella. This was a disaster. I searched the building and managed to find a bright yellow golf umbrella with Schweppes written all over it. Great. That would complete the look nicely. I didn't want to mess up my hair, so I had no choice but to use it.

Ten past six and no text from Tom. Well he had said sometime after six. That could mean half past eight for all I knew. The rain eased and I went outside. I went to the cashpoint. Walked around the block. Contemplated nipping in a bar and knocking back a couple of shots of something strong. Twenty past six and still no sign. Where was he? Had he bottled out? I looked at myself in a couple of windows and tried not to poke anyone's eye out with my man umbrella. I checked my phone several hundred times to ensure it was switched on. Nothing. I was just about to call Vodafone to ask if there was a fault on the line when at last, 6.32 and a text came though.

*Virtual Tom: Hi. In the Crown & Anchor quaking in my boots.*

*Jo mobile: OK. On my way. Large G&T please!*

This was it. The moment of truth. I took a deep breath. When I got to the pub door, I didn't have time to be nervous. I was faced with the dilemma of putting the umbrella down and getting my new hair wet, or trying to manoeuvre my way through the door with it still up at the risk of looking like a bumbling idiot. I opted for the latter, but the brolly got stuck as I tried to put it down. Talk about making an entrance. After a fight with the door, I turned round and eyed the bar. I saw Tom straight away. He was sitting at the other end, watching me and my great umbrella struggle, with a wry grin on his face. Good start. I mustered some fake confidence and strolled on up.

"Hello. So this is what you look like?" Was my fantastic opener. The words just fell out of my mouth. He laughed. I wasn't sure whether it was nerves or pity.

"I got you a drink," he said, and passed me what I hoped was a double gin and tonic.

We looked at each other nervously and exchanged a few pleasantries. Despite knowing everything about Tom, I was finding it difficult to find words. I was too busy thinking that the anti-climax I'd half expected hadn't arrived. He looked even better in the flesh. Although not traditionally handsome, his face was boyish and smooth. And he was tall and skinny. Exactly what I like. You can keep your body builders and blokes who look like they're carrying an invisible bucket of water in each hand. Give me skinny any day. I felt the fabled chemistry instantly.

He was quite scruffy. His cardigan wouldn't have looked out of place on my grandad, and his jeans hung awkwardly from his lanky frame. I didn't dare look at the shoes. He'd mentioned he wasn't going to be making an effort as that was 'trying too hard'. I'd assured him I wouldn't be either. If we ended up together, I'd just have to get my hair done professionally every day.

After the second drink the ice was broken and the nerves subsided. He thanked me for my sophisticated opening line and admitted he'd been just as nervous. Neither of us had ever done anything like this before and we both found it rather embarrassing. He hadn't told his friends either. I felt safe in the knowledge that he'd been through the same emotions as me and was showing no signs of wanting to leg it just yet.

Conversation was soon flowing. Just as it had online. We moved on to another bar after a while. It was a cocktail bar he knew. Tom took charge and ordered two of the most potent concoctions imaginable, which I pretended to enjoy. The waitress brought some nibbles over which was good, because I was starting to feel light headed. Suddenly, Tom put his glass down, leaned towards me and looked into my eyes meaningfully. I hoped I didn't have houmous on my face as I tried to engage his stare. His eyes were unusual. I'd never seen eyes like them before. Deep green and like glass. I hoped they weren't.

"I think you're great," he announced. "In fact you're perfect for me."

I didn't know what to say. This was too good to be true. Luckily I didn't have to say anything. He leaned in a bit further and kissed me perfectly on the lips as if to seal the deal. It couldn't have felt more right. I didn't want to leave that table. I could have sat there forever staring into Tom's eyes and drinking revolting cocktails just because he said they were nice. I was hypnotised.

But of course we had to leave eventually. It was closing time and the staff wanted rid of us. It would have been easy to jump in a cab together and carry on the introductions somewhere more comfortable, but something stopped me and I got in a cab alone. It was difficult. Finally I'd met someone on my wavelength and the feeling was mutual.

As I fell into bed, sweet dreams ahead, my phone bleeped and startled me.

*Virtual Tom: Thanks for tonight. You didn't disappoint.*

*Jo mobile: Nithrev dud youjd 4 a bloek of teh intrenet*

———— ❤ ————

I paid a visit to Mario on the way to work. My head wasn't feeling too clever. I guess I was paying the price of too many confidence cocktails.

"Ah. Jo is very happy this morning," he said. "What make-a the smile on the face?"

"I don't know what you mean Mario!" I grinned. I couldn't help it.

"I thinka that Jo is in love," he teased as he put my already cooked bacon in the deep fat fryer.

"Don't be ridiculous. You know me!"

"Ah yes. I know you, Jo. Every morning you come-a here. No happy. No smiling. Tired. This morning you come here, happy and can't-a stop-a smiling. Who is lucky guy?"

God was it that obvious? Was I in love? I was certainly in something. I got to my desk and tried to wipe the smile off my face. I had to invent a story about how I'd met Tom before I announced our love to the world. There was still a stigma attached to internet dating, although I'd met someone nice, so why did I care?

| | |
|---|---|
| *Tom says:* | *Hi. Missing you already!* |
| *Jo says:* | *Ahhh. How American! – how you feeling?* |
| *Tom says:* | *Rough. But good. You?* |
| *Jo says:* | *Same. Can't wait for the day to be over! Those cocktails were evil.* |
| *Tom says:* | *Yeah – but a necessary evil! I had a good night. I can't stop thinking about you.* |
| *Jo says:* | *I'm the same. I can't quite believe it.* |
| *Tom says:* | *I know! It's very odd. Have you told anyone about me?* |
| *Jo says:* | *No. Not yet. I will do though. Have you told anyone about me?* |
| *Tom says:* | *No. We better get a story together. Don't want our friends knowing the awful truth!* |

We concocted a story and arranged to meet again. I was less nervous this time, but still had the odd butterfly. I did my own hair, which frankly could have gone one way or the other. It looked kind of acceptable. We met in Soho in a trendy bar. Who were we kidding? We soon ended up at the Dog & Duck. He looked even nicer this time in a blue shirt and white jeans. They could have been chinos actually, but I wouldn't have cared if they were tracky bottoms.

We had another great night which culminated in Tom

trying to get in my cab home. Hard as it was, I declined him again. It was still only our second meeting after all.

On the third date we went to the Portrait Gallery. There was something on he wanted to see, which I pretended to have heard of. I did a bit of research on the internet in a bid to sound like I knew what I was talking about. We still ended up in a bar drinking two bottles of champagne, before heading back to his in a cab. He said he was going to cook for me, but the champagne put paid to that and we ended up getting a take-away. I had visions of his place in my mind. I knew it would be nice, but it was nothing like I'd imagined. Far more swanky. It was in Maida Vale proper (as opposed to Kilburn), and it was enormous. A loft-style apartment with slate floors and Smeg appliances. I'd landed on my feet here!

As we sat on the designer sofa quaffing champagne, eating pizza, and comfortably chatting, one thing suddenly lead to another and... well let's just say that the last remaining piece in the acquaintance puzzle slotted naturally into place. Tom definitely ticked *all* my boxes.

I left his place the next morning walking on air. I'd met the man of my dreams and it felt good. Who said internet dating was for freaks and weirdos?

———— ❤ ————

I started to tell my friends I'd met someone. How excited were they? It was a revelation. Jo had made it past the first month with no signs of faltering from either party. I wasn't quite ready to unveil him yet, but maybe in a couple of weeks' time...

My parents came to London one night. We had tickets for the ballet. I wanted to be a ballerina when I was about five, and they were treating me. It was four short ballets, nothing heavy. Principal ballerina Darcey Bussell was in the first one. The seat next to me was empty, which was strange. As I watched Darcey dazzle the audience, I imagined Tom sitting in it, accompanying me to the ballet with my parents. They'd like him.

When the second ballet came on I was lost in thought. Tom was in the audience and I was the ballerina on stage. He was watching proudly, staring at my arabesque in wonderment. Then someone interrupted me from my day dream when they took the empty seat next to me. 'How rude' I thought. 'This isn't the Odeon you know.' I looked at my mum and dad. They were engrossed in the performance. I wondered if I should really make their day later. Tell them I'd met someone. That I wasn't actually a lesbian, and that I too had joined the world of happy couples. Perhaps the word 'grandchildren' wouldn't be banished forever after all.

As I sat pondering the issue in the posh seats at the Royal Opera House, I was suddenly brought back down to earth with an almighty bump. My mobile phone rang. OH MY GOD. My mobile phone was playing *Mambo Number Five* in the middle of a performance by the Royal Ballet. Could there be a more mortifying experience?

I could have sworn I'd switched it off. Oh god. I was stuck. Surrounded by diamond necklaces, the whiff of Chanel No.5, loud tuts and icy glares, I panicked. The phone was in the bottom of my bag and it was still going off at ascending volume. Please somebody rescue me from this nightmare. Louder and louder it rang, as I leapt from my seat and tried to throw myself and my bag out of the auditorium. I was then faced with further embarrassment. The empty seat next to me had been occupied by Darcey Bussell herself. Humiliation of the highest degree. I looked at her. I think she felt sorry for me. Either that or she was wondering when the Royal Opera House had started admitting heathens.

I manoeuvred myself outside as my parents pretended they didn't know me. *Mambo Number Five* sprang to life again as my phone told me I had a voice message. I never want to hear that bloody song again. However, I had some time to kill, so I listened to the message. It was Tom. I felt slightly better on hearing his voice.

"Hi there Jo. Only me. Just remembered you're at the ballet tonight so you're probably on silent. Gimme a ring later if you can. Looks like I have to go to LA tomorrow for a week. Anyways. Call me. See ya."

I phoned him straight back. I told him about my horrendous faux pas, and that I couldn't possibly return to my seat until after the interval, if at all. He laughed his head off and said ballet was stuffy. He was still at work. There was a problem and he was trying to resolve it. That meant a visit to LA and he was leaving tomorrow morning. He told me he'd miss me. I told him I was sure our love would endure a week apart, secretly wishing I was going with him. I contemplated the thought of us moving to LA one day. He'd probably want to go back eventually, which would suit me fine. We could get a nice house by the beach and I could learn to rollerblade. Eventually we'd have dogs and children.

———— ❤ ————

The week he was away, everything went back to just the way it was before we met. Boring. I hadn't bothered checking my messages on Digital-Cupid for ages, although they kept insisting I should. Several men were looking for someone just like me. But Tom occupied most of my thoughts and I really wasn't interested. It was the longest week ever. He sent a couple of emails saying a quick 'hi', but apart from that, contact was temporarily defunct.

At last, Thursday came and I was excited at the prospect of seeing him again, but I was surprised when he didn't log on to MSN first thing. He was supposedly back in the office and I was expecting an email. Or perhaps a phone call. But he was probably busy after his trip. We had tentative plans to go out that night if he wasn't too jet-lagged. Maybe he was and he hadn't made it to the office yet. Understandable since he'd only landed late the night before.

I waited until late afternoon and called his mobile. It was switched off. He was no doubt asleep and didn't want disturbing, so I decided to leave it until the following day when he was back at work and far more with it. Anyway, he'd probably call me later when he woke up.

Friday morning and I was getting worried. I still hadn't heard from Tom and there was no sign of him online. What if something had happened to him? He could've been dead for all I knew. Not knowing any mutual people, how would I ever find out? I could phone his work I suppose, but who would I speak to? What would I say? I tried his mobile again. It was still switched off, but according to the ringtone he was definitely in the country, so I sent him an email.

| From: Jo Elliott | To: Tom Evans |
|---|---|
| Subject: Are you back? | Date: 29.06.01 |

Hi. Just wondering if everything's OK? I've been trying to call you but to no avail. We were meant to catch up last night and I didn't hear from you. I was just a bit worried. Let me know you're still alive.

Jo x

About three hours later I got a response. It wasn't really what I'd been expecting.

| From: Tom Evans | To: Jo Elliott |
|---|---|
| Subject: Re: Are you back? | Date: 29.06.01 |

Everything is not OK no. I found out our UK office is closing and I have to make everyone redundant. I'm being moved back to LA. It's not a good time.

My heart sank to my boots. Well it would have done if I'd been wearing them. It's hard to describe how I felt. Kind of virtually knocked out. I went from elation to rock bottom in three seconds flat. I couldn't believe what I was reading. His tone was totally cold, like a different person. What was he saying? Was that it? OK, making people redundant wouldn't be particularly nice, but was it the end of his world and everyone in it? Did it render me obsolete? Reading between the lines of his curt message, I certainly wasn't part of the equation. My subconscious knew that pretty quickly, but my conscious wasn't prepared to accept it. But rather than question his sudden personality transplant, I pandered.

| From: Jo Elliott | To: Tom Evans |
|---|---|
| Subject: Re: Are you back? | Date: 29.06.01 |

That's terrible. You poor thing. You should have called me. Sounds like you need a drink. Do you want to go for one after work.

| From: Tom Evans | To: Jo Elliott |
|---|---|
| Subject: Re: Are you back? | Date: 29.06.01 |

I can't. I have shit to do here. I have to leave in two weeks. I haven't got time for anything else. Sorry.

I'm surprised I didn't offer to help him pack, the poor love. Whatever he was saying to me, it wouldn't compute. I think I'd have preferred it if he'd said he'd met someone else. He might be able to switch off his emotions for a career move, but I certainly couldn't. I needed it spelling out loud and clear.

| From: Jo Elliott | To: Tom Evans |
|---|---|
| Subject: Re: Are you back? | Date: 29.06.01 |

So you're going back to LA for good in two weeks and that's it? As if the last few weeks just didn't happen. Do you have any feelings for me at all?

| From: | Tom Evans | To: | Jo Elliott |
|---|---|---|---|
| Subject: Re: Are you back? | | Date: 29.06.01 | |

Of course I have feelings for you. I just can't deal with this at the moment. I have to go now. Got a meeting.

How could he be so distant? I found it beyond belief. What had I done to deserve this? How could things change so much in the space of a week?

I left work early and wandered the streets like a zombie. I didn't know where I was going but I ended up in Topshop, where I bought several totally inappropriate items I didn't need. I caught sight of myself in a mirror. Face like a slapped arse. I went home and devoured the contents of my fridge and then some. The phone rang and I leapt up, hoping it was Tom and he'd seen the error of his ways. Was he ringing to apologise for his nonchalant behaviour and beg for forgiveness? It was Claire. I burst into tears.

"What's up mate?" she asked full of concern. "What's happened?"

"The lovely Tom Evans," I sobbed. "He's not so lovely after all."

Claire, Lucy and Jane were on my doorstep within the hour, armed with a bottle of wine each and a bunch of flowers. I loved them for it. They listened to the whole sorry tale amid tears and a severe outbreak of Tourettes. They hadn't met Tom so they had nothing to go on as to what kind of person he was apart from what I'd told them.

Three bottles of wine later and they came to the conclusion that all was not lost. Tom was a man, they reminded me, and he had a crisis on his hands. Men couldn't deal with more than one thing at once and he was probably just as gutted as I was, but he had his hands full with the work issue. They advised me to give him some space and see what happened in a few days when he'd had more time to get his head round the situation. They were right. It could be as simple as that.

I had to restrain myself from contacting him for the next few days until I could bear it no more. I emailed and asked him how he was. He replied saying 'busy'. I emailed again with some pointless banter which before he would have laughed at, but now he had a conference call. I phoned him one night and he didn't answer. I texted him and he didn't reply. I sent a couple more emails and his reluctant answers were excruciating. I felt like a stalker. I'm not sure why I put myself through the shame of it, but I guess I needed answers. I was finding it impossible to get my head around this Jekyll and Hyde behaviour. He was still Tom Evans on a pedestal in my head.

He humoured me for two weeks, then said he was leaving in two days' time. Back to LA LA land from whence he came. No suggestion of us meeting. He was leaving, just like that, as if nothing had ever happened. I was out of my depth. I'd fallen for one person and ended up with another. I didn't tell him I was going crazy. I could do blasé too, but only on the outside. I carried on with the jovial Jo act and wondered when he'd remember to pack me in his suitcase.

I had to see him before he left, so practically begged him to meet me for a drink. Once he saw me again he'd remember I was perfect for him and everything would be OK. Pathetic really, looking back. He said he could spare me half an hour after work but he still had a lot to do. It was kind of him to find me a window in his busy schedule. He even suggested we met at the Crown & Anchor where we had our first date. The romantic fool.

As I walked down Neal Street I phoned him to say I was on my way. *"This number is no longer in use"* said the monotone voice at the other end. He'd changed his number and he hadn't even told me. At that point I wondered if he'd even turn up. I doubted it very much and began to think all sorts of things. Perhaps he'd been murdered and someone else had taken on his identity. The person who'd come back from LA certainly wasn't the person who went.

There was no sign of him in the pub. It seemed like an

eternity since we'd met there on the first date, but unbelievably, it was just two months ago. I felt stupid. Then he walked through the door, all tanned and looking like a new man. He certainly didn't look like someone on the verge of a nervous breakdown. Quite the opposite. He couldn't have looked more refreshed if he'd tried. His clothes were different and his hair was better. He'd been shopping in HMV.

"Hi. How are you?" I asked with fake buoyancy.

"Yeah. Getting there. It's been hectic," he replied without actually looking at me.

"Been buying music?" I said, stating the bleeding obvious.

"Yeah."

At least he'd found time to stock up on CDs before going back to the States where they were half the price. I got the drinks in. It was painfully obvious he didn't want to be there. It baffled me that he'd actually agreed to this farce. There was clearly a lot more to this than a change of job, I just wished he'd find the decency to tell me. I looked at him and he looked rather pathetic. Like a schoolboy who'd been naughty but didn't want to confess. After about twenty minutes of uncomfortable conversation, he said he had to go. He needed to finish packing because the shipping people were coming in the morning.

I still didn't want this to happen. Say something, I thought, but nothing would come out. I was bewildered and upset, but wearing a mask of indifference. As we left the pub he checked the screen on his trendy new mobile. Was he expecting someone?

"Guess this is it then," I sighed, lingering outside the pub with this stranger.

"Guess so," he replied, with no emotion whatsoever.

I wondered which way he was going. He wondered which way I was going and chose the opposite, before reluctantly embracing me as he flagged down a passing cab.

"Keep in touch won't you?" I said, still convinced there was a chance that this was all a big mistake. Or a wind-up.

I was half expecting Jeremy Beadle to jump out of the cab.

"Yeah. Course."

"Take care," I added, prolonging the agony.

"You too."

With that, he climbed in the cab, slammed the door and off he went, taking my heart and my dignity with him. I noticed it wasn't Jeremy Beadle at the wheel.

———— ❤ ————

I wish I could re-live that twenty minutes. I'd do things differently. Demand an explanation and stamp on his new CDs. The truth would hurt, but it would be better than this. I clearly had a lot to learn.

I saw his name every day on my contact list and sadly I couldn't bring myself to delete it. He never logged on anymore. Naïvely I thought that might be the time difference, but Claire phoned his London office a few weeks later and he answered, bright and breezy as you like. At least it confirmed what I already knew. It was all a big lie. I felt an overwhelming compulsion to confront him but what was the point? Instead, frustration ate away at me. My head was saying 'forget it! He's just not worth it', but my heart was having none of it.

# five

## *New balls please*

A couple of months later and Claire had found a new boyfriend, Jane had got married and Lucy had signed up with Digital-Cupid. I was still moping around in the throes of despair and listening to a lot of REO Speedwagon. Strange, it had hardly been the love affair of the century. Several weeks of internet flirting and a two-month relationship, followed by a couple of weeks of psychotic nonsense. I wasn't in love. I was infatuated. According to the dictionary, infatuation is the state of being blindly in love. Blind to the faults of the other person. I was certainly that, but at least I had a new pair of Kurt Geiger wedges to look forward to.

I'd been to several weddings that summer, including Jane's. I was never even the bridesmaid, let alone the bride, and always seated at the back on the table of token singles who get drunk and heckle during the speeches. I met a nice man at one of them. Our relationship just about saw out the last dance, but it was a useful catalyst. Slowly the feeling of being consumed by madness began to subside, and I returned to the planet, albeit with a protective layer of cynicism on the subject of romance.

Digital-Cupid were still flogging their wares by daily email. Several men were still apparently keen to meet me, but I couldn't bring myself to look. It brought back bad memories. After all, my idea of blokes on the internet hadn't exactly been proved wrong. Lucy's attitude was somewhat more positive, as I found out a few weeks later on a night out with the girls. She hadn't particularly clicked with anyone yet, but it hadn't put her off. She said she was having a great time experimenting.

"So what were they like?" I asked, intrigued. "Did you chat for long online or dive head first into the dates?"

"Well. A bit of both really. With the first one, we chatted online for about a week I think. He was Italian. Giovanni..." she sighed.

"Lucy! You don't like foreigners!" Jane pointed out with horror.

"I'm broadening my horizons," she protested. "Anyway. I quite liked the idea of having a fella from Florence, or Rome. It sounds romantic."

"Did he have an accent then?" Claire asked.

"No! He'd gone on and on about his Italian background, but he was born and bred in Peckham!" she giggled. "There's probably more Italian in a jar of Ragu!"

Oh dear.

"His pictures weren't bad and he was really funny on email. The accent would have just been a bonus."

"So what happened once you realised you'd made a date with Del Boy?" I asked.

"Well! When we got round to actually meeting up..." She couldn't keep a straight face.

"Yeah...!" we were all chomping at the bit for the dramatic conclusion.

"He was vertically challenged, with a mullet and a bad case of dandruff."

Raucous laughter followed and Lucy went on to tell us about Darren. He'd spent the whole evening talking in a mock Jamaican accent about his ambition to be a DJ, before offering to show her his decks. He lived with his mum in Muswell Hill. I was beginning to think I'd got off lightly.

"It gets better," she said with a big grin.

"Go on!" we screeched, eager for more.

She then relayed the story of her date with Perry Valentino, the resting actor. It was lust at first sight for Lucy. She thought things were looking up. That it might be a case of third time lucky. The date was going smoothly until they ended up in a late bar in Soho and he confessed that he thought he might be gay.

"Oh my god!" said Claire. "What the bloody hell did you say to that?"

"Well I was gobsmacked! I fancied him. But it was clear he didn't feel the same, so I told him to join gaydar.com and stop wasting my time."

And she was having a great time experimenting?

———————❤———————

It was food for thought. I wondered if I could adopt Lucy's positive attitude and throw myself into the dating game properly. Despite a healthy array of male friends and hanging out in B&Q of a weekend, my real life encounters with prospective men were sparse.

After dithering for several weeks and getting through Christmas and New Year in New Zealand without so much as a sniff under the mistletoe, I decided there was no harm in logging back on. I had nothing to lose, and there might be lots of messages awaiting me. Would it be love at first click?

---

### Digital-Cupid ❤

Due to inactivity your account has been suspended.
*Click here to reactivate your account*

---

Suspended? Oh great. Did this mean I had to go through the rigmarole of filling in the questionnaire about what I eat for dinner and the state of my facial hair again? I clicked on the link anyway and was relieved to find that I just had to answer a couple of multiple-choice questions about why

I'd been away so long and we were back up and running. Simple as that.

---

### *Digital-Cupid* ♥

Welcome back jo-to-go! It's always good to see you.

( Click here for your latest matches )

---

I did as I was told. Unfortunately my number one match was coming up as AustinPowers from Newcastle, 5ft 6, caucasian, bald head and built like a brick shit house. Perhaps it was time to alter my profile. I couldn't remember what it said anyway. I had a quick look and made a few changes. I was now here for romance/relationship with men aged 30 to 40, who lived within a 50 mile radius of London. I tweaked the 'In my own words' bit to make it sound like I was vaguely open to meeting someone, although I was still extremely dubious.

---

### *In my own words*

Hi. I'm Jo. Down to earth, sociable, confident, unconfident, funny, solvent and various other adjectives which I can't think of at the moment.

I enjoy travelling, socialising, pretending to be a pop star, and laughing at my own jokes (and sometimes other people's).

I thought I'd give this a go and see if anyone is on the same wavelength as me. I'm not sure what frequency that is, but try tuning in and we'll see what happens.

( Submit )

---

I read it back and wondered what the hell I was talking about, but I submitted it anyway. I also added a couple of new photos for good measure. One of me up a mountain in New Zealand, and one of me dancing on a table in a bar with the girls. I'd now realised that pictures really do speak louder than words. At least people could see I lead a relatively exciting life and know how to have a good time. It seemed to pay off. The very next day I had several new messages waiting to greet me.

| From: | Lewisham_John | To: | jo-to-go |
|---|---|---|---|
| Subject: | Happy new year | Date: | 23.01.02 |

How are you? Hope your christmas and new year were blinding. Do you have a dog?

I'm a 30 year old cracker looking for a special girl to develop a happy fun loving relationship with. I am 5ft 10, well built, blue eyes, receding and work in sales.

I dont take life too seriously which I think is a good thing. I've looked down the miserable stress road and it didn't do me no good so I won't be going down there again.

Have a look at my profile. I think we have plenty in common. If you think I'm up to scratch then reply and we can arrange a date and take it from there.

John

| From: | Squirrel_Nutkins | To: | jo-to-go |
|---|---|---|---|
| Subject: | Wow | Date: | 23.01.02 |

You look great – fancy a natter with a married man? I'm happy at home, but looking for a bit extra. I have a pic I can send you. If you like the look of it, we could meet for some discreet fun at a location convenient to you. Hope to hear back from you.

Nutkins. x

| From: | Your_Hero | To: | jo-to-go |
|---|---|---|---|
| Subject: | Hi! | Date: | 23.01.02 |

I'm Andy from Milton Keynes. I'm 26, single and I work in IT. I have 2 girls Britney and Chelsea. I'm tactile, love to play pool and go bowling.

Come say hi, i wont bite xxx.

| From: | want-a-baby | To: | jo-to-go |
|---|---|---|---|
| Subject: | I WANT A BABY | Date: | 23.01.02 |

Hello.

I am looking for a woman who's main concern is not a career or travelling the continents, but who just wants to have a baby.

I'M ALRIGHT – JUST DIDN'T LEARN HOW TO SEDUCE A WOMAN. I'm 43, 5 foot 9 tall and well built. I'm not ashamed of who I am either. I want that baby. I don't want my brothers kid to get my 2 houses and 8 acres of land, as much as I love her. So I need a volunteer woman to bear me a child (we can have a relationship if we get on). Can I put it any simpler or directer than that?

I won't write any more coz it dilutes the message, which I stress again is: I WANT A BABY. Get back to me ASAP if you are willing.

Dean

| From: | Mick-67 | To: | jo-to-go |
|---|---|---|---|
| Subject: | Hello | Date: | 23.01.02 |

Hope you are well. Just a message to get to know you and maybe have a chat sometime and then hopefully meet up for a meal and then a trip to the cinema. All the best for now hope to hear from soon.

Mick

---

| From: frog_monkey | To: jo-to-go |
|---|---|
| Subject: Ciao bella!!! | Date: 23.01.02 |

Today, I would like to be born in England but now it's too late, I think. I waited for you 48 years but I made a mistake, I choose to live in Brasil under a very big and dark forest, where I only meet parrots.

Please write me xxx

---

Wow! Spoilt for choice. Obviously it was tempting to have discreet fun with Squirrel_Nutkins, or bear the intellectually impaired Dean's child. But I didn't know which of these lucrative offers to reply to first, so I decided to sleep on it.

Part of me was secretly pleased that there was no potential as it was safer that way. The other part wanted to get back into circulation as soon as possible and go on a few dates. Surely there were some 'normal' men on the site?

I did a search for eligible males around my age. There certainly wasn't a shortage. Plenty of attractive men with interesting profiles came up. They just weren't contacting me. Was I going to have to switch tactics and start contacting *them*? I guess it couldn't hurt. It wouldn't be too embarrassing if they didn't respond, because they didn't know me. It wasn't like asking someone out in the real world and being turned down flat. At least I could blush in privacy. While I deliberated about the trials and tribulations of contacting a few quality candidates, at last one of them contacted me.

---

| From: Jake_1970 | To: jo-to-go |
|---|---|
| Subject: Hey Jo | Date: 04.02.02 |

Greetings from the States!

I just saw your profile and it stood out from the rest. You seem pretty cool. Do you still have the beard? Hope to hear back from you.

Jake

---

Oh no! I'd forgotten to change the facial hair bit on my profile. I still had a long haired-beard. No wonder I was having problems attracting suitable men. It looked like it had raised a laugh with Jake_1970 though, and judging by his photos, that was fine by me.

'Greetings from the States' should have probably had me running a mile under the circumstances, but he was gorgeous. Short dark hair, tanned skin and an amazing smile. In one picture he was water-skiing, in another he was on the beach, and in another he was surfing. Then there was a close-up in which I could really see his rugged good looks. Was he too good to be true? I decided to overlook the fact that he was from across the pond in this instance, and furnish him with a reply.

| From: jo-to-go | To: Jake_1970 |
|---|---|
| Subject: Re: Hey Jo | Date: 04.02.02 |

Hi Jake.

Thanks for the message. Your profile's interesting too. Are you a keen water-skier?

I don't have the long haired beard any more by the way. Just a goatee these days. What about yourself? I note that on your profile it says clean shaven, but on one of your pictures you have some stubble. Where do you stand on this issue? And whereabout's in the States are you from? I look forward to your reply.

Jo

| From: Jake_1970 | To: jo-to-go |
|---|---|
| Subject: Re: Hey Jo | Date: 05.02.02 |

Hi Jo.

You could say I'm a keen water-skier. I make a living from teaching it and also compete a bit. I live in Florida so it's all right here on my doorstep.

Where are you in London? I was born there and lived there until I was 5. Been back a few times since.

By the way – I'm clean shaven at the moment. I must admit you look gorgeous in your pictures, where you are also clean shaven!

Jake

---

I look gorgeous? Coming from this tall, dark and handsome water-skiing pro, that was one hell of a compliment. I pictured myself on the beach in Florida, watching Jake skilfully skim the waves. Sunning myself and eating oranges.

---

| From: | jo-to-go | To: | Jake_1970 |
|---|---|---|---|
| Subject: Re: Hey Jo | | Date: 05.02.02 | |

Wow. Must be great to live in Florida and have the beach on your doorstep. It sounds like a brilliant lifestyle. I imagine that waking up, strolling to the beach and strapping on your water skis is slightly more pleasurable than trudging to work on a packed train (if it's working) and sitting at a desk all day.

I live in Wandsworth (south west London). Do you know it?

Jo

---

| From: | Jake_1970 | To: | jo-to-go |
|---|---|---|---|
| Subject: Re: Hey Jo | | Date: 06.02.02 | |

My mother is from the south London area. Wandsworth rings a bell. I think I remember it. There's a KFC on the high street right?

So what brings a stunning girl like you to a place like this?

Jake x

---

Another amazing compliment from Mr Perfect. And a kiss.

I didn't even feel the need to point out there was a KFC on practically every high street in the world. I was too preoccupied by this beautiful being, showering me with compliments like never before.

| From: jo-to-go | To: Jake_1970 |
|---|---|
| Subject: Re: Hey Jo | Date: 06.02.02 |

Yes – you're right. There is a KFC in Wandsworth. And a McDonalds. What brings me here? I'm not sure really, but I seem to get far more attention here than I do in the real world. On second thoughts, I probably shouldn't have said that – it doesn't say a lot about my personality does it! I do have one – honest.

What about you? What brings you here? You must get heaps of attention from the bronzed, size 6 bikini clad babes on the beaches of Florida?

Jo x

| From: Jake_1970 | To: jo-to-go |
|---|---|
| Subject: Re: Hey Jo | Date: 07.02.02 |

There are plenty of those kind of girls here, but after a while it gets boring. There's nothing challenging about a beach bum, no matter how pretty she is. Most of them are shallow. I prefer women with something to say.

Actually, I'm coming over to the UK soon. My mother is back over there visiting and I'm coming for a month in the summer. Maybe we could catch up?

Jake x

Oh my god. I might be able to hold a conversation and scrub up OK on a low resolution photo, but I couldn't compete with the Florida beach babes, no matter what I had to say for myself. I suppose I could starve for the next couple of months and block-book the tanning booth. If he looked anything like his photos in the flesh, which presumably he did, I'd be speechless. I imagined walking in the Slug & Lettuce with him on my arm, Claire, Lucy and Jane aghast at my fantastic catch. It was too funny.

| From: | jo-to-go | To: | Jake_1970 |
|---|---|---|---|
| Subject: | Re: Hey Jo | Date: | 07.02.02 |

That would be great. I can introduce you to the delights of sunny London.

Are you into anything other than surfing and water skiing? There's not much surf here I'm afraid, but we do have a brown river.

Jo x

| From: | Jake_1970 | To: | jo-to-go |
|---|---|---|---|
| Subject: | Re: Hey Jo | Date: | 08.02.02 |

LOL! No problem.

I do like other things. There's plenty to see in London that we don't have here. It would be good to check out a few cool bars too. I have some friends over there. It will be good to catch up with them as well.

I'll leave it up to you to show me around. I'm already looking forward to it

Jake x

Mmmm. Me too! The time difference was annoying. If I was online, Jake was in bed and vice versa. Communication was slow. One email a day and no instant messaging, but it certainly gave me something to look forward to of a morning. I had other messages, but no-one came close to Jake. He was a one-off and he was coming to London in the summer. I couldn't wait.

I was reading his latest message one morning. He'd sent me another photo and I was swooning over it when Lisa, my Aussie friend at work, walked in.

"What you smiling at Jo?" she asked.

"Nothing," I replied. I hadn't realised I was.

"Still looking at boys on the internet?" she teased.

"Shhh..." I gestured her over to my desk.

I hadn't told anyone else at work that I was signed up with an internet dating site. It was far too embarrassing. But Lisa had tried it too. The fact that she was looking for a female and me a male made no difference. We'd both had no luck and we'd both attracted a bunch of absolute no-hopers.

"You may laugh, but wait 'til you see this beauty," I whispered proudly. "He's a cut above the rest, make no mistake. Slight problem in that he lives in Florida, but he's coming over soon and wants to meet up."

"Sounds good. Nice one Jo. Let's have a look at him."

I enlarged his picture on my screen and waited for her to gasp in appreciation at Jake's handsome good looks.

"That's Mark Philippoussis," she said a bit too loudly.

"No. It's Jake from Florida," I corrected her.

"It's Mark Philippoussis!" she repeated.

"Mark Philippoussis? What are you talking about? It's Jake – the guy I've been talking to in Florida!" I scoffed at her silly mistake.

"Jo. Those pictures are of Mark Philippoussis. I'm telling you. Google him. You'll see!" She was cracking up. People were looking.

"OK. I will," I said confidently. Lisa usually knew what she was talking about, but Mark Philippoussis was a tennis player, not a water-skier.

After spending ten minutes trying to spell Philippoussis, hundreds of sites came up. I went to the one that looked official and as I clicked on the link, my heart was pounding. Doubts were creeping in as I prayed she was wrong. Oh god. What if she was right? Everyone in the office was gathered round my desk now, waiting to see if I'd been duped by a sad internet loser who'd taken on the identity of Mark Philippoussis.

The opening page came up. The first thing I saw was a picture of Mark Philippoussis water-skiing. Apparently he's very good. Then there was Mark Philippoussis on the beach. Mark Philippoussis surfing, and a rather familiar close up of his handsome face.

My boss stuck his head in the room at this point and said a collective "are you winning?" His timing was immaculate. As the realisation sunk in that I most definitely wasn't winning, I began to wonder how this could have happened. It wasn't as if I didn't know who Mark Philippoussis was. I'd just never seen him without a tennis racket in his hand and wearing whites. Jake had seemed so real. So believable. I pictured him now – a sad, geeky loser in a trailer park whose only chance of marital bliss was to wed his cousin.

I wanted the ground to swallow me up. To make matters worse, everyone in the office knew and judging by the hysterics going on, it had made their day. Would I ever live this down? I looked up mortified in the dictionary and it didn't even come close to how I was feeling. No more heart flutters when I looked in my inbox and no visit from the American dream. I couldn't believe I'd fallen for it.

Humiliation turned to anger, which soon subsided when I logged back on to Digital-Cupid. I clicked on his profile to look over the evidence and he'd added another picture since my last visit. Mark Philippoussis getting out of a Ferrari wearing a pair of bright white trainers. Caption: *'Me in my new sneakers.'* I decided that whether Lisa had intervened or not, that would have been it. I couldn't possibly go out with someone who used the word sneakers so proudly.

Reluctantly, I began to see the funny side. Well I didn't have much choice. I'd been well and truly had, but that was no reason not to send my daily email to 'Jake'.

| From: | jo-to-go | To: | Jake_1970 |
|---|---|---|---|
| Subject: | Strawberries & Cream? | Date: | 27.02.02 |

Morning!

How are you today? I'm feeling great and I can't stop thinking about your visit. I'm so excited!

I've told my friends all about you and I think they're looking forward to meeting you as much as I am. I showed a couple of them your pictures and they thought they recognised you.

I guess you'll be over around June then will you? Would you like to stay at my place? I'm literally down the road from Wimbledon and my one bed flat is very cosy. I could help you with your backhand if you like, and perhaps you could serve me up a couple of aces in return. You never know, the score could reach love all.

Let me know what you think. Anything I can do to make your stay in London as comfortable as possible will be my pleasure. Could I just ask one favour of you though? Do you think you could arrange for me to meet Sir Cliff?

Thanks,
Steffi xxx

# six

## *A bit of a conundrum*

By now my initial thoughts about the kind of man looking for love on the internet were well and truly confirmed. What with Tom Evans and his amazing disappearing act, followed by the Mark Philippoussis tribute show, I was beginning to think I'd joined the circus.

The thing was, I was intrigued and I lived in hope. Jane's friend was still with her man and they'd just got engaged. She'd met him on Digital-Cupid. Proof it *can* happen. What if the love of my life was winging his way into my inbox that very minute? I was compelled to keep checking those messages. The thrill of what I might find was like an adrenaline rush. Usually quickly extinguished the minute I logged on, but compulsive nonetheless.

---

| From: JOHN_SINCLAIR | To: jo-to-go |
| --- | --- |
| Subject: HI | Date: 06.03.02 |

MY NAME IS JOHN IM 36 AND HAVE A BOY CALLED
JAYSON I AM HAPPY WITH MY LIFE BUT NEED TO
SHARE IT WITH SOMEONE I WORK HARD AND PLAY
HARD AND WANT TOO MEET AN ATTRACTIVE
PERSON WITH LONG HAIR TOO SPOIL AND HAVE
FUN WITH IF YOUR INTERESTED LET ME NO
JOHN

---

I was interested alright. Interested to know where the full-stop key had gone on John's keyboard.

| From: | hanky_panky | To: | jo-to-go |
|-------|-------------|-----|----------|
| Subject: | Hi!!!!!!! | Date: | 06.03.02. |

Hey good looking! What you got cooking?!! I'm Barry, 49 year old carpenter from Swindon. I love Swindon football club, my 3 kids and my mum – in that order! LOL.

How was your weekend? Mine was fantastic!! Went out dancing, got lashed and ended up on the karaoke!!! This weeks aim is to get drunker than last week – LOL!!! Hopefully with you as I reckon you're my perfect woman. Hope you agree.

Barry xxx

Sorry Baz, but this week I will be mostly sticking pins in my eyes.

| From: | Up4it | To: | jo-to-go |
|-------|-------|-----|----------|
| Subject: | Wow!!!! | Date: | 08.03.02 |

Hi Jo-to-go,

How are you this fine day? When I seen your profile I was surprised your single coz you look very pleasing to the eye indeed.

About me, I love kissing (with tongues) and I like women that smell nice. I can't stand bad breath, thongs with skids in, or mutton dressed as lamb. I don't like people that chat shite either. Drop me a line – this could be your lucky day. I'm a diamond geezer – straight down the line.

Bill

Gosh. Bill sure had a way with words. I could hardly hold myself back.

| From: | monkeyboy | To: | jo-to-go |
|---|---|---|---|
| Subject: Welcome to my world! | | Date: 11.03.02. | |

Hi Jo, Hows you?

33 year old virgin here (not including dead animals and ladyboys LOL!!!). I'm successful and clever with a very warped sense of humour and I'm up for anything. When was the last time YOU set fire to your pubes? LOL!!!!

If you like the sound of me and fancy FUN FUN FUN, get in touch and let me entertain you!

Luv n laughs!

Graham :)

---

When was the last time I set fire to my pubes? I couldn't remember to be honest. They all merged into one...

---

| From: | Frodo-fan | To: | jo-to-go |
|---|---|---|---|
| Subject: Hello Jo | | Date: 12.03.02 | |

I saw your profile and I think we go well together.

I am 36 years of age and live in Luton (not Luton airport though – LOL). I am 5'7" and I think you'll agree, really nice looking. I have a good lifestyle. I just bought my own house which I have been renting off the council for 16 years. I work for the post office and like reading all the Harry Potter books and Lord of the Rings. I am really into Dungeons & Dragons and my hobby is going away on weekends in forests where we dress up and do role play.

I enjoy eating out. There is a Harvester near me and I eat there at least once a week as I think it's lovely and I'm addicted to the scampi. Anyway – it would be great to hear back from you and hopefully arrange to meet for a dinner. I could come into London or you can come to Luton – I don't mind which. Speak soon.

Rod x.

Well that was something to look forward to. Dinner for two at the Harvester in Luton with Role-play Rod.

---

| From: | Bruce_53 | To: | jo-to-go |
|---|---|---|---|
| Subject: Hello Jo | | Date: | 14.03.02 |

How are you?

My name is Bruce. I am 53. I am 5 foot 7 inches tall and of medium build. I like playing badminton, going to the cinema and eating out. My hobbies are keeping fit, computers and reading about medicine and astronomy. I am a non-smoker and non-drinker.

I live in Essex which is just outside east London. I am a Chartered Accountant and I am English. I separated from my ex-wife in 1997 and I have been divorced for about four years.

I have one brother who is older than me and is married with one son and one daughter and also lives in Essex. I am serious about finding a relationship. Please contact me soon as I think we have a lot in common and could be good for each other.

Bruce.

---

Well they say you learn something new every day. Today I learned where Essex is.

———— ❤ ————

I've often wondered where the writers of soaps get their inspiration from. Some of the characters are so implausible, I never thought such people could possibly exist. But I'd been living in my own world, with my own people. I was beginning to realise that there were other worlds, with other people. Strange people. Maybe some of those soap characters were more realistic than I thought. Finally someone from my world showed up.

| From: | pauls_alright | To: | jo-to-go |
|---|---|---|---|
| Subject: | Jeeeezuz | Date: | 30.04.02 |

Hurrah. Like your style! Someone normal. I'm in the west end too by the way. What are you doing on here?

Paul

---

I realised it tended to be the ones that didn't write a waffling life story that caught my eye. I looked at Paul's profile. All present and correct. He was a writer. His profile was very witty and his picture was nice too. He wasn't posing in his boxer shorts or flexing his muscles. He was sitting at a bar, drinking a pint of beer and looking pretty normal.

| From: | jo-to-go | To: | pauls_alright |
|---|---|---|---|
| Subject: | Re: Jeeeezuz | Date: | 30.04.02 |

I'm not actually sure what I'm doing here. I ask myself that most days and I never get an answer. I think I'm waiting for something exciting to happen. Are you it?
What are you doing here?

| From: | pauls_alright | To: | jo-to-go |
|---|---|---|---|
| Subject: | Re: Jeeeezuz | Date: | 30.04.02 |

I'm just prostituting myself for kicks. It's actually pretty appalling so far. Have you met anyone in the flesh yet?

Paul

| From: | jo-to-go | To: | pauls_alright |
|---|---|---|---|
| Subject: | Re: Jeeeezuz | Date: | 30.04.02 |

I met one. But it turned out he was from a different planet. What about you? Been on any dates?

| From: | pauls_alright | To: | jo-to-go |
|---|---|---|---|
| Subject: | Re: Jeeeez | Date: | 30.04.02 |

I've met a couple of people. But they were from other planets as well. One was from planet lard, and the other from the planet of the apes. I'm constantly amazed. You appear to be more human than most.

My virtual rapport with Paul was instant. He was funny, sarcastic and on my wavelength. It seemed he had brains too. Apparently he'd won *Countdown* a few years earlier. Either that or his photoshop skills were very good as he sent me a fetching snap of him, Carol Vorderman and Richard Whiteley, flanked by a complete set of Encyclopedia Britannica.

I started to look forward to his messages. I was well aware of the fact that he could be anyone, but for now he was Paul the freelance journalist who was getting articles published, but struggling to make a living. I asked him what he lived on, which is when he told me about his day job.

| From: | Paul-Lovely | To: | jo-to-go |
|---|---|---|---|
| Subject: | Re: Jeeeez | Date: | 03.05.02 |

I'm the editor of a low rent porn mag. Does that bother you?

Well I wasn't expecting that. I was a bit surprised to say the least. I'd never met anyone from the porn industry before, but it didn't bother me. Actually, it intrigued me. I used it as the perfect opportunity to ask the questions I'd always wondered about such as *'why do they have to censor that orifice and not that one?'* And *'is that stuff real or do they put it on afterwards?'* It was fascinating and I learned a lot. He said I could go on a photoshoot with him sometime if I wanted. I declined and said a drink would be fine, but a porn shoot was pushing it.

| From: | pauls_alright | To: | jo-to-go |
|---|---|---|---|
| Subject: Re: Jeeeez | | Date: 10.05.02 | |

OK. Lets live dangerously. I dare you to sneak out of work for half an hour. It's 3 o'clock on Friday afternoon. Who cares? We're 10 minutes apart. Lets meet for a quick drink. Now. All Bar One. Cambridge Circus.

He was probably right. No-one would notice if I disappeared for half an hour. It felt right that we should meet, but I was still very wary. He would be my second 'eyeball'. And coincidentally, almost a year to the day after my first. If I thought about it for too long I'd find an excuse not to go. I decided to bite the bullet.

| From: | jo-to-go | To: | pauls_alright |
|---|---|---|---|
| Subject: Re: Jeeeezuz | | Date: 10.05.02 | |

What the hell. I'm on my way. See you there in 5 minutes.

"I'm just nipping to the bank," I mumbled to no-one in particular.

I put my coat on and ran down the stairs, stopping in the toilet to look in the mirror. I had a strategically placed spot in the middle of my forehead that looked like a bindi. I tried in vain to cover it, realised there was nothing I could do, and headed outside towards Charing Cross Road. I thought spots were meant to disappear with your youth?

I didn't have time to panic or change my mind, and I was in the bar in less than ten minutes. I couldn't see Paul though. It suddenly dawned on me that I might not recognise him easily because, on his Digital-Cupid picture, some of his face was obscured by his pint glass. There was always the *Countdown* picture but that was years old. Then someone at the bar gestured me over and I realised it was him. He was already halfway through a pint of lager.

Thirsty work this internet dating. My immediate thought was 'you don't look at all like I imagined'. There was nothing wrong with him. He just didn't look like the picture I had in my head. He was taller, more broad and paler skinned. He also looked more serious (or perhaps disappointed). I wondered if I looked anything like the image in his head.

He stood up to greet me. A strong sense of unease surrounded us as he asked what I wanted to drink.

"Gin and tonic please," I said, and willed it to arrive as fast as possible. There was a rather awkward silence, followed by the exchanging of niceties and the over-riding feeling that neither of us could wait to get away. I must have sunk that G&T quicker than you can say conundrum. And it was a large one.

"Do you want another one?" I asked, sure he'd decline.

"Go on then," he replied.

I wasn't sure about dating etiquette these days. Not that this was your average date. Well, it was quite average so far come to think of it. And very quick. Had we invented a new concept in Speed Dating? I liked the idea of this. Perfect for the chemistry-free couple on an internet gamble. We left the pub within fifteen minutes of arriving and as we said goodbye on the street corner, Paul handed me a large plastic bag.

"Here you go," he said. "Thought you might want these."

"Hey?"

"There's a few things in there to keep you entertained."

"What is it?" I asked, bemused as I opened the bag and looked inside.

"Samples!" he shouted as he turned on his heels and headed down Shaftesbury Avenue.

The bag, I discovered, was full of hardcore porn and sex aids (still boxed). I contemplated life for a moment. I never expected mine to be like this. Meeting strangers on seedy Soho street corners to be given bags of porn. My parents appeared in my mind and they were shaking their heads. I couldn't work out whether it was deeply repugnant, or bloody hilarious. It must have been the latter because I couldn't stop laughing as I made my way back to work. Should I send an all-staffer like they do when there's left-over sandwiches after a meeting? *"Explicit porn and sex toys on my desk if anybody wants them..."*

I was still laughing with disbelief when I walked in the office and presented my colleagues with some very early Christmas presents. There were a few strange looks but the blokes thought I was the best thing since sliced bread. Apparently you couldn't get some of those magazines in this country. And as for the DVDs...

---

❤

---

Come Monday morning it was all a bit of a blur. I wasn't sure if that was the two double G&T's in quick succession followed by a heavy weekend, or the whole experience. I hadn't really thought any more about Paul. He was a nice bloke, but I suspected he didn't fancy me and I was pretty certain I felt the same. Then I got an email from him, confirming my suspicions.

| From: | pauls_alright | To: | jo-to-go |
|---|---|---|---|
| Subject: | Nice... | Date: | 13.05.02 |

... to meet you on Friday, but I thought it was a no, and I think you did too.

Paul

I hadn't completely decided that, but I guess he'd done it for me which was fair enough. I replied thanking him for the kind gifts and wishing him luck for the future.

But that wasn't the last I heard of Porno Paul. A couple of weeks later I got a phone call from Lucy.

"Guess what?" she gushed. "I've just been to lunch with this bloke called Paul from Digital-Cupid."

"Yeah. How was it?" I asked. "Do you think you'll see him again?"

"I think so. He was a nice guy. But Jo! You'll never guess what he does for a living!"

"Errrm... he's not the editor of a porn mag by any chance is he?" I stole her thunder.

"Yeah. How did you know?"

Small world, the virtual one. I told Lucy the story of my date with Porno Paul and the loot I'd come away with. Lucy, it transpired, had come away empty handed, but with the prospect of a second date. I guess it was a matter of opinion as to who'd got the booby prize. Me or her?

# seven

## *Little Lord Fauntleroy*

---

### *Digital-**Cupid*** ♥

Hi jo-to-go! Great news! Several men are
looking to meet someone just like you!
Here are some of their details for your perusal.
Could one of them be the man of your dreams?

---

BRAD-ALIKE is 39 and lives in the north east.
He describes himself as very attractive. He is
approximately 6ft and weighs 180 lbs. BRAD-ALIKE
has brown hair, blue eyes and has one or more tatoos.
You are currently number 4 in BRAD-ALIKE's list of
desirable women.

---

SLK-DRIVER is 34 and lives in Greater London.
He describes himself as stunning. He is approximately
5ft 6 in. tall and weighs 175 lbs. SLK-DRIVER has
receding hair and brown eyes. He wears glasses
and does not smoke. SLK-DRIVER takes pride in his
appearance and is spontaneous, passionate and
sexy. He enjoys the cinema, drinking in bars and
curry. Good news! SLK-DRIVER is online right now!

---

MC UNDRESS is 32 and lives in the West Midlands.
He describes himself as attractive. He is approximately

5ft 11in. tall and weighs 190 lbs. <u>MC UNDRESS</u> has a shaved head and hazel eyes. He wants to meet women between the ages of 18 and 45. He is looking for fun. He smokes and has three or more piercings.

Hold me back! I couldn't contain my excitement as I logged on to read my new messages. If these credentials were anything to go by, there were fun times ahead.

| From: | Imran | To: | jo-to-go |
|---|---|---|---|
| Subject: greetings from Egypt | | Date: | 04.06.02 |

Where to start with such a special beauty queen? I am egyptian businessman, I lives between london and egypt. I am 43 year old, 177 cm, black hair and with average body. I am a man that you can really trust, romantic and have a lot sence of humer, and very stylish.

Please let us keep the rest down to chemistry and communications. Would you please send me picturs. Really you are the person I have been looking for. I will be cunting the stars, waiting for you reply.

Imran

P.S. I can gives you cash

| From: | PlayStation | To: | jo-to-go |
|---|---|---|---|
| Subject: Happy? | | Date: | 07.06.02 |

Hi there. My name is Ian. I'm 45, single and live in London. I have greyish hair, and am an average build, and 5ft 9 and a half inches tall.

I'm on here to find a serious relationship, not a happy-go-lucky sponge with no commitment. I'm not very sporty or fit, but I don't mind if you go to the gym. I need someone to love, but they need to be able to to entertain themselves sometimes coz I can't be there 24/7.

I also want to make a difference to the world and am looking for someone to help me do that. In my spare time I like watching sitcoms and action movies.

I do not have mind reading skills, so I'd prefer it if you just said when I make you happy and when/if I don't.

Ian

---

No need for mind-reading skills with me Ian. Let me spell it out for you: NO CHANCE.

---

| From: KINKYGUY | To: jo-to-go |
|---|---|
| Subject: Are you kinky? | Date: 10.06.02 |

I know the subject heading is a bit direct, but I ain't into beating about the bush. No point kidding anyone I'm here for marriage when I'm not. I'm happy being single, got plenty of friends and I like my own company.

I get my share of offers from women believe me, but it aint just about looks for me. Looks are important to a degree but I'm more after a girl who's a bit kinky. If you wanna know more, write back.

Dx

---

Computer says no...

---

| From: Wildbeast | To: jo-to-go |
|---|---|
| Subject: <none> | Date: 18.06.02 |

Hi babe. Do you want dinner for 2? For desert we can have a bottle of champaine in the jacuzi and I'll hit you wit my magic stick! I'm a carefree black guy with a bouncers build, sexy bum, 9 inches uncut.

I know how to enjoy myself and can show you a good time. Friends say i look like 50 cent. Get back to me and maybe we can go for that dinner. You won't regret it.

---

| From: Funtime-Frankie | To: jo-to-go |
|---|---|
| Subject: Wanted! FUN!!!! | Date: 28.06.02 |

I absolutely love your profile!!!!!! I'm a fun loving chap who's been working in the entertainment industry for the last 15... oh my god has it been that long!!!!! Just finished on the cruise ships and settling back to life off the ocean wave! LOL!!

I live in Kent but I'm in London loads as I just LOVE musicals!!!! I think I've seen them all and I'm starting from the beginning again!!! Mamma Mia is my favourite ever!!! I love cooking and my fave pudding is lemon merangue pie!!! Just one nibble and I'm all yours! LOL!! I do hate talking about myself but seeing as you ask...!!! I'm tall, slim and athletic, cheeky, oh – and modest too!!!! tee hee!!! : )

Why am I here I hear you say!!!??? Well, we're here for a good time, not a long time!!! And I am such a nosey parker. I love to find out about people. I'd love to find out more about you Jo, so yes – it's your lucky day!!!!! LOL.

Hope to chat soon!!!!!! I'm waiting!!!!!

Funtime Frankie xxx

---

Funtime-Frankie was clearly way too much fun for me. Punctuation is a wonderful thing, but there's a time and place for it. Instead of getting my pulse racing, my messages just made me laugh. Who'd have thought that joining a dating site could provide so much amusement? There was one message that stuck out. Probably because it didn't involve body parts, desperation or bad punctuation.

| From: Trust-Fund-Baby | To: jo-to-go |
|---|---|
| Subject: Hi Jo... | Date: 03.07.02 |

I liked your profile. Somehow it stood out from the others. Have a look at mine and see what you think.

Luke.

I liked his handle. I thought Trust-Fund-Baby was quite funny. Obviously anyone who was one wouldn't have been shouting it from the rooftops. He was no doubt just as skint as the rest of us. He looked attractive in his pictures, with wavy black hair and blue eyes, so I had a look at his profile and took down his particulars. He was 24 years-old and 5ft 8. Far too young and only an inch taller than me, but an inch all the same. Despite these fundamental flaws, for some unknown reason I responded to his message asking what an attractive young man like him was doing in a place like this. He told me he found girls his own age immature. Said he met them all the time but they just wanted him for his money and looks. I wondered whether he was taking the Trust Fund Baby thing a bit too far.

| From: jo-to-go | To: Trust-Fund-Baby |
|---|---|
| Subject: Re: Hi Jo... | Date: 10.07.02 |

So the girls all want you for your money. Lucky you!
How come you're so loaded at 24?

| From: Trust-Fund-Baby | To: jo-to-go |
|---|---|
| Subject: Re: Hi Jo... | Date: 10.07.02 |

And looks. But I don't like talking about it to be honest.

Could have fooled me. But I assumed he was joking. No-one was that conceited were they?

| From: jo-to-go | To: Trust-Fund-Baby |
|---|---|
| Subject: Re: Hi Jo... | Date: 10.07.02 |

And rightly so. So what's the real story? Renting a room in a flatshare because you can't afford to live in London, like most people?

He insisted it was true and went on to tell me how he was voted the UK's 76th most eligible bachelor in a magazine last year. He had to be winding me up. I asked him what he was doing on an internet dating site if he was such a fabulous catch and he told me to look it up if I didn't believe him. I did, but it didn't go as high as 76.

I wouldn't normally have carried on conversing with someone with such an obviously large head, let alone agree to go out with them, but I was intrigued. And despite sounding like a pretentious idiot at first, he somehow reeled me in.

Luke lived in Richmond and worked for a publishing company in Kensington. Was it the family business? Perhaps the trust fund hadn't kicked in yet. After a while, I started to look forward to hearing from him because strangely, he made me laugh (admittedly I wasn't sure if it was with him or at him at first). Apart from telling me about his newly landscaped garden and his brand new Mercedes convertible, he didn't go on about his so-called wealth too much.

We exchanged emails for a few weeks and it seemed that aside from my initial doubts about his status, we did have a few things in common. Most of the time he was down to earth and funny in a subtle kind of way. And according to him, at 24 he was ready to meet someone and settle down. We spoke on the phone a few times. He was well spoken but his voice was quite shaky. It had probably only just broken. Anyway, we struck up an unlikely friendship and without warning I was alarmed to find I suddenly had feelings for virtual Luke. So when he said we should meet for a drink one night after work, I readily agreed and suggested he could pick me up in his Merc. He said he got the train to work.

We arranged to meet outside Henry's bar near Green Park at seven o'clock. It was a warm Thursday night in late August, and strolling down Piccadilly I felt nervous about meeting Luke, my third internet eyeball. As I crossed the road just after the Ritz, wondering why he hadn't suggested going there, I couldn't see him waiting outside Henry's. And I was late. What if he wasn't going to turn up? Or maybe he was watching me from behind a pillar somewhere? I casually played with my phone for couple of minutes before deciding to call him.

"Hi. I'm here. Where are you?" I asked.

"Sorry," he sounded breathless. "Left work a bit late. Nearly there. Just gone past Boots. I think I can see you. Are you wearing a red top?"

I looked to the left.

"Yes. I can't see you though. What are you wearing?"

"Lilac shirt. Cream trousers," he said.

I could see someone in a lilac shirt and cream trousers walking towards me. He was carrying a tan leather bag. Not really a briefcase, but a bag. With a shoulder strap. And he was talking on a mobile phone. He was getting nearer and he was looking at me in a familiar way and smiling. The whole thing seemed to be happening in slow motion. I recognised the wavy black hair and the blue eyes. He stopped in front of me. All 5ft nothing of him.

"Hi!" He grinned expectantly, exposing the best advert for a trip to the dentist I'd ever seen.

My heart sank. Illusions shattered in a split second. This wasn't the person in the profile. The one I'd been corresponding with for the last few weeks. Well it certainly wasn't the person in my head. I felt cheated instantly. He'd deliberately misled me. I could run, I thought, but it's too late to hide. And did he deserve that just because he was vertically challenged and sporting a pair of fangs? But we were meeting on the basis of a possible romance. Millions of thoughts bombarded me. I had the time it took for the doors to revolve to make up my mind. Oh god.

———❤———

"After you!" he gestured, still grinning. Did he honestly think I hadn't noticed the blatant eight-inch lie?

I managed to muster a false smile as he lead the way to an empty table. I wondered what would be an acceptable amount of time to hang around. Half an hour? An hour? You never know, I told myself in an attempt at being positive. It might be fun. I hoped against hope that he didn't like me. Then we could breathe a collective sigh of relief, safe in the knowledge that our six-week virtual relationship had culminated in total anti-climax.

The waitress came over and took our order. "Large red wine please," I said. That should dull the disappointment.

Luke ordered a beer. I imagined a little chap like him would probably be hammered after that. While we waited for the drinks to arrive, he put his man bag on the table and started rooting around in it with a perplexed look on his face.

"Are you OK?" I asked, keen to make conversation.

"Hold on..." he answered "Just want to prove something to you."

I wondered if he was looking for a magic tape measure, but was surprised when he pulled out a set of car keys.

"See!" he said triumphantly. "I do drive a Mercedes."

I wasn't sure how to react. Should I stand up and applaud? Or perhaps throw my arms round him and say "hooray! I don't care that you're a little liar. You drive a Mercedes!"

If only I'd had my car keys with me. I could have got them out to prove I drive a Renault Clio. Thank God the waitress arrived when she did because I thought I was going to die of discomfort.

After a fabulous cringe-worthy start and two large glasses of red, things didn't look quite so bad. Luke was a nice enough person, but with a warped view of his own self-importance. I quickly came to the conclusion that he was hiding a massive inferiority complex under his lilac shirt. I asked him about the trust fund again.

"I can't tell you," he said.

"Why not? Is it another lie?" I said, unexpectedly.

"What?" he looked shocked.

I'm not sure he heard me right. If he did, he pretended he hadn't. I had every right to take him to task for lying about his height, but I didn't have the heart. I could either get through the evening and I'd never have to see him again, or I could hurt his feelings by explaining that dwarves with bad teeth just don't do it for me.

"Look. I just can't tell you about it," he said.

"Hey?" I was confused. "So you're the lucky recipient of a trust fund, but you can't tell anyone how, or where, it came from. Sounds a bit dodgy to me," I pointed out. By now he was getting irate.

"Can we change the subject please?" he said petulantly. "Let's go for something to eat. Are you hungry?"

I was actually. And after a third large glass of wine I thought it was probably a good idea. I could have made a hasty exit at this point, but perversely, I was starting to enjoy myself.

We left Henry's and headed back towards Piccadilly Circus. I felt a bit wobbly when the air hit me. Eating was definitely a good idea. I wondered if Luke was going to suggest the Ivy. No doubt he could wave his car keys and get the best table. No such luck. We found ourselves in Chinatown in a "great little restaurant" where he proceeded to take control of the food order because he'd been to China when he was twelve and was an authority on Oriental cuisine. That was fine by me. I was in the mood to throw caution to the wind and try something different to my usual lemon chicken. I took care of the drinks. A large glass of Chinese restaurant house red for me and a Tiger beer for Luke. I couldn't believe he was still standing, but then I was drinking two to his one.

I saw glimpses of the virtual Luke every now and again. It may have been the wine, but when he stopped trying to prove himself, he was fine. And he looked just like his photo when he was sitting down with his mouth closed. It was amazing how his image had been distorted via email and one big fat lie. I wondered what he thought about me. I couldn't tell one way or the other how he thought it was going.

The food arrived. Lots of boiled onions and red peppers, with the odd piece of meat thrown in. I wasn't complaining.

It filled a hole. After we'd eaten, Luke said he'd take me to a "cool little bar" he knew. I really should have gone home at this point but I think he must have put something in my prawn crackers because I was happy to carry on, blissfully unaware of the hole I was digging. I wondered where we were going as we made our way down Charing Cross Road. An exclusive members bar perhaps?

"Let's climb on the lions!" I exclaimed as we got to Trafalgar Square. Why I thought it was a good idea to climb a London landmark late at night whilst under the influence I'm not quite sure.

"You're mad. I'm not going up there," argued Luke. But I was already on my way.

"Come on shorty – I'll give you a leg up!" I yelled. Oops. I might have overstepped the mark there but he didn't say anything. Well, what could he say? Reluctantly he joined me on the plinth. He looked terrified as we surveyed London with all its lights. It would have been so romantic had I not been with Little Lord Fauntleroy.

We went to Gordon's. The dingy little bar that he, and everyone else knew. Much as I love Gordon's, I began to wonder why I hadn't taken the earlier opportunity to go home. My carefree mood was slowly waning and I was conscious we had a table for two in a candle-lit corner and Luke was folding his arms and leaning towards me.

"You're crazy," he said, staring at me with sparkling blue eyes and a shit-eating grin. "But I like you."

Oh no. Was he getting romantic on me? As I tried to think of something to say in return, like "thanks but I don't feel the same and I never will", he swooped in and locked his lips on mine. Rather than pull back and shriek in horror, I had a momentary lapse of reason and returned the kiss. It just seemed like the easiest thing to do. As his fangs banged against my teeth for several seconds, I wondered how on earth I was going to dig myself out of the crater I now found myself in. Should I assume unconsciousness? Or just go along with it and have a relationship with the bloke rather than hurt his feelings?

"I don't feel too well. I think I need to go home..." I finally announced.

"No problem," he said lovingly. "Let's get a cab."

Thank god for that, I thought, oblivious to what he meant by "let's". We left our drinks and stumbled up the stairs and onto the Strand. I really did feel queasy and I just wanted to get home as quickly as possible. Luke flagged down a cab and I thanked him for a 'lovely' evening and got in. I was surprised when he got in with me. Then I assumed he was going on to Richmond, which I guess made sense. I just wanted this evening to end *now*. I would tell him the coward's way, via email, that we didn't have a future.

He put his arm round me but I was too tired to care. When the cab pulled up at the end of my road I was so pleased to be home I practically fell out of it. My bed wasn't just calling me, it was positively screaming my name. But as I fumbled with my purse to pay the fare, the cab drove off, minus Luke.

"What are you doing?" I asked him, suddenly feeling very sober. "I thought you lived in Richmond?"

"What?" he said, looking totally bemused.

"Why did you get out here?" I said, the penny finally dropping.

"Why do you think?" he replied haughtily.

My patience was wearing thin now, and not hurting his feelings was fast becoming less of a priority. I should have legged it outside Henry's when I had the chance.

"You can't stay here," I said with disbelief at the fact that he clearly thought he could.

"I beg your pardon?" he spat. Was I not making myself clear or something?

"How dare you treat me like this?" he added.

"Like what?"

"God, you're a prick tease," he told me. "I thought we were getting on fine. You seemed to be enjoying yourself anyway. Especially in Gordon's."

"What?!" I almost laughed. Which planet was he on?

"And now you've dragged me all the way back here under some pretence," he continued. "How dare you treat me like this?"

Was this really happening? Someone wake me up from this nightmare. It was nearly one o'clock in the morning and this poor little rich boy was having a tantrum in my street.

"I never asked you to come here. I thought we were just sharing a cab," I told him. "I said I wanted to go home. I didn't ask you to come with me."

"Well that's not what it looked like to me," he yelled. "You've just *used* me tonight. I've never been treated so badly in my life."

Lucky you, I thought, unable to understand exactly what crime I'd committed, other than to drink too much wine.

The whole thing was surreal and I was in danger of telling him what I really thought, but I still couldn't. It would have scarred him for life. So I turned to walk away and my 'relationship' with Luke culminated with him huffily throwing his man bag (with Mercedes keys) over his shoulder and storming into the night in an absolute rage.

Once he was out of view, I ran home as fast as I could and collapsed into bed, vowing never to drink wine on a date again. That's if I could bring myself to go on a date ever again after this ordeal. I'd have to be more careful. Let's face it – the clues had been there at the beginning. I'd just chosen to ignore them.

# eight

## *If at first you don't succeed...*

After a while I realised I couldn't let the poisoned dwarf put me off. Internet dating was a learning curve. I decided that as my date with him had probably been the worst date in the history of dating (well, my history), things could only get better. However, I was reminded that it wasn't quite so simple when I revisited my inbox.

| From: | Happy_Chappy | To: | jo-to-go |
|---|---|---|---|
| Subject: hiya! | | Date: | 05.09.02 |

First off, I keep getting messages from guys! I don't know why! I don't mind them checking out my pics but I must stress – I am not a bummer! I'm here to find a lovely girl and you look just the ticket. I'm well educated and love a political argument. And I usually win – LOL!

You won't need to house train me coz I already put the lid down on the bog and the cap on the toothpaste! LOL! I'm quite up for meeting an older girl like you, but I dont want a pensioner!!! I have a wide taste in music. Anything from Shania Twain to Westlife to Guns n Roses.

I take pride in my appearance. I'm mad for Calvin Klein. I don't wear any other pants and I like the waistband to show so people know I don't shop down the market!

Penny Smith is my ideal women and if I was a car I'd be

a Mercedes SL Sports with alloy wheels and ergonomic seats. I love going out, but don't mind a night in with a bottle of German wine and a good film. Look forward to hearing back from you.

Lee. x

Penny would be flattered. Clearly a man of impeccable taste and contradiction. German cars and German wine. Too high a spec for a merlot-drinking Clio driver like myself.

| From: | Personal_Slave | To: | jo-to-go |
|---|---|---|---|
| Subject: An offer you can't refuse? | | Date: | 23.09.02 |

I loved your profile and photo and I would like to dedicate myself to YOU. I am a submissive looking for a superior and beautiful Lady to control and own me.

I would love the opportunity to pamper You. Run a bath when You get in from work, serve You wine, cook your meals, wash up, then worship every inch of You. I am very successful, intelligent & confident. I'm based mostly in Coventry, but would be prepared to give up all my free time to be at Your beck and call.

Since being introduced to my submissive side, I realise that my role in life is to serve. I have a high pain threshold and am pleased to be marked and humiliated for Your pleasure. I am not interested in a straight relationship and I think about submission all day. My wish in life is to follow my desire to serve. I beg You to consider me for any way in which I can serve You. I assure You that I am 100% genuine and will not waste your valuable time.

Humble regards
Slave Stephen

Hmmm, hang on a moment. Let me think... "Run me a bath Slave Stephen..."

Having thought about it for three seconds I decided the dominatrix role wasn't for me. Nope. Best I continue in my search for a common or garden bloke.

| From: Richee_Rich | To: jo-to-go |
|---|---|
| Subject: Hey Jo, | Date: 02.10.02 |
| I'd like to sweep you off your feet – got a dustpan? | |

Richee_Rich, it transpired was a down to earth guy who'd travelled, lived in my vicinity and had a decent job. His picture was slightly pixelated but he was definitely the best prospect for a while, so I responded. Banter started flowing straight away and when the question arose as to what we were doing on an internet dating site, we both made light of it and insisted we were just curious. Neither of us admitting to the secret hope that we might really meet someone in this virtual meat market. Could this be it?

A week later, he invited me to his house warming party. It was fancy dress and the theme was Jimmy Savile. When I'd finished laughing at the prospect of meeting a prospective date dressed in a shiny tracksuit, jingly-jangly jewellery and a dodgy wig, I declined the invitation. I told him I'd be happy to meet under more conventional circumstances, so we arranged to meet in a pub. I wasn't nervous. It would be a breeze. Rich seemed easy-going and obviously had a sense of humour.

As it turned out, I was wrong (again). Rich only had a virtual personality, which shut down with his computer. I bought the first drinks and tried to make conversation. He was more interested in peeling off his Bud label. I then sat with an empty glass for twenty minutes before reminding him it was his round. Chemistry is a very powerful thing. It was clear we had none, so when could I leave?

❤

There were plenty of new and exciting opportunities landing in my inbox. Next up was Simon. He sounded nice and his picture was even nicer – 6ft 3, lived in Southgate, worked in the city and no sign of a tash. We only corresponded for a couple of days online before swapping phone numbers. What had happened to the overly cautious Jo who was never going to meet anyone from the internet? I was fast becoming a dab hand at this.

We arranged to meet in a pub near Liverpool Street. I was kind of immune to the nerves now and getting my hair done specially was a thing of the past. Everyone in the pub looked the same – suit and tie, holding a pint. Not what you need when you're on a semi-blind date. It was only when he whistled from the other side of the bar and followed it up with "over 'ere Jo", that myself and the rest of the pub clocked him.

Although Simon's photos were definitely genuine, once again, in reality he hardly resembled them at all. I'd come to understand how much a bit of movement changes someone's appearance. And not always for the good. Give him a chance, I thought. Don't judge a book by its cover.

"What's yer poison?" he asked, after greeting me with an over-familiar kiss on the lips.

"I'll have a gin and tonic please."

He got the drinks and we stayed where we were. Standing at the bar with all the other geezers. I couldn't get a word in edgeways as Simon proceeded to tell me all about himself in the manner of a stand-up comedian.

He'd started out as a shoplifter, but he'd come a long way since his days as a juvenile delinquent. He used to have a problem with alcohol but he had it under control now. Yes, he had a drink every day and thought it "rude not to have a beer for breakfast", but he knew when to stop. He could still get drunk without being an alcoholic and at least he wasn't doing the charlie anymore.

He worked in the back-room of some financial house and he was proud of his job in the city and his studio flat in

Southgate. Proud that he'd dragged himself away from a possible life of crime, and even more proud, it seemed, that his boss was oblivious to the fact that he was half-cut most of time. He was positively "crazy".

Congratulations, I thought, but you're not really selling yourself. He hadn't sounded like this on the phone. Or had I not listened, too busy focusing on the 6ft 3 and the attractive picture on his profile? I couldn't endure a whole evening of it. I managed three drinks before coming down with a sudden headache. I blamed it on the pollen count despite it being November. Simon didn't notice.

"I'm taking tablets for it and I'm not really supposed to be drinking," I lied.

"Not a problem," he assured me as he downed his pint in one. He'd been too busy talking about himself to notice that the yawn factor was so high I was nearly asleep.

"I'll give you a call sometime," he said as we left the pub. With that, he did a 360-degree spin on his snakeskin-clad heels before pointing at me and swaggering off down the street. The only thing missing was a cane and trilby.

———❤———

I began to wonder about the internet again. Obviously it was too easy to misjudge people. To build up an image of Brad Pitt, only to be presented in real life with the pits. If I met these guys in a bar I wouldn't look twice. I wouldn't look once to be honest. But hope springs eternal and with all those messages landing in my inbox, temptation was never far away. Plus, I was on a roll now. Why quit when you're not ahead?

Adrian was a producer on a cable TV show I'd never heard of. His picture was by no means gorgeous, but that meant nothing by now. He probably didn't resemble it one iota anyway. And using reverse psychology for a moment, perhaps it meant he was gorgeous in real life.

Again we had the basic stuff in common. And by

coincidence, we'd also lived in Sydney at the same time and celebrated Christmas Day on Bondi Beach in '92. I scoured my photos one evening to see if I could spot him. Not very likely amongst ten thousand lager-swilling backpackers doing the conga, but worth a shot.

He asked me if I fancied exchanging some digits, which I gathered was TV speak for "can I have your number?" So I obliged and we arranged to meet on Saturday night. At first the realisation that I was free on Saturday night gave me a mild panic attack. Shouldn't I have something better to do than meet an almost stranger from the internet? Well on this occasion I didn't, but if it was unbearable I'd make some excuse and be home in time for Parky.

It wasn't unbearable. It wasn't anything really. Adrian was wearing a black suit, with a black shirt, a black tie and smart black shoes. Perhaps he'd been to a funeral. I felt like I was at one. He'd aged somewhat from his photo and reminded me of Skeletor. Decent bloke. No spark. I caught the second half of Parky.

❤

Steve replaced Adrian as my interest *du jour*. He caught my eye by way of a good old fashioned passport photo and a forgettable one liner. I'd learned that photos usually counted for nothing. I should have learned that personality is much more important, but instead I was learning that I'm as shallow as the next person in the first instance, and Steve looked like my cup of tea. Six foot, slim, blonde-ish hair, slight stubble and a nice smile. After emailing back and forth for a couple of days, I discovered he was a nice bloke too. And dare I say it – had the ability to make me laugh.

He lived in Earlsfield and he was a consultant, which I thought was the person at the top of the hospital hierarchy. But it turned out he wasn't that type of consultant. He was the ambiguous type. Consulting whom about what, I'm not sure, but he must have been doing OK because he was in the process of buying a four-bed house in Clapham. He'd also done a lot of travelling, which seemed to be a common area with most of my Digital-Cupid encounters. Always a good ice-breaker, and a sense of adventure can only be a good thing. We'd both done Australia and South-East Asia. That was *so* last millennium. Steve was planning on taking three months off the following year to do South America. Something I'd always wanted to do but never got round to. It got me thinking. We could do it together. I could take a sabbatical. It would be so romantic. Sunsets in Mexico... reaching Machu Picchu... cocktails on Copacabana Beach...

Running before I could walk again, but I got excited about him rather quickly. Perhaps he had that rare combination of everything. Intelligence, sense of humour, looks, decency, solvency, zest for life. Or perhaps I should take my head out of the clouds and reserve judgement until when and if we ever met.

Steve had been on two internet dates so far. Well, one and a half. The first was obviously desperate and twice as old as she'd implied on her profile, and the second didn't turn up. It was interesting to note the other side of the coin; that women could be just as deceitful as men when it came to their profiles. So he was understandably dubious about the whole thing, but like me, oddly addicted.

We clearly had to meet, but it was a question of when. Steve had a mate over from the States for a few days. He said they'd be in The Puzzle in Earlsfield on Friday night. I was going out with Lucy in Wimbledon that Friday night. Just around the corner in fact. That could work. We could meet them for a drink. A cosy foursome perhaps?

Lucy was still going full steam ahead with the internet dating, but she hadn't met the man of her dreams either. She'd got to the fourth date with someone who'd seemed really promising. A 32-year-old doctor called Ryan. Very good looking, if a bit shy. He seemed keen, taking her out to fancy places, but he never made a move. At the end of the fifth date, and tired of mixed messages, she'd dragged him under duress to the bedroom, where things went completely tits-up. He couldn't perform. Didn't want to perform. Had never, it seemed, performed. A baffled Lucy watched as he buried his head in the pillow and sobbed at the sheer embarrassment, disgust and shame of it all. Sadly Ryan disappeared off the face of the world wide web after the 'incident', and Lucy was back to square one. It hadn't put her off though, and if we could help each other out, then all the better.

"What's his mate like?" she asked, when I phoned to see how she felt about Friday.

"Haven't a clue," I told her. "I don't even know what Steve's like but he seems too good to be true. Knowing my luck he'll be a caricature of his photo with no personality, and his mate will be gorgeous," I added, covering myself just in case. I didn't really think that. His photo was pretty clear and the camera never lies apparently. Although it had told a few fibs recently.

"No – I bet the mate's a geek. Let's go along anyway. It'll be a laugh."

So go along we did, once we'd had a few rounds of Dutch courage after work. When he texted me at eight o'clock to say they were in The Puzzle, we were still in Soho at the Crown & Two Chairmen. So we finished our drinks, flagged down a cab and made our way to Earlsfield. I was looking forward to meeting Steve. I had a good feeling about him. He was a nice, attractive, successful businessman in the process of buying a house in Clapham. I didn't know anyone who owned a house. Well, none of my London contemporaries anyway. The most any of us owned was a two-bed flat, and that was with a lodger in the spare room and mortgaged to the hilt.

As we made our way into the pub, I wished I'd found out exactly where they were. It was packed and I couldn't see for looking. Two middle-aged blokes in leather bomber jackets leaning on the cigarette machine leered at us as we walked past. What had Steve brought us to? And more to the point, where was he?

"Can you see them?" asked Lucy as we stood in the pub, simultaneously craning our necks and trying to look inconspicuous. We headed for the bar and as Lucy ordered the drinks, my phone bleeped in my pocket.

*Steve Consultant: I can c u!*

Well that was helpful! It was disconcerting knowing they could see us looking for them. I turned towards the bar and texted a reply.

*Jo mobile: So where r u?*

"He's just texted me!" I filled Lucy in. "Said they can see us." My phone bleeped again.

*Steve Consultant: By the cig machine.*

Lucy looked at me, eyes wide, waiting for me to inform her of our destiny. Successful Steve and his equally successful American counterpart, who so far had remained nameless. Meanwhile, the expression on my face had changed from eager suspense and excitement, to downright disappointment in the bleep of a text message.

"You alright Jo?" Lucy asked innocently.

"I don't believe this," I replied. "It's those two in the bomber jackets by the fag machine."

She burst out laughing. I wished I could see the funny side. They were looking at us. I tried to feign a friendly wave but it was bloody difficult. My fake grin only fuelled Lucy's fits of laughter, which probably looked like a welcoming smile from where they were standing. They made their way over. Steve was tall and hunchbacked with not much hair and even less chin. He'd certainly piled on the pounds since his photo was taken. His passport must have been due to expire any time now, if it hadn't already. Why, oh why, do these people insist on putting old photos on their profiles? You're going to get found out!

"Hi," said Steve appreciatively. "We meet at last!"

"Yeah. Hi," I replied. "This is Lucy." They shook hands, her smile probably a lot more welcoming than mine.

"And this is Jim," he gestured towards his diminutive friend. "Please excuse him. He's been drinking all day."

"Hey!" said Jim loudly. "How's it goin'?"

Jim looked like Hank Marvin on acid. He couldn't stand still and was clearly smashed. I looked at Lucy. I could tell she was finding the whole thing highly amusing. I was finding it highly irritating that I'd been duped yet again. Although he might still be an extremely nice man, his deception had killed my enthusiasm. I'd just have to grin and bear it.

Steve was very quiet. I soon realised that was because he was totally overpowered by his loud friend. Lucy held court, but was laughing at him as opposed to with him. Steve seemed uncertain and embarrassed as Hank (aka Jim), proceeded to dominate the evening with his hilarious one-liners and dazzling wit. It was the most fun I'd ever had without laughing.

The conversation I swapped with Steve was brief and my virtual impression of him couldn't have been more inaccurate. Was this the same bloke I was planning on joining for a romantic trip to South America only an hour ago? He was dull as dishwater and his body language was, well... non-existent. There was nothing animated about him *whatsoever*. Funny, I thought again, how personality can be distorted by email. Was I guilty of it too? On my profile I was a blonde-haired, blue-eyed, tall-ish, solvent, amusing, single 30-something girl, with my own London pad and a busy social life. Why was a fabulous catch like me still single? Was I dull as dishwater in reality too?

We endured Hank's cabaret some more, and then alas and alack, last orders were called.

"I'm hungry," I said to Lucy as the place suddenly went

quiet. "Fancy going for something to eat?" Huge mistake. "GRRRREAT IDEA!" exclaimed Hank. "I could really kill for pizza!"

I tried my best to steer the situation in any direction other than one that involved spending more time with Hank, but the next thing I knew, the four of us were sitting in an Italian restaurant perusing the menu.

Hank was narrating the description of every pizza, adding the odd *"oh my gahhhhhd"* for good measure. After practically salivating at the Meat Feast and doing the waitress's head in, he managed to place his order. Lucy was laughing, Steve was bright red, and I was thinking "what on earth am I doing here?" I was tempted to slope off to the Codfather for takeaway fish and chips but thought I should see it through. I felt sorry for Steve.

Things calmed down for five minutes when Hank went to the 'bathroom'. Steve apologised profusely on behalf of his irritating friend. He realised that jet-lag and an afternoon of drinking was no excuse for his behaviour, but he was usually a really nice guy. Said he hoped it hadn't put me off and that we really should go out again under different circumstances. I wasn't convinced.

Luckily we were interrupted by the American idiot's return, and Steve soon realised the fat lady had sung when Hank sat down, dipped his head in a plate of bruschetta and started singing *Thriller*. It was like a scene from *One Flew Over the Cuckoo's Nest*. Lucy looked at me, shaking her head in disbelief and having hysterics at the same time. The waitress looked horrified and disappeared into the kitchen, presumably for back-up. You could say that things weren't quite going to plan. Call me intolerant, but I'd had enough at this point and no amount of cheap red wine was going to rescue the situation.

"Right, I'm off," I announced, ceremoniously slamming my empty glass on the table with far more gusto than intended. I stood up and put my coat on. Lucy obediently followed suit, pretty much hyperventilating by now.

"Come *arrrrrn*. Have some more wine!" protested Hank loudly, his face dripping with chopped tomato. "Jeeeeez! What's *wrong* with you guyzzz?..."

# nine

## *Déjà vu and a bottle of rum*

OK. It hadn't proved particularly fruitful so far, but I was now throwing myself wholeheartedly into the internet dating scene. I clearly hadn't mastered the art (if there was such a thing), of reading between the lines and sifting the wheat from the chaff. However, despite the lack of romance, I was determined not to class all my encounters as failures. I'd had a few 'interesting' nights out which made for good stories around the dinner table if nothing else.

But some of my friends weren't so sure. Though amused at my constant tales, they urged me to give it up. Claire thought it was only a matter of time before I met someone dangerous and Jane regretted the day she ever put the idea in my head. David, who's a close male friend, told me after each disaster "forget it, there's plenty more fish in the sea," which was helpful. Was I was focusing too much on the internet to notice the sea?

Around this time, I rediscovered the joys of MSN messenger. I'd avoided it since the Tom Evans affair, as I'd come to the conclusion that it was psychologically damaging. The Tom on my contact list was still the nice Tom I'd fallen for over the keyboard, not the complicated weirdo who'd dumped me so cruelly, and I'd find myself staring at his name, willing him to message me. I could have deleted him of course, but I obviously enjoyed the mental torture.

But Fiona, the fifth member of Wandsworth's answer to *Sex And The City*, had recently moved to New Zealand. She was working nights, so what better way to keep in touch? At the tips of our fingers and at someone else's expense.

It was lunchtime in London and I was waiting for her to sign in for our daily chat. I was dying to hear all about the guy she'd met last week at a cricket match (of all things). She'd left me hanging on yesterday, with the information that he'd cooked her dinner the other night. Before I'd had a chance to find out what (if anything) was for pudding, she'd logged off suddenly and never came back.

> **Tom Evans has just signed in**

Oh my god I nearly had a heart attack. Talk of the devil. Although he was long gone, old emotions came flooding back as I sat at my desk, staring at his name once again.

One click. That's all it would take for me to say hello. Find out what he was doing. But would he respond? And besides, did I want to communicate with him after the way he'd behaved? Perhaps he'd message me in a minute. It must have been hard living a lie. He was only human. Well at least I assumed he was. He must have felt guilty. Perhaps he was seeking redemption. Could he see me online, or had he deleted my name from his contacts? Why did I care? It was well over a year ago. After ten minutes of staring at the thing, the suspense and temptation were too much to bear.

*Jo says:*   Hi.

Pregnant pause.

*Tom says:*   *Oh my god. Hi Jo! Great to hear from you.*
                 *Most unexpected! How are things with*
                 *you these days?*

A bit enthusiastic, I thought. My heart pounded and I didn't know why.

Jo says:    Things are fine thanks. How are you?

Tom says:   Yeah. Good. I'm fine. This is weird. It's been
            a while huh?

Jo says:    Yes. It has. How are things going over there
            in the States?

This would be interesting. He didn't know that I knew he was still here. Presumably he still thought I was stupid.

Tom says:   Well. Actually I'm over here in the UK

Jo says:    You are? Really? How come?

Tom says:   Well it's a long story.

Jo says:    I have some time.

Tom says:   Well I ended up getting another job here at
            the last minute. An offer I couldn't refuse,
            so I stayed in the end!

Jo says:    Gosh how funny! Good for you. And you
            were in such a hurry to get back to LA.

Tom says:   I know. It all happened very quickly.

Jo says:    It must have done. You were practically
            on the plane when I saw you last.

Tom says:   Kind of... Anyway – I thought of you the
            other day actually.

He thought of me the other day. He hadn't forgotten about me then. Did he care, after all?

Jo says:    Did you? How come?

Tom says:   I walked past your place – it was a couple of
            weeks ago.

Jo says:     *My work? Are you working near me?*

Tom says:   *No – not work. Past your home.*

What was he doing walking past my home? I was surprised. But not as surprised as I would have been had I looked out of my front window one day to see him strolling casually down the street. I didn't know what to say.

Jo says:     *I see. Well you should have called in for a cup of tea.*

Tom says:   *Errrrmmmm.... I was with my g/f.*

Oh.

Jo says:     *What's a g/f?*

I asked sarcastically, keen to lull him into a false sense of security with the impression that it didn't bother me at all. I was annoyed and frustrated to find that it did.

Tom says:   *My girlfriend. She lives round that way.*

Jo says:     *Oh right. What a coincidence.*

Tom says:   *I know. It's cool round there. We're looking to move in together somewhere bigger.*

Jo says:     *That's nice. Been together long?*

Tom says:   *Quite a while. I've known her a couple of years. We went out before.*

Jo says:     *The one before me?*

Tom says:   *Well, yes. But there was no overlap. I wasn't with her when I was with you.*

Yeah right. And I'm Princess Anne.

Tom says:   *Got a meeting now, sorry. Great to chat. Lets chat again soon. Bye!*

And with that, he disappeared. Back into cyberspace or wherever it was he came from. I was left staring at the screen, wishing I'd never initiated the damn conversation.

————— ❤ —————

"Forget about him!" said Lucy. "We already know he's got a slate loose."

"I know that," I tried to explain. "It's not him I'm bothered about as such. It's the complete disregard for anyone but himse–"

"Park it, Jo," warned Claire. "There's no point going into one about it again."

We were at Jane's having a girls night in. She'd just got back from the Caribbean and instead of the usual bottles of wine, we were drinking her new speciality – rum punch. On a Wednesday night as well.

"I'm not going into one," I assured them. "I'm just telling you what happened. I can't believe the audacity of–"

"I really think you should knock the internet dating thing on the head," said Claire firmly. "It's not making you happy. You're not meeting anyone decent are you?"

She could talk. Tony was at least twenty years her senior, totally eccentric, and lived on a barge. Not to mention a bit on the large side.

"Oh I don't know," said Lucy. "What about Hank and the chinless wonder?"

"Oh yes," I gushed with fake lust. "They were ideal. Such a shame they weren't interested!"

"There's so many blokes on there, sooner or later we should hit the jackpot," she laughed. Thank God I had an ally. If only I shared her optimism.

"I couldn't be arsed with it," said Claire.

"Yeah. It can be pretty painful," I admitted. "But it's so addictive. Where else can you get a date that easily? I never seem to meet anyone in real life..." the familiar line came tripping off my tongue.

"Have you ever thought about doing a night class?" suggested Jane innocently.

Oh god. Not the night class line. If I'd heard that once, I'd heard it a thousand times. It had briefly flitted through my mind once, but what would I do if I joined a night class? There were always people handing me leaflets outside the station for salsa lessons, but I couldn't think of anything worse. Could I ever be attracted to someone who attended a salsa class? Something in my head couldn't quite connect with the idea.

As the rum punch quickly diminished, so did any sign of coherence and the four of us spent the rest of the evening dirty dancing around Jane's lounge with the contents of her vegetable rack.

———————— ❤ ————————

"*Don't* even go there Mario," I pleaded, as I stood at the counter with my head in my hands. I wasn't even sure if a Mario special would shift this hangover. It occurred to me that it might be time to grow up. I was 33 now, not 23. Trouble was, I didn't feel it. And it always seemed such a good idea at the time. Not so good when you're sitting in a meeting nodding your head aimlessly to indicate that you understand the brief: "*do something creative with a brochure about pensions*".

My mind wandered. I knew what Claire was saying about internet dating, and maybe Jane was right. I could sign up for a car maintenance night class. Or plumbing. I quite fancied learning a language. French appealed to me. Maybe I'd look into that. Or other ways of dating. I hadn't tried speed dating (apart from my date with Porno Paul), and I hadn't tried those dinner party things. All a bit too engineered for my liking. Once you were there, I imagined you were stuck there for the night. If you suddenly left, you'd mess up the numbers. At least with the internet it was one-on-one and if you were having a bad time and wanted to leave, you'd only ruin one person's night.

It was just a case of finding the right chemistry. I say just, but that's the hardest part. A lot of people find it easy going from relationship to relationship, seemingly falling in love at the drop of a hat. Do these people really have the right chemistry? Are they really in love, or are they just afraid of being on their own?

I did a bit of research, and discovered that being in love is a scientific state involving the production of 'stuff' in the brain. Adrenaline and dopamine to be precise. I wasn't prepared to settle for anything less than the right chemistry, and decided that I must be severely lacking in the adrenaline and dopamine production department. So where could I get some from?

———❤———

It seemed I'd just have to be patient. Digital-Cupid were still insisting that hundreds of men were keen to meet me in their limitless pool of prospects. Surely they couldn't all be wrong? In amongst the clichés, pixelated photos and cropped out ex-girlfriends, there had to be some potential. I couldn't help feeling a glimmer of hope that at least one of them would eventually produce the right chemical reaction.

| From: | Ken_Goldstein | To: | jo-to-go |
|---|---|---|---|
| Subject: 2nd attempt – please read | | Date: | 08.03.03 |

I emailed you some time ago and you haven't replied.
I realise you may be busy, but why use this service if
you're not prepared to play the game – please have the
decency to respond this time.

I'll tell you a bit more about me anyway. I'm 51 and have
had a varied and interesting life so far. Have quite a
successful career and am up to junior management.
Been married twice and have 4 kids. First wife walked
out taking 2 kids with her. Haven't seen Esther and
Jacob for 19 years.

Remarried straight away and we had Ben and Elizabeth.
Ben is dyslexic and Elizabeth has special needs. I tried
my best but wife was on medication. I left as I thought I
might hit her. She got the police involved and took me
to the cleaners financially so now I don't trust anyone.

Am renting a 2 bed semi in Brent Cross area and need
someone to help decorate and fill it with furniture and
affection. Have Sky Plus and a great sound system. Will
have two cars by early next year. A Citroen Saxo to run
around in and a Renault Espace for longer journeys.

I want to share my life with someone again. Wouldn't say
no to starting a new family or marriage. Looking for a
younger lady up to 45 and am willing to take into
account your previous mistakes (within reason), and work
through them with you.

I have practical experience in dealing with disabilities and
illness. My estranged wife has kidney problems and
needs dialysis and my first wife had asthma, diabetes
and Epilepsy. My father had Alzheimers.

In my spare time I like doing Mystery Shopping. I love
complaining about people not doing their jobs properly.
I can play the piano but not professionally. I think I'm a
good catch and having read your profile think we go well
together. Please re-read my profile and respond this time.

Ken.

---

Well Ken was certainly full of the joys of spring. I couldn't
believe I'd missed him last time. I'd have been sure to
respond if his first message was as upbeat as this one. The
word 'nutter' sprang to mind as I clicked the link to his
profile. Judging by his photo, he was fairly near the back of
the queue when it came to handing out looks. Poor Ken.
Had he really led such a tragic life?

# ten

## Dinner on the President and a sticky situation

| From: Legal_Alien | To: jo-to-go |
|---|---|
| Subject: Fancy a change? | Date: 19.03.03 |

Hi Jo,

Forgive my directness, but I just read your profile with great interest. I think you seem really refreshing and stand out from the crowd.

I'm an American in London for a year, and looking forward to making the most of my time here.

I am looking for someone mature and wise, to spend time with. I have ample means and want to share it with the right person. I enjoy first class dining, theatre, and sometimes just conversation. If this is you, then we should hook up.

Best regards,

Kurt Richard Williams

---

Ample means? I assumed he meant his bank balance and not the contents of his trousers. It was a nice message. Factual and to the point. But another American? Well I couldn't tar them all with the same brush, could I? I clicked the link to his profile. There was a picture of an ordinary looking man standing in front of the White House. How very patriotic.

| From: jo-to-go | To: Legal_Alien |
|---|---|
| Subject: Re: Fancy a change? | Date: 19.03.03 |

Thanks for your message. I'm not sure whether I'm either mature or wise, but I do like eating, theatre and conversation, so that could be a good start.

Anyway – what brings you to London for a year?

Jo

| From: Legal_Alien | To: jo-to-go |
|---|---|
| Subject: Re: Fancy a change? | Date: 20.03.03 |

Your pictures and profile are great by the way. Sure seems like you know how to have fun. I would love to meet up for a drink with you. I'm in the States this week and next, but are you free any time the week after?

Best,

K

He didn't answer my question. Am I free for a drink? Wasn't it a bit soon to be arranging a date? Maybe he wasn't into long online relationships and would rather cut to the chase. I guess there was something to be said about that. Long online relationships can mess with your head. I'd learned that the hard way. Spend too long getting to know someone over a keyboard and you're setting yourself up for a rather big fall. Your perception of them becomes so deep-rooted and your expectations so high, chances are they'll never live up to them. Perhaps getting it over and done with as quickly as possible was the way forward.

| From: jo-to-go | To: Legal_Alien |
|---|---|
| Subject: Re: Fancy a change? | Date: 21.03.03 |

I'm free a week on Thursday if that's any good.

---

| From: | Legal_Alien | To: | jo-to-go |
|---|---|---|---|
| Subject: Re: Fancy a change? | | Date: 21.03.03 | |

Fantastic! Thursday works for me. I've been staying at One Aldwych while my new place gets sorted out. You know it? I usually gravitate towards the Lobby bar after work. What say we meet there about 7pm?

Best,

K

---

I'd never been to One Aldwych, but I'd heard a lot about it. Somewhat more upmarket than the Crown & Anchor by all accounts. I checked out the website. *'Contemporary and luxurious, fabulous and happening'*.

---

| From: | jo-to-go | To: | Legal_Alien |
|---|---|---|---|
| Subject: Re: Fancy a change? | | Date: 24.03.03 | |

Yes – I know it well. I'll make my way there on the Thursday for 7 o'clock then. Drop me an email beforehand to confirm. See you there!

Jo

---

| From: | Legal_Alien | To: | jo-to-go |
|---|---|---|---|
| Subject: Re: Fancy a change? | | Date: 24.03.03 | |

I look forward to it. In all likelihood I'll be wearing a dark suit (charcoal or navy), white shirt, and a solid dark green tie. I'll manoeuvre toward the bar for 7pm. (I'm around 6ft, 180 lbs.)

K

---

How did he know what he'd be wearing in ten days time? It sounded like a military operation. Manoeuvres at seven hundred hours. One Aldwych. Central London. I almost replied saying *"and I'll be in a black balaclava hanging from the ceiling,"* but I left it. I didn't have a clue what I was going to wear yet.

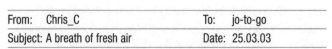

| From: Chris_C | To: jo-to-go |
|---|---|
| Subject: A breath of fresh air | Date: 25.03.03 |

I really loved your profile. Sharp and to the point. And you don't want to save the world! As the subject header says – a breath of fresh air.

Am I on your frequency? Who knows? I'm down to earth and have been known to amuse, particularly when filled with enough booze. And that's just my dancing.

Chris

Two emails in one week that raised a flicker of interest. Things were looking up. I felt a surge of near excitement as I read Chris's message and the feeling of 'a breath of fresh air' was mutual. With baited breath I clicked on the link and checked out his profile: 6ft 2, living in London, originated in Melbourne and appeared to have a sense of humour. He was a TV and film director no less. There were two black and white photos of a handsome looking man who was definitely worthy of a reply.

| From: jo-to-go | To: Chris_C |
|---|---|
| Subject: Re: A breath of fresh air | Date: 25.03.03 |

Thanks for your message. A welcome breath of fresh air for me too. I'm intrigued to find out more. Not so much about any films you've directed, but about your dance skills.

Jo.

P.S – It's not that I don't want to save the world.
I just don't think I can do it single-handedly whilst modelling swimwear.

| From: | Chris_C | To: | jo-to-go |
|---|---|---|---|
| Subject: Re: A breath of fresh air | | Date: 26.03.03 | |

Whoa Miss World!

It would be kind of misinformation to say I've directed any blockbusters. In fact it would be a downright lie.
I have worked on film and am currently reading several scripts. Always reading scripts. But most of the work I've done lately is TV. Eastenders, Holby, Murder Mystery... that kind of thing.

Oh dear. I've just read that back and its not particularly amusing, or indeed interesting. Only a few paragraphs and already such a disappointment. Perhaps I need to ask you out for a drink and show you my piece de resistance. My dancing.

Chris

---

| From: | jo-to-go | To: | Chris_C |
|---|---|---|---|
| Subject: Re: A breath of fresh air | | Date: 26.03.03 | |

I wouldn't say that directing some of the country's most popular TV shows is a disappointment. So what's Dot Cotton like?

You're really selling the dancing. I'm not sure it's wise to build it up too much. I'd love to see it with my own eyes, but I'm not into clubbing. How about carpet dancing in the local pub? In the meantime, can you describe it? I'm not sure I can wait.

Jo

---

| From: | Chris_C | To: | jo-to-go |
|---|---|---|---|
| Subject: Re: A breath of fresh air | | Date: 27.03.03 | |

Ah yes. Carpet dancing in a pub will only enhance my moves, especially if said carpet is sticky from beer spillage. I'm no longer into clubbing either. Those days are long gone. How to describe my dancing? I guess it can only be described as standing still, only faster.

I've got so much work to do. I shouldn't be writing to you but you provide me with much more amusement.

So we should meet for a drink. Ease in gently before the dance-off. I'm a member of a club in Soho. If you play your cards right, you may get an invite. It's no different than anywhere else really except you can listen to people making loud media deals.

Chris

---

I liked Chris already. He was funny. A 6ft 2 attractive, successful Aussie, who'd rather laugh at himself than pretend to be perfect. He sounded like my ideal man. I tried not to get excited, but it was easier said than done. He wanted to go for a drink. I'd forgotten all about my date with the mysterious American at One Aldwych.

---

| From: jo-to-go | To: Chris_C |
|---|---|
| Subject: Re: A breath of fresh air | Date: 27.03.03 |

That sounds good. I like eavesdropping and people watching. I hope I'm deemed worthy of an invite to your special club at some point.

The description of your dance moves made me laugh out loud. If fact, I nearly wrote LOL, but I couldn't bring myself to. I'm allergic to internet speak. Whereabouts in London do you live by the way?

Jo

---

| From: Chris_C | To: jo-to-go |
|---|---|
| Subject: Re: A breath of fresh air | Date: 27.03.03 |

LOL! I know what you mean : )

I live in Acton at the moment with a friend. The apartment

is huge but it's a bit crap. I've been away a lot this year, so couldn't be arsed to move, but I want to get somewhere on my own.

Thing is, there's a good chance I'm making a movie in New York next year, so it's hardly worth it at the moment. Plus I find moving such an ordeal. For some reason I seem to have so much stuff!

Chris

---

Hmmm. A movie in New York. Suddenly there I was, strolling across Times Square in my Manolo Blahniks. Rollerblading in Central Park. Hanging out in coffee shops with my unusually attractive friends...

---

| From: jo-to-go | To: Chris_C |
|---|---|
| Subject: Re: A breath of fresh air | Date: 27.03.03 |

That sounds exciting – making a movie in New York. Do you need an assistant? Perhaps I could make the teas or something?

---

| From: Chris_C | To: jo-to-go |
|---|---|
| Subject: Re: A breath of fresh air | Date: 28.03.03 |

Well if you're up for moving to the other side of the world, we should arrange that drink so we can discuss what kind of job description I'd have for a cute blonde assistant.

I think you have more ambition than making the teas and doing what I tell you. The feisty nature I've noticed reading between the lines suggests few people tell you what to do and live very long. But I like a girl with something to say. It's so refreshing. There's nothing worse than a subservient wallflower.

Chris

---

'Cute blonde assistant.' Flattery would get him everywhere. But I wasn't sure about the ambition bit. I'd be more than happy to make the teas and go shopping.

---

| From: jo-to-go | To: Chris_C |
|---|---|
| Subject: Re: A breath of fresh air | Date: 28.03.03 |

That's not true. I do as I'm told all the time!

Not being funny, but do you think it's early days to be talking about moving to another country together?
I mean, it is something I'd consider with the right person, but perhaps we should meet first!

---

| From: Chris_C | To: jo-to-go |
|---|---|
| Subject: Re: A breath of fresh air | Date: 28.03.03 |

Yeah I figure we might actually want to go for a drink or something before agreeing to emigrating together.
Call me crazy but it's just the way I prefer to operate.

How is your social calendar looking? When are you free to go for that drink, should I decide to ask you? In fact why don't you give me your phone number, then I can call and ask you out properly.

Chris

---

I thought he'd never ask. We swapped numbers and arranged a window in our hectic schedules for a call that night. Right on cue the phone rang. I was sitting on top of it, but I let it ring a few times before casually answering like I didn't know who it was. Who was I trying to kid? His name came up on the screen.

He had a nice voice. Deep, and with only a mild Australian twang. We over-ran the allotted window by about two hours as we chatted like we'd known each other for ever. We shared stories about the internet dates we'd been on and I was pleased to discover it wasn't just me who'd met some freaks. Chris had been on three dates and they'd all been pretty disastrous. One's ex-boyfriend apparently showed up halfway through the date, one was completely miserable, and the other was obsessed with karma. I listened in disbelief as he told me how she'd paid to get his stars read before they met and proceeded to refer to the results throughout the date.

Chris was a Virgo like me. After ripping the karma woman to shreds, I couldn't help thinking that was a good thing. Taking into account the characteristics of a typical Virgo, I wondered if perhaps Virgos should only go out with other Virgo's. Then we can all be anal together.

We decided that by the law of averages, whatever that is, we should be OK to proceed, and arranged to meet the next Wednesday at his club in Soho. He told me he'd be at his usual table and I just needed to ask for him. Couldn't he meet me outside? Would I recognise him from his black and white photos?

———————❤———————

I was nervous as I walked through the door on Wednesday night. I didn't know the drill in these kind of places, but I stuck my head in the air and pretended otherwise.

"Hi. I'm here to meet Chris," I told the perfectly groomed girl at the desk. It suddenly occurred to me that I didn't even know his second name. That was a bit disorganised. What if there were lots of Chris's at lots of tables, all expecting guests?

"Oh yes, Jo. He's expecting you," she smiled. "I'll take you through."

She led me through to a dimly lit table in a corner. A strawberry blonde guy wearing glasses was sitting there musing over some papers with a pen in his mouth. I'm sure I saw him glance up, but he pretended he hadn't.

"Hi. Chris?" I said quietly, hoping it was the right Chris.

"Hi! Jo." He jumped up and shook my hand, as if my being there had taken him my surprise. He was the right person at least.

"Sit down," he gestured. "What can I get you to drink?"

He called someone over and ordered two Kir Royales. Chris was nice looking, but he wasn't much like the picture in my mind. Quite different from his photos again, but I wouldn't say I was disappointed. I'd imagined him to be laid back and a bit scruffy, but he was quite businesslike and serious. Perhaps it was the glasses. They made him look studious. He wore expensive-looking dark jeans and a patterned shirt tucked in at the waist, with a tan belt, and matching tan brogues. All in all, the first impression was fine, though pretty different to how I'd imagined.

I sat down and Chris cleared away his papers. We made small talk until the drinks arrived. I wondered what he thought of me. He wasn't giving anything away. His face hadn't exactly lit up when he saw me, but it hadn't fallen either. The conversation certainly wasn't flowing as it had on the phone yet, but the dynamics were so much different in the flesh. There were facial expressions, and body language to consider and Chris wasn't showing much of either. He was very controlled. I was all over the place. This was a man, not a boy. It seemed different to the norm – almost like a business meeting.

Thank God the drinks arrived when they did. I needed something strong and it worked. I started to feel more comfortable and Chris began to chill out. With the help of a few more drinks, everything became more relaxed and it all fell slowly into place. By the end of the evening I'd secured a cameo in his film and an admission that he'd been just as nervous as me. As we left, he put his arm round me and told me I needn't have worried.

"Do you want to go somewhere else?" he asked. "Maybe I can show you those dance moves."

I conjured up an image of Chris in his patterned shirt, busting some moves on the dance floor. It didn't have quite the same effect as the image I'd had in my mind before we met. That of a tall, grungy, laid back Aussie with no sense of rhythm and no worries. As we stood on Shaftesbury Avenue in the freezing cold, the fresh air hit me and I decided my best option was to go home. I looked at my watch. It was midnight. What on earth had we talked about for five hours?

"I think I've had enough excitement for one night," I told him. "Let's save the dancing for next time."

"Good idea," agreed Chris. "And a good excuse for there to be a next time."

Was it the Kir Royales, or had I met someone decent here? I flagged down a cab. Chris pulled me towards him and I noticed now that we were out of the dimly lit corner, just how red his hair was.

"Thanks for a nice night. It was good to meet you," I told him.

"You too," he grinned, as he planted his lips firmly on mine with the tenderness of a wet fish. It took me by surprise.

A few slobbery seconds later, I clambered into the waiting cab and bid him farewell. Apart from the last few seconds, it had gone well. He wasn't as easy-going and funny in the flesh as I thought he'd be, but I liked him and wanted to see him again. And he, it seemed, felt the same. The slobbering was a technicality. We could work on that.

---❤---

| From: | Legal_Alien | To: | jo-to-go |
|---|---|---|---|
| Subject: Tonight. | | Date: 03.04.03 | |

Hey Jo! I was thinking – the best way to really know what someone's like is to know what their favourite drink is.
I'm a coffee in the morning, Manhattan in the afternoon, Bourbon in the evening kind of guy. What about you?
Best
K

Oh my god. It was Kurt Richard Williams and his ample means. And I was supposed to be meeting him at One Aldwych tonight. Shit, shit, shit.

---

| From: jo-to-go | To: Legal_Alien |
|---|---|
| Subject: Re: Tonight | Date: 03.04.03 |

I like a nice cup of tea in the morning, or champagne at any time. My favourite cocktail is Mojito and I'm partial to a glass of good red wine. I usual just drink G&T though. It might have been easier to ask me what I don't like!

Jo

---

I felt like death warmed up, and I didn't look much better. I couldn't possibly go on a date with a stranger at One Aldwych looking like this. And besides, I'd met Chris now. Admittedly I'd only been on one date with him. Probably shouldn't take it as read that he's the one, but it had gone so much better than all the others. I suppose it's a natural reaction to put all your eggs in one basket, but I decided the sensible thing to do here was to keep my options open.

---

| From: Legal_Alien | To: jo-to-go |
|---|---|
| Subject: Re: Tonight | Date: 03.04.03 |

Sounds like you have an eclectic taste. Great! As for tonight – there's a sculpture of a man in a boat in the middle of the lobby bar. I suggest we meet there at 7pm.

Best
K

---

| From: jo-to-go | To: Legal_Alien |
|---|---|
| Subject: Re: Tonight | Date: 03.04.03 |

That sounds great. See you there at 7pm.

---

I avoided the temptation to make a rude joke about the man-in-a-boat. I was too busy wondering how on earth I was possibly going to scrub up for this one. I decided I'd go to the gym at lunchtime. It was about time my membership card had an airing, and the showers were great. I could duck into Topshop on the way and buy something to wear. Any excuse.

I got back from lunch feeling pristine and new, happy to see Chris in my mailbox.

| From: Chris_C | To: jo-to-go |
|---|---|
| Subject: Afternoon! | Date: 03.04.03 |

I just got back from checking out some locations for a shoot. Not ideal with a sore head. I think I might have just agreed to something totally inappropriate.

Hope you got home OK last night, and thanks again for a good night. Are you free tonight? I've just realised I have no plans and I don't have to work. I'm in Covent Garden for a meeting this afternoon. Fancy picking up where we left off?

Chris

Tonight! Blimey – he was keen. But I was otherwise engaged. I'd have preferred to go out with Chris again, but I'd arranged a date with the Bourbon-drinking-kind-of-guy and it seemed wrong to let him down now. Chris would keep. I told him I was shattered and I needed an early night. He told me I could sleep when I'm dead. I apologised for being a killjoy and we arranged to go out next Saturday.

———❤———

I'd bought a skirt at Topshop and I found a pair of high heeled shoes under my desk. I remembered why they'd been under my desk for the last six months as I made my way towards the Strand. They were absolutely excruciating and

I could hardly walk in them. Must have been going through a classy phase when I bought them as I rarely wear heels. I looked quite smart apart from the coat. I wasn't going to buy a new one, and it was too cold to go without, so I was stuck with the scruffy parka I'd thrown on as I flew out the door that morning.

"Can I take your coat?" said the host.

"Please do," I agreed, thankful to get rid of it.

I spotted the man-in-a-boat sculpture straight away. You couldn't really miss it. There was a figure in a dark suit hovering next to it. He was looking at me and I knew instantly it was Kurt due to the attire, although he'd fibbed about the colour. The whole ensemble was bottle green. I made my way over.

"Kurt?" I said, as if I wasn't sure.

"Howdy Jo. Can I git you summinga drink?" came the reply in a strong southern American drawl. He looked pretty much like his picture. Tall, smart and perfectly average.

"Erm. Yes please. What are you having?" I asked. The thought of alcohol didn't really appeal after last night, but what else do people drink in bars?

"I'm just gonna git mahself a beer," he said. "Hey. Whah don't you check out the carrrktails. They're absolutely arrrsome in here."

I looked at the menu. The cocktails did look awesome, but so did the price tags. It felt a bit presumptuous ordering something so expensive considering I'd only known him two minutes.

"I'll just have a beer as well," I said.

"Don't you worry your priddy lil' head 'bout the prahce or who's payin' " he said, as if to read my mind. "You just have whatever you want and enjoy it."

"Are you sure?"

"Sure as the day I was born ma'am."

Quite sure then. And did he just call me ma'am? He got me a Kir Royale and it reminded me of Chris. I had a Mojito next, followed by a Cosmopolitan and a Banana Daiquiri.

Kurt stuck to beer.

"So what do you actually do for a living?" I asked. He'd avoided the question so far and I was intrigued.

"Based at the American Embassy, ma'am. You know the American Embassy? Big gates. Eagles. Down there at Grosvenor Square." At last I was getting somewhere.

"Anyways. You have one cute accent and I was right about you," he added.

"Right about me? What do you mean?"

"Well I'm not a gambling man, but I guessed that you'd be fun and I was right. You are fun with a capital F." That was a bit over the top. All I'd done was drink four 'carrrktails' and rave about the venue.

"And I hope you don't mind but I've taken the liberty of booking a table for dinner at 8.30," he carried on. Subject expertly changed. He really didn't want to elaborate about his job.

"Errm. No. That's fine," I said, realising I was starving. "Where are we going?" I prayed it wasn't far. The shoes wouldn't get me far. And as for the parka...

"Upstairs at the restaurant here. Indigo. You'll like it."

The staff knew Kurt by name and seemed keen to cater to his every whim. No money changed hands for the drinks but presumably they were being charged to his room. By the time I'd finished my Banana Daiquiri, I'd convinced myself he was FBI. I wasn't attracted to him at all. We were worlds apart, but I was having a good time and I was going to enjoy the hospitality of Mr Bush.

"Mr Williams. Your table is ready at Indigo," a member of staff informed him.

"Thank you, sir," said Kurt, with a follow-up wink.

I looked down on the busy Lobby Bar as we made our way up to the restaurant. The website was right. It certainly was fabulous and happening. And with Kurt by my side I felt like I was at the oil barons' ball.

He ordered some wine and I studied the menu. I was too ashamed to admit I didn't know what half the dishes were, so I didn't. *'Tasty Tagine of lamb served on a bed of wild rice with something or other jus.'* Lamb casserole in other words. Kurt said he could recommend the lobster, but I ended up playing it safe with a fillet steak and home made fries.

The food was gorgeous, the wine lovely and Kurt was very nice. He was overly polite, a great listener, and generous to a fault, but getting information out of him was akin to pulling teeth. I wondered when would be an appropriate time to leave. I guessed after coffees, but Kurt had other ideas. He said he had some champagne in his room and he'd be honoured if I'd help him drink it. Although I was unsure as to whether I could drink anything else, I found myself agreeing as if it was the best idea I'd ever heard. Given that I'd just enjoyed a sumptuous evening that didn't cost me a penny, I felt kind of obliged.

The first things I noticed when we got to the room were three pairs of cowboy boots neatly lined up and a stetson on top of the telly. There was champagne in an ice bucket on the side. Had he prearranged this?

"I don't think I want another drink actually," I said. "Sorry, but I think I should get going." I came to my senses. Anything could happen. I could be stuck in this hotel room with a clone of JR Ewing for the rest of my life and no one would ever find me.

"No prarblem ma'am," said Kurt. "Let me get the concierge to call you a cab." And he did. Just like that. His intentions, it seemed, were entirely honourable. He'd just wanted some company.

"You've been a fine dining companion and if I'm ever lonesome at the dinner table again I'll have you back, make no mistake," he told me.

As I waited for the cab, I used his bathroom. I nicked the soap as a souvenir of my evening as a high-class escort, and by the time I was done, my cab was waiting. Should I kiss him goodbye or shake his hand? In the end I just said thanks and went to retrieve my parka.

———— ❤ ————

---

| From: BigCock4U | To: jo-to-go |
|---|---|
| Subject: yo baby | Date: 08.04.03 |

hi there i saw ur pic and fort i would say hi and see how u was doing. if u fancy a chat pls dont b put off by my silly name and pls reply. hope to hear from u soon.

Dave x

---

| From: Tony-Malone | To: jo-to-go |
|---|---|
| Subject: <None> | Date: 09.04.03 |

I don't want to beat about the bush so I won't.

I have looked at your picture and I think you look quite sweet and I would like to have a relationship with you.

Maybe we could meet for a coffee or tea or a drink. Sorry if you think this is forward but I'm not interested in lying on email to impress. That's for kids which I am not.

Stay Sweet

Tony

---

| From: dirk-diggler | To: jo-to-go |
|---|---|
| Subject: Hold me, thrill me, kiss me... | Date: 10.04.03 |

... But don't kill me!!!

How are you today anyway? I'm fine, thanks for asking! I'm 29 and I live in Reading. Muscular, good looking and funny (not in the head, but some may beg to differ! LOL!!)

I'm also partial to the odd alcoholic beverage or ten! I enjoy going out, getting drunk, and ending up on the nearest dancefloor. I'm looking for a lady who's not afraid to speak her mind and knows how to have fun. Someone with a great body, beautiful face and nice hair (on her head, not chin). Personality is important as well. I couldn't have a relationship with a bullfrog pig with a decent personality any more than I could a beautiful woman with no personality.

I must confess, I am a boob lover. I've never experienced the joys of really big ones. Nothing over a C cup so far. but that doesn't mean to say I dont like small boobs. Any boobs are fine by me! I can't see yours from your pics.

Do you like larger men (I'm not talking about waistlines!) I would say that the rest of my body is in proportion to my size. That's a polite way of me trying to warn you I have a big C@*k!!! That's not a wishful boast – picture available on request to back it up. Look forward to your reply!

Dirk xxx

---

I was still keeping an eye on Digital-Cupid. What made these people tick? Why on earth did 'Dirk' in Reading think I was remotely interested in his anatomy? Thank God I had my second date with Chris on Saturday.

It was over a week since the first date and I was looking forward to seeing him again. We met in a pub in Notting Hill. He looked kind of different this time but I couldn't put my finger on why. Maybe his hair was different or something. I'm sure it wasn't in a side flick last time. Another loud shirt and stonewashed jeans finished off the eighties look quite nicely. I didn't have a problem with it. Maybe one day I could take him shopping.

"I had fun the other night," he mused, as we sat in a cosy corner of the pub re-familiarising. Another one using the F-word. God if I was this much fun I should have been snapped up years ago. Or is fun all I am, I wondered?

At last orders, Chris informed me he had to be up at 6am to go to Manchester for work and he'd be away all week. I was disappointed he was cutting the night short, but if he had to work, he had to work. I could wait a bit longer to see his dancing.

"How about I make it up to you next weekend?"

"OK. I think I'm around," I said vaguely.

"Well why don't you come over to my place and I'll cook you my signature dish?"

"That sounds nice," I agreed, excited at the prospect of having Chris cook for me.

"So what is your signature dish?"

"It's a fish curry," he announced proudly. My face fell.

"What's up? You don't like it?"

"I'm really sorry. I just don't like curry..."

"You don't like curry? Are you abnormal?" he laughed.

"It would seem so," I admitted. "I don't know anyone else who doesn't like curry."

They threw us out of the pub eventually and we made our way on to Notting Hill Gate for another slobbering session in a cab rank. There was still masses of room for improvement but I wasn't sure how to bring it up yet.

Chris went to Manchester and we kept up communication with the odd midnight phone call. He got back to London a day earlier than expected. His work was done up north, so we made a date for Friday night at his place.

We'd made it to the third date. I rang the buzzer at the front door, wondering where was this going to lead?

"Hi. Push the door and come on up the stairs," said a voice on the intercom. It was an enormous door in an old Victorian house and it weighed a tonne.

The communal area was about the size of my flat and I decided it could do with a lick of paint. His apartment was lovely, if in need of a bit of TLC. High ceilings and period features. I had ideas for the lounge already. And as for the roof terrace – it could be fantastic with a couple of plants and minus the rusty fridge. Still, I guess he was only renting. This time next year, we'd be in New York.

"What's on the menu?" I asked.

"Fun," said Chris, as he popped a bottle of champers.

There was a delicious smell coming from the kitchen, which turned out to be a very tasty, if unimaginative spag bol. It was the longest cooking spag bol of all time. I think we ate about 11 o'clock, by which time we'd had two more bottles of champagne and I was about to die of hunger.

After dinner I cracked open the mediocre bottle of plonk

that I'd bought. Then it was time for Chris to reveal his infamous dance moves. I had a rummage through his CD collection. Bruce Springsteen, Bob Dylan... various people with beards that I'd never heard of.

"Got anything good?" I thought out loud.

"Whaddaya mean?" he slurred. "It's all classic stuff I'll have you know."

We finally settled on some Roxy Music, and Chris turned the lights down. If he wasn't winding me up, he was right about the dancing. It was terrible.

"Enough already!" I shrieked after about ten bars of *Love Is The Drug*. Probably not the best song to choose as it's jerkiness only accentuated his dreadful moves. I was doubled up with laughter when Chris took the opportunity to wrestle me to the ground in mock fight. I promised never to laugh again, and with sweat dripping from his forehead, his lips descended on to mine and the dreaded slob-fest began. I thought this would be the ideal opportunity to say something and see if we could improve things. Perhaps lose a bit of spittle. But all I could do was mumble. I realised it was a lost cause as the slobbering intensified. His tongue drilled open my lips and he started doing an impression of a fully loaded washing machine inside my mouth.

I wanted to scream *"I'm celibate... Get me out of here!"* and be magically transported out of this urban jungle. If only it was that easy. Oh God – this was awful. He was grunting and moaning and sweating and shaking and I was trapped. Did he think I was enjoying myself? Did he care? When he came up for air briefly to tell me how good it felt, I seized the opportunity.

"I need the bathroom," I lied, desperate to break up the world's most unpassionate clinch. A big drip of sweat landed near my eye as he panted like he was in the middle of a full-on cardiovascular work-out.

I ran to the bathroom and looked at myself in the mirror. The breath of fresh air that had kicked off this union a few weeks ago had suddenly gone well and truly stale.

This wasn't how it was supposed to be. I'd sobered up rather quickly, but was shocked when I looked at my watch to see it was nearly three o'clock in the morning. I stayed in the bathroom far longer than necessary before realising I couldn't stay there all night. I reluctantly made my way back to the lounge where I then did a double-take. There was porn on the telly. Chris was lying on the sofa. Eyes half closed, trousers undone, hands down his pants and a look on his face that suggested I'd just missed the real life money shot. Who said romance was dead?

Premature evacuation was called for here, but how the hell did I get home from Acton at this hour? Hank and his *Thriller* impression, Luke and his fangs, Paul and his porn – it all paled into insignificance compared to this. I hid in the kitchen and tried to find a cab number on the noticeboard. It was then that I saw the letter addressed to Mr Chris Clutterbuck. Things were going from bad to worse.

I couldn't get a cab for love nor money, but in a few hours it would be daylight. Chris walked in fully dressed as if nothing had happened and asked if I wanted a cup of tea. For want of something better to say, I said yes. Was I dreaming? I was so tired, I wasn't sure. I fell asleep on the sofa shortly afterwards, and was awoken a few hours later by a dressed and showered Chris, blow-drying his hair at the mirror. With the light streaming through the window, his hair was practically orange and his skin was almost translucent. He had a weird look about him and I felt sick.

"I've got to go into work," he announced.

It was only eight o'clock, but that was fine by me. I couldn't get away quick enough, so I splashed some water on my face and squeezed some toothpaste into my mouth. I looked like someone from Cell Block H but I really didn't care.

"I'm ready," I declared, eager for him to buzz me out.

"I'm driving," he replied. "I can drop you at the station."

"Don't worry. I could do with the walk."

He was still preening himself in the mirror. Spraying his hair and adjusting it as if it made a difference. A couple of

squirts of Davidoff Cool Water later and he was ready to roll.
"Sure you don't want a lift?" he asked. "It's raining."
"Positive," I told him. I'd have walked even if there was
a monsoon outside.

He buzzed me out, saying he'd call me later. Don't
bother, I thought, but I must have been suffering from shock
because all that came out of my mouth was "cool". Would
I ever have the guts to be brutally honest?

I went straight home and straight to bed. I buried myself
under my duvet and cringed myself to sleep. I wanted to
hibernate. I was never going on another date again. Internet
or otherwise. Thankfully Chris didn't call. But he did email
on Monday morning.

| From: Chris_C | To: jo-to-go |
|---|---|
| Subject: In the cold light of day... | Date: 21.04.03 |

Hi Jo.

Good to see you on friday. It was a bit out of control
though. It's been ages since I had such a crazy night
Sorry I wasn't in touch the rest of the weekend. Been
working loads and no time to recover and take stock.
But in the cold light of monday morning, reality has set
in and here I sit, wondering if it's all too much too soon.

I don't know. Maybe I'm doing what girls usually do and
freaking out when things go too quickly. I did enjoy friday.
I just wish we'd stuck to the original plan and had dinner,
with no pudding, if you know what I mean.

I'm so busy at work at the moment, I don't think I can
deal with it and you. Sorry.

Chris

I nearly fell off my chair. Did I read that right or was I going
mad? Was he totally oblivious to the events of Friday night?
He might have had pudding, but I certainly hadn't! I wasn't
sure whether to laugh or scream so I did both, then read the

message again. Whichever way I looked at it, he appeared to be passing off his creepy behaviour as mine. He was implying that we'd enjoyed a night of wild abandon and debauchery instigated by me, which a nice girl like him just wasn't ready for.

At least he didn't want to pursue it. The feeling was mutual on that score. The thought of those slobbering lips going anywhere near me ever again filled me with dread. I couldn't help thinking it should be me writing the Dear John letter, but I wasn't going to look a gift horse in the mouth.

| From: jo-to-go | To: Chris_C |
|---|---|
| Subject: Re: In the cold light of day... | Date: 21.04.03 |

Dear Mr Clutterbuck

Gutted as I am that you seem to be having second thoughts about moving forward with this relationship, on reflection I think you may be right.

I'm sorry that I jumped on you like that. Sometimes I get a bit over excited and find it difficult to hold back. Especially when it's been a while, if you know what I mean. Apologies for any stains (sweat or otherwise) you might find on your carpet.

Thanks for the spag bol. Better late than never, but I think you forgot to serve the pudding while I was in the room. What was it? Spotted dick and custard?

Onwards and upwards.

Jo

# eleven

## *Curiouser and curiouser*

Staying single was looking more and more appealing. It was painfully obvious that a lot of men on these sites were after one thing and one thing only. And it wasn't love. Could I ever trust anyone's profile again? And more to the point, could I trust myself not to fall for it again? Anyone could be forgiven for asking why on earth I ever logged back on to Digital-Cupid, but I couldn't help myself. I was addicted.

| From: Sexy_Errol | To: jo-to-go |
|---|---|
| Subject: I need you | Date: 07.05.03 |

Jo,

i love your picture, mainly your sexy eyes. i will certainly give you the best of romance and the future will be bright for us. i am a handsome, sexy, big black guy and i want to share many sexy and tender moments with you. i am at your service and i promise i will call you everyday.

You are well lucky i have contacted you today sweetheart, so write back soon.

Cheers honey

Errol

I wouldn't say I felt lucky exactly...

---

| From: Fernando | To: jo-to-go |
|---|---|
| Subject: Taurus for a virgo | Date: 12.05.03 |

How's life treating you Jo?

Can I add anything to it? Can I make you happy, because when you are the happiest lady in the world, I am the happiest guy. Please check out my profile. We have much in common. This could be a romance for life.

I see you as an intelligent, elegant lady, who although independent financially, would like a man by her side.
If you feel a bit uncertain sometimes I will comfort you.
At this moment I'm single, but I am not without offers.
I have a busy life, and spend my spare time enjoying art, opera, literature, theatre and Salsa dancing.

So dear Jo, are you the special lady who can tame this raging bull? Are you the lady who will make me proud when you walk next to me? I want to experience the good things in life with someone special. Your place or mine?

Fernando xxxxx :)

---

The offers flooded in thick and fast for the next few weeks and I was like a kid in a sweet shop. Or should I say a joke shop. At least I was getting my money's worth in comedy value if nothing else.

---

| From: 7OAKS_LEDGEND | To: jo-to-go |
|---|---|
| Subject: HIYA! | Date: 22.05.03 |

Hey there Jo!

I'm Ronnie. I'm a 27 year old lad from Kent. An ex salesman, now in the exciting world of accounts *Yawn*. And hey, before you start getting an image of me in a grey suit and glasses PLEASE DONT! *Smiles* : )

I'm looking for a relationship. I dont sleep about. I believe in respecting a woman and treating her like a princess.
I love making women laugh and being a clown. I can be

quite clumsy at times and come out with stupid things. My nickname is Donut Boy – simply because I AM THICK sometimes. I would describe myself as funny, caring, honest, genuine, unique and charming. Oh – and did I mention clumsy! *Smiles*. I have a husky soft voice a bit like Beppe from Eastenders.

I love running and playing football, although people pick on me as I am a joker. They sometimes pull my shorts down or kick the ball at me on purpose : (

I love watching really scarey films which sometimes make me swear out loud in fear! I also love going to concerts. Been to Craig David, Will Young and Dizzy Rascal – mostly with women, so don't call me a soft lad!

I like cooking and I even enjoy washing up. Want to know why? My Mum brought me up well and before you think "oh sugar – a mummys boy", dont, cos I aint.

I love wearing black (my fav colour), or cream. I love my black suit or black levis and white top. I dont really wear trainers coz I'm more into my loafers or dressy shoes. My fav aftershave is hugo boss and i like galtier even though the man in the ad is gay!

I'm looking to meet someone with a nice smile, pretty face, lovely eyes and wicked personality. If you like what you hear and want to know more – YES – THERE IS MORE! then drop me a line. Hope to hear from you.

Luv Ronnie x : )

---

You couldn't make it up. You really couldn't. I seriously thought that message was a joke, but then I decided it was far too unreal not to be real. Who could come up with that stuff? I clicked on Ronnie's profile. He was of Asian persuasion and fully blinged up. I didn't need to drop him a line to find out more. I already knew all I needed to know. 7OAKS_LEDGEND was – and still is – a legend.

And then there was Daniel.

| From: Daniel_1973 | To: jo-to-go |
|---|---|
| Subject: Hi | Date: 03.06.03 |

Hi there Jo.

I like your profile. It definitely stands out which is refreshing. Well done. Nice pic too.

I'm 29, 6ft tall and live and work in London. I'm a regular guy, but I'm not here for the reasons you may think. I am here because I want to fulfill a dream I've had for a long time. Intrigued? Want to know more? Message me and I'll tell you what it is.

Dan

He sounded nice in theory, but what was he talking about? I clicked on the link to his profile, hoping to find out more. First things first – see what he looks like.

But he didn't have a picture. In its place was a random cartoon. What's the point of that? I guess it's better than a blatant photo of George Clooney. I could only assume he was extremely unfortunate in the looks department, or married. However, I was of course intrigued as to why he was here if it wasn't for a date.

| From: jo-to-go | To: Daniel_1973 |
|---|---|
| Subject: Re: Hi | Date: 04.06.03 |

Hi Dan,

I'm glad you like my profile. You don't say much on yours though, and you look like a cartoon character.

But yes. I am intrigued as to what this dream is you want to fulfil. I look forward to hearing about it.

Jo

What could it be, this dream of his? And how could I help him fulfil it?

| From: Daniel_1973 | To: jo-to-go |
|---|---|
| Subject: Re: Hi | Date: 04.06.03 |

Thanks for getting back to me so quickly Jo. I'm not here for a long term relationship, just to fulfil my dream as I mentioned before. Allow me to explain.

I'm looking for someone (hopefully you) to meet me at a hotel, where I'll be waiting in one of the rooms. There will be no contact or conversation between us beforehand, and at a pre-arranged time, you will knock on the door. The door will be unlocked, and when you hear me say 'enter' you'll walk in wearing a mac and a trilby hat.

I'll be lying in the bed, but it's not what you think. On the floor, you will see a row of ten custard pies. I simply want you to pick them up one by one, throw them in my face, and walk out again without saying a word. What do you think? Are you up for it?

Dan

To say I was stunned is an understatement. I thought at worst he was going to be just another bored, married bloke with a penchant for danger. But no. He was a self-confessed 'regular guy' with a penchant for the phantom flan flinger. Surely he was winding me up? Was this his way of breaking the ice? Trying to win me over with his charm and wit before revealing his shortcomings in the looks department. Who knows with the internet. With tongue placed firmly in cheek, I decided to pursue it for my own amusement.

| From: jo-to-go | To: Daniel_1973 |
|---|---|
| Subject: Re: Hi | Date: 06.06.03 |

Well that's certainly a new one on me Dan! I've had some strange messages in my time on Digital-Cupid, but nothing quite like yours!

I must admit though, despite my initial surprise, having

re-read it and given it some thought, I find myself seriously considering the idea. It sounds quite exciting.

Can I just clarify that I've got this right though? You want someone to come to a hotel where you'll be waiting in a bedroom, and all they have to do is come to your room wearing a mac & trilby and throw custard pies in your face? Nothing sexual? Just the custard pies? What's in it for me by the way?

Jo

---

| From: | Daniel_1973 | To: | jo-to-go |
|---|---|---|---|
| Subject: Re: Hi | | Date: | 08.06.03 |

Yep – that's it. That's all I want you to do. Without saying a word. And as for what's in it for you... well... excitement! And the knowledge that you'd be making someone very, very happy.

I'm so glad that you're considering it. It's been a dream of mine for as long as I can remember but it's been pretty impossible finding someone to fulfil it. I realise it's a bit different, but if you were to accept, it would be truly fantastic for me.

Dan

---

**I think he might be serious. I should probably leave it now. But that would be boring.**

---

| From: | jo-to-go | To: | Daniel_1973 |
|---|---|---|---|
| Subject: Re: Hi | | Date: | 09.06.03 |

It surprises me that you've found it difficult to find willing participants. I would have thought that with us being from the Tiswas generation, it'd be everybody's fantasy.

So when were you thinking of doing this?

Jo

---

From: Daniel_1973           To:   jo-to-go

Subject: Re: Hi              Date: 10.06.03

---

The sooner the better really. Are you up for it then?
I will book a hotel which is convenient to you and let you
know the details on the day.

Dan

---

Am I up for it? Who did he think I was? Jim'll Fix It? I still
couldn't believe he was serious. But how far could I take it?

---

From: jo-to-go            To:   Daniel_1973

Subject: Re: Hi              Date: 11.06.03

---

Yeah. I think I'm up for it. I could certainly do with some
excitement in my life. Will you be supplying the mac &
trilby or is that up to me? If so, is there any chance I can
substitute the trilby for a cowboy hat and save a couple
of quid? (I already have one you see).

Jo

---

From: Daniel_1973           To:   jo-to-go

Subject: Re: Hi              Date: 11.06.03

---

Brilliant! I'm so glad you're up for it. How are you fixed for
next Wednesday?

Just one thing, I would prefer to stick to the original plan
and for you to wear a trilby. It's been such a dream for so
long, I don't want to change a single detail, no matter
how small. Don't worry though. I'll supply the outfit. I'll
leave it at reception in a bag with your name on, then you
can get changed in the toilets before coming straight up
to the room. I'm really looking forward to it now! You've
made my day.

Dan x

---

Classy. Donning a mac and trilby in the hotel bogs, before undertaking a secret custard pie mission. It was like a scene from *Allo Allo!* Listen carefully... I shall say zis only once...

———————❤———————

"Oh my God! You have to go," said Lucy. "Just to see if he's for real!"

"You've got to be joking," I replied. "He's obviously a bloody weirdo!"

"Or a wind-up merchant," said Jane.

"I know. I'm intrigued," I admitted. "But I don't know who's winding who up or what's going on. All I know is I'm not really going to do it!"

"I will!" yelled Lucy.

"I've got it!" exclaimed Jane. "Tell him you're up for it and we'll all come with you. We'll all get a mac and a trilby and we'll all throw custard pies in his face. Whether he's joking or not!"

"Brilliant," Claire laughed. "Safety in numbers!"

"He wouldn't know what had hit him," I added.

"Can you imagine?" said Lucy. "It would be hilarious!"

"Come on, Jo. You know you want to..."

———————❤———————

I had a dream that night. And it felt uncomfortably real. Four girls dressed in macs and trilby hats, driving through London in a Renault Clio 1.2, Led Zeppelin's *Custard Pie* blaring on the stereo. We got pulled over by the police for acting suspiciously. I was let off with a caution and a custard pie to the face. Eventually we got to the hotel. It had long, wide corridors with thick red carpets and gilt framed mirrors. It certainly wasn't a Holiday Inn. I couldn't remember Daniel's room number so we knocked on the door of every room and launched custard pies at anyone who answered. The whole thing degenerated into madness, with security chasing the four of us up and down corridors with their own, far superior custard pies. We never did find Daniel.

I was glad when I woke up in my bed and not in a prison cell. A sense of relief washed over me that it was *only* a dream. I hadn't really been running amok in the corridors of some plush hotel, dressed in full Daniel-fantasy-custard-pie-throwing regalia.

It was then that I knew I couldn't take it any further. Hilarious as it may have been, it was best to leave Daniel and his fantasy in room 101 where they belonged.

# twelve

## ...then try, try again

**VIRGO**

*Your stars for week commencing 23rd June 2003.*

*You are lost and you want to find a safe path, but you are beginning to worry that you'll never find it. What you don't realise though, is that each awkward encounter is ruling out one more road of false hope. By a process of elimination, you are being guided in the right direction. You will find what you are looking for. Be patient. Sit back and relax, Virgo.*

Thank God for that. Despite my tenacity, I could be forgiven for getting despondent. But now it all made sense. Although I hadn't met Mr Right yet, or even Mr Maybe, I still shouldn't think of my *'awkward encounters'* as failures. More like the necessary tools to help me on the road to success. Everything was happening for a reason. The false hope, the wrong dates, the slobbery kisses and the weirdos. All a necessary evil. I'd strike gold eventually, it was obvious. It said so in the stars.

Armed with this knowledge, I logged back on to Digital-Cupid with a renewed sense of optimism. I had several new messages waiting and the suspense was killing me. Would there be a new potential love interest to occupy my mind, or just another bunch of illiterate martians?

| From: | Enchanting_Being | To: | jo-to-go |
| --- | --- | --- | --- |
| Subject: The right elements? | | Date: | 23.06.03 |

Dear Jo,

We are all here to seek a union, but there are many levels. Lets explore them together...

Does your heart feel at one with nature? Do your eyes soak up the beauty? Wouldn't it be great to experience what is in your heart and mind, to explore the magical mystery tour of this life and beyond, within the embrace of your beloved. In an ideal relationship, we must work at seeking equilibrium. My Heart is open like a rose, so embrace me in your ocean. I am an unusual guy. In control of my masculinity, whilst very in touch with my feminine side. I'm into yoga, wholesome food, meditation, spirituality, the universe and beyond.

I see you were born in 1969 and are an earth sign. Get in touch. I'm looking for a Goddess who is willing to overcome barriers and unite alchemically on every level. Preferably with blonde hair and blue eyes. Must be open for a spiritual journey.

Om.

---

Well that was a new angle. There was a picture of a bloke sitting up a tree in the lotus position. Sadly I couldn't unite alchemically on that level, as I suffer from vertigo.

| From: | David_John | To: | jo-to-go |
| --- | --- | --- | --- |
| Subject: Hi Jo | | Date: | 24.06.03 |

I know its a naughty question, but have you ever given a guy a golden shower?

David xxx

---

No. And I'm not about to start now David.

---

| From: | Garcon_Francais | To: | jo-to-go |
|---|---|---|---|
| Subject: hello jo-to-go | | Date: 30.06.03 | |

I am a Frenchman living in london. I have been here only 2 month. Before I work in Paris. I do not know many person in London so I join this site.

I am liking london. There is so much to do. I like music and going to live gig. Please look at my page. Sorry – my english is not good!

Didier

---

Didier caught my eye. Let's face it, that wasn't difficult with the competition in my inbox. Besides, I've always liked a Frenchman. I'm not sure why. Probably the accent, or the whiff of Gitanes. Maybe it's the effortless sophistication (some call it arrogance), but I like them. I'd often fancied myself living in a chateau, dans le South of France. Baguette for breakfast, long lingering lunches and wine for tea. So I immediately took an interest in Didier and checked out his profile. His picture was small, but he wasn't bad apart from the flying jacket. He was tall, thin and rather good looking, but he didn't look French somehow. Did I expect him to be wearing a beret with a string of onions round his neck? I imagined he'd have olive skin and black hair, but instead, he was pale and interesting. He was 34 and worked in Camden as a web designer.

---

| From: | jo-to-go | To: | Garcon_Francais |
|---|---|---|---|
| Subject: Re: hello jo-to-go | | Date: 01.07.03 | |

Thanks for your message. Your English is much better than my French. Maybe you could give me lessons sometime. I've spent a lot of time in France, but I can't seem to master the language.

Bonjour,
Jo.

---

| From: | Garcon_Francais | To: | jo-to-go |
|---|---|---|---|

Subject: Re: Hi        Date: 01.07.03

Au revoir! Ha ha. I like very much your funny. I am happy
to help you French lessons. You can help my English.
I learn every day at work but it takes long time.
Do you have MSN messenger?

This would be interesting. Conversing in Franglais on MSN
messenger. I added him to my contact list and he was
already online.

*Jo says:*      *Bonjour!!*

*Didier says: Ah. You are here. Bonjour.*

*Jo says:*      *Ouvrez la fenêtre!*

*Didier says: Porquoi?*

I love school book French.

*Didier says: Would you like to go to lunch one day?*

*Jo says:*      *Oui. That would be très bien merci.*
                   *Which day?*

*Didier says: How is Friday for you? 1pm?*

*Jo says:*      *Oui. Friday at 1pm. Magnifique.*

*Didier says: Tottenham Court Road tube station is OK?*
                   *Vous parlez vachement mal le francais!*

Things were moving fast, but I thought it was best to meet
Didier sooner rather than later. A long online relationship in
this instance could be painful for different reasons.

Apart from the odd hello, the next contact we had was
on Friday morning to confirm we were still on for lunch.
It was only then that I started to really wonder what he'd be
like. Maybe the communication problem would be a blessing
in disguise. If I said something stupid he probably wouldn't

understand, and his accent was definitely going to overide any faux pas from him.

As lunchtime approached I felt nervous to be meeting this tall, French stranger that I knew hardly anything about. I brushed my hair and did a spot check before leaving the office. Would I be able to pick him out amongst the heaving throng of people at Tottenham Court Road? We hadn't even established which exit to meet at.

I needn't have worried. As I walked up Charing Cross Road I spotted a flying jacket through the crowds. In it was a tall, pale redhead looking worried. As I got nearer, and he got clearer, the flaws that a low resolution photo can hide became apparent. Our eyes met. He didn't smile. It was more of a sneer. His eyes were narrow and close together. He looked more like 54 than 34.

"Hi," I said. "Nice to meet you." I fixed my face with the best grin I could muster. Disappointment engulfed me, but I tried not to show it.

"Yes. And you," he replied. He didn't look like he meant it. I sensed a difficult hour ahead.

"Where do you fancy going?" I asked.

"I do not know. You know zis area better I sink? I leave it up to you." He hadn't taken his hands out of his pockets yet.

I felt the pressure. It was up to me to find somewhere to go, and to keep the conversation flowing while Didier walked beside me adding absolutely nothing. Admittedly Oxford Street was hectic and not the best place to hold your first conversation with a potential date. Perhaps he was nervous, I thought. Give him a break. OK, he wasn't what I'd imagined, but he hadn't exactly lied. I'd taken a chance on a few exchanged sentences and a poor quality photo, purely because I had a romantic vision of a sophisticated Frenchman. That illusion was now a distant memory and we hadn't even found a restaurant yet. Thank God it was only a lunch date. We veered off into Soho.

With it being Friday lunchtime, everywhere was packed.

This was a totally disorganised rendezvous. After fifteen minutes of awkwardly walking the streets, we ended up in Pizza Hut. How romantic. To top off the ambience perfectly, we were put on a tiny table at the back, next to a group of German tourists with lots of luggage and very loud voices. Then I was faced with another dilemma. Should I go for à la carte, or all-you-can-eat for £4.95? I decided that the latter wouldn't be very graceful, so I compromised and went for all-you-can-eat from the salad bar. Didier did the same. He didn't seem to have a mind of his own so far. Or was it the language barrier?

Once we'd loaded our plates and got back to the table, I had a chance to have a proper look at him. His photos on the website were definitely real, but he looked so different close up. I'd never seen such dry, pale skin. Nothing a good moisturiser and a couple of sunbeds couldn't sort out, but his eyes were narrow and empty. He kept looking at me strangely. Kind of staring. I felt uncomfortable and decided he could turn if provoked. So I tried to keep things moving, but just found myself scraping the barrel for conversation.

"So do you usually fly to Paris or take the Eurostar?"

"Eizer way. Whatever is cheapest."

That killed that conversation dead. His English wasn't bad when he actually spoke. I asked about his job, where he was from in France, how long he was here for, what he'd done in London, whether he'd been on many dates from the website. All the usual conversation starters, but I couldn't generate a flowing response to anything. He asked me nothing. I gave up after a while and concentrated on my salad. It was more interesting.

It was a long hour. I don't know what he was thinking. Probably that I was extremely dull bombarding him with inane questions. I was so relieved when it was time to go, I could hardly hide my delight. We went Dutch with the bill – about a fiver each – then made our way outside. I'd never been so pleased to see Oxford Street in the school holidays. I wondered which way he was going. The opposite one to me preferably.

"It is nice to meet you. And nice lunch. I must go now. I will talk wiz you on email later," he said.

Wow. What's with the sudden monologue, I wondered.

"Nice to meet you too. Au revoir."

After an awkward goodbye involving no touching of any kind, I went one way and he went the other. Thank God it was over. It was hard work. That's not how a date should be – it should be fun and interactive. I breathed a sigh of relief and decided that lunchtime dates were definitely the way forward. It's not easy pretending to enjoy yourself, but I thought I'd done a pretty good job of it. I was sure he felt the same and I didn't think I'd ever hear from him again. But I did, and sooner rather than later.

| From: Garcon_Francais | To: jo-to-go |
|---|---|
| Subject: Hello | Date: 04.07.03 |

Nice lunch? I am wondering what you are thinking of me? Are you wanting to go out with me again?

Had he been on the same lunch as me? The one where he'd hardly said a word and looked at me coldly throughout? And he was asking if I wanted a repeat performance. Frankly I couldn't think of anything worse. I could have told the truth but that would have been far too rude. I'd have to try and be diplomatic.

| From: jo-to-go | To: Garcon_Francais |
|---|---|
| Subject: Re: Hello | Date: 04.07.03 |

It was nice to meet you, but I don't think there was any spark. We're not really compatible so I don't think we should go out again. Good luck in the future.

Jo.

| From: | Garcon_Francais | To: | jo-to-go |
|---|---|---|---|
| Subject: Hi | | Date: 04.07.03 | |

That is all? You would not like to go out with me again?

Without spelling it out that I found him extremely unattractive and more than a little bit creepy, there was nothing else to say. I'd known him for an hour. I wasn't bound by contract. I'd told him how I felt and that was it as far as I was concerned. Any normal person would have taken it on board and moved on.

I thought he had because he didn't contact me again. Well, not straight away anyway. About a month later when I'd forgotten all about Didier, he reappeared in my inbox out of nowhere. His English was certainly coming on.

| From: | Garcon_Francais | To: | jo-to-go |
|---|---|---|---|
| Subject: ... | | Date: 06.08.03 | |

Ugly bitch.

I was gobsmacked. What on earth was I supposed to say to that? *"Why, Monsieur Didier, you are really spoiling me..."* It probably would have been better to say nothing, but I replied thanking him for his kind observation, and asked if it was a compliment in France.

| From: | Garcon_Francais | To: | garcon_Francais |
|---|---|---|---|
| Subject: Re: ... | | Date: 06.08.03 | |

It is obvious you are not interested in me. You are horrible rude nasty ugly bitch. Be careful treating people like shit. You do not deserve to be happy you whore.

Well it sure looked like he was having fun with a thesaurus.

151

C'est la vie. Needless to say, I didn't accept any further correspondence from the suave and vitriolic Frenchman.

———————❤———————

And so, back to the grindstone. There was Martin and there was Pete, both raising some interest in my mailbox. Martin worked in the city and wore a suit in his photo. He wasn't handsome, but he was nice looking. He lived locally and was into rugby.

Pete worked down the road from me, but there was some confusion as to exactly what he did. Even he didn't seem to know. Something to do with health and safety as far as I could gather, but in a building above a pub, which in retrospect I think he spent most of his time in. Pete had split from his wife a few months earlier and had decided he was ready to meet someone else. He lived near Croydon and obviously wasn't meeting the right kind of girl in Sinatra's.

I'd been exchanging messages with both Martin and Pete for a couple of weeks and now they'd both asked me if I wanted to meet for a drink. I decided to kill two birds with one stone and arranged to meet Martin for lunch and Pete in the evening.

Martin was a really sweet, unassuming, nice person. We had lunch in Covent Garden and it was pleasant. He didn't make me laugh and he didn't make my heart miss a beat, but I wasn't watching the clock or scraping the barrel for conversation. It was all very nice and *safe*. Nothing risqué, and nothing particularly exciting. I went back to work feeling neutral about Martin. But neutral was better than nothing. And neutral was better than most of my internet dates so far, so I filed him in the positive box and wondered if Pete would provoke more emotion that evening.

Looking back, I have no idea why I actually agreed to meet Pete. We had nothing in common, but I was trying, like Lucy, to broaden my horizons. Not just wait for the non-existent handsome ones with no baggage, good jobs and amazing wit. Well if that was my rationale, I couldn't have made a better choice.

We met in The Moon Under Water on Charing Cross Road. Brightly lit and crowded, it wasn't exactly ideal for a romantic interlude, but I needn't have worried about romance. I spotted Pete straight away. He was wearing a black leather jacket and wet-look gel in his spiky hair. The very beginnings of what looked suspiciously like a tash and black loafers with tassels finished off the mid-life crisis look a treat. He certainly wasn't handsome, and as I found out, had baggage-a-plenty.

He asked what I wanted to drink. He was on his second pint already. Did I want a bowl of chips with my drink? He'd already ordered some as he was "bleedin' starvin'". There were no tables, so we had to stand. I decided against the chips on that basis, and went for a spritzer.

I spent the next two hours passive smoking and learning the ins and outs of his relationship with his soon-to-be ex-wife and the custody battle he was embroiled in for their three children. Plus his resentment for her new boyfriend living under his roof, while he was roughing it in a one-bed flat in the same block as Dane Bowers. I understood his point, but couldn't help wondering if I could get home in time for *ER*.

It wasn't bad. It wasn't even boring. We just had absolutely nothing in common. Even if we had, the chain smoking would have put me right off. He must have got through a whole packet of Benson & Hedges. His breath smelled like an ashtray and his fingers were yellow. Not to mention the sallow skin. I guess the poor bloke needed some pleasure in life, and if that was his, then who was I to knock it? I just didn't want to share it. I made my excuses about ten o'clock and left, wishing him good luck in resolving his marital issues and advising him that he probably wasn't as ready as he thought to meet someone else. More like a therapy session than a date really.

———— ❤ ————

I'd also been exchanging messages with a bloke calling himself The-Hairy-Cornflake. He sounded really funny, and despite having no picture on the site, he'd reeled me in with his witty repartee. Martin wanted to go out again, but I ruthlessly told him there was no spark. I didn't want to string him along. I was more interested in The-Hairy-Cornflake and I didn't even know what he looked like. A prime example of how virtual reality can play tricks with your mind. A nice reliable real bloke, or a faceless comedian?

We'd bonded over all things eighties, me and The-Hairy-Cornflake. Especially music. He told me it was perfectly fine to be a Duranie, even in this day and age. Of course I already knew that – it was positively über-trendy, but it was nice to meet fellow eighties throwbacks.

Turned out his name was Jason. He said he'd been on a few dates from Digital-Cupid, but the quality so far had been average to below zero. I could certainly relate to that. He had what sounded like an amazing job in PR. If what he said was true, most of his time was spent quaffing champagne and schmoozing with clients at various star-studded events. But reading between the lines, these 'stars' were all Z-list desperados and tabloid tarts. All except the former A-list sports star I'd always thought was rather nice and wouldn't have said no to meeting. Apparently, he and Jason were practically best friends, and if I were to meet him for a drink, he'd tell me some juicy stories.

But I still didn't know what Jason looked like. All I had to go on was what he'd written on his profile, which in my experience, wasn't worth the keyboard it was typed on. I really needed to see a photo before agreeing to meet. In the past I'd been accused of being shallow for asking for a picture. *'It's what's on the inside that counts, not what you see on the outside,'* was a familiar line with those too scared to show their face. Well that's all very well, but what if you look like Shrek's ugly brother? Let's be realistic. You're probably not going to win me over with your charm and wit. This ain't no fairytale.

| From: | jo-to-go | To: | The-Hairy-Cornflake |
|---|---|---|---|
| Subject: Picture? | | Date: 26.08.03 | |

I'm not meeting someone with no idea of what they look like! Why don't you upload a photo? Or email me one. Go on... it's only fair.

Jo.

| From: | The-Hairy-Cornflake | To: | jo-to-go |
|---|---|---|---|
| Subject: Re: Picture? | | Date: 26.08.03 | |

I haven't got a picture! Honestly. Even if I did I wouldn't know how to get it on the website. I'm a complete technophobe me.

I can assure you I'm normal. I'm tall with a full head of dark blonde hair and my mum said I'm good looking! Don't worry – I'm not some 50 year old in a string vest perving at blonde stunners. Find out for yourself. Meet me for a drink.

Jason

Blonde stunners? Well I was flattered, even though it was plural. And I was curious. He was obviously very comfortable with himself. I don't think I'd have the audacity to assure someone I was attractive enough to date with no need for proof. A lot of people do seem to have magic mirrors, but at the end of the day, beauty's in the eye of the beholder.

Jason seemed to be on my wavelength though. He made me laugh. And I might get to meet the A-list sports star. Could I break the no-picture no-date rule? I was becoming more accomplished at this internet dating thing, but let's face it, this was still the internet and if I could fall for a fake Mark Phillippoussis, anything could happen.

But of course, curiosity got the better of me in the end. I figured I'd probably endured worse. As long as he didn't have a crazy mate with him or insist on playing custard pies,

I could handle it. So I threw caution to the wind and arranged to meet him on Thursday at a pub in Brixton. What was I letting myself in for? I told myself whatever happened we'd have a laugh.

We weren't meeting until 8.30, which was just as well as I ended up working late. Just as I was finishing up and getting ready to leave...

> **Tom Evans has
> just signed in**

It made me jump. Something about his name still provoked a reaction. I had no idea why – I'd pretty much forgotten all about him. While I reflected upon this quandary, he was busy typing a message.

*Tom says:*   *Hi! How are you?*

Don't answer Jo. Just log off. And better still, delete him.

*Jo says:*   *Hi. Fine thanks. How are you?*

*Tom says:*   *I'm good thanks. Working hard, playing hard, you know!*

*Jo says:*   *Yes. I know.*

*Tom says:*   *Got something to tell you actually*

*Jo says:*   *What's that then?*

*Tom says:*   *Are you sitting down?*

*Jo says:*   *No. I'm typing standing up.*

*Tom says:*   *LOL – that's what I always liked about you - your sense of humour.*

Oh God – spare me the sentimental bollocks. Just get on with telling me about your wedding plans.

*Tom says:*   *You won't believe it.*

| | |
|---|---|
| *Jo says:* | *Try me...* |
| *Tom says:* | *I just got married!!! In Vegas!!!* |
| *Jo says:* | *Wow. Congratulations.* |
| *Tom says:* | *It wasn't planned. I got a ring and surprised her. Luckily she said yes!* |
| *Jo says:* | *Yes! Very lucky.* |
| *Tom says:* | *It's weird to think I'm a married man!* |

Married yes, man no. Why was he telling me all this?

| | |
|---|---|
| *Tom says:* | *How about you? How's your love life?* |
| *Jo says:* | *Oh fantastic. Orgies every night.* |
| *Tom says:* | *LOL! Tell me more!* |
| *Jo says:* | *I'm not sure your wife would like it. Anyway, I have to go now. Need to get some furry handcuffs for tonight. Bye!* |

I quit the pointless conversation and deleted him from my contact list once and for all.

———— ❤ ————

I didn't feel like going out, but I had to go and catch the Victoria Line to meet the invisible man. I must have nodded off on the train. It's a good job Brixton was at the end of the line because I jerked awake to the words *"This train terminates here. Everybody off please. This train terminates here..."* OK, OK! I texted Jason.

*Are you there yet? If yes where?*

*Jason Mob: Just by door at bar. Blue shirt and jeans.*

As I walked towards the pub, I tried to muster up some psychic powers to manifest myself a gorgeous adonis in a blue shirt and jeans. Unfortunately it didn't work. Instead I got Tin Tin's dad. About my height, reddish hair teased into a quiff at the front. Cheeky grin with a gap between the two front teeth and carrying a few extra pounds.

"Hiya! How's it goin'?" he shook my hand firmly like we were closing a deal.

"Hi. Fine thanks. How are you?"

He clicked his fingers at the barman and ordered some drinks before the usual chit-chat ensued. I quickly deduced that he was one of those cocksure types. Very sure and a bit of a cock. Despite that, he was quite entertaining and told me several fascinating stories about so-called celebrities. Were there any reality TV stars he hadn't met?

He went to the toilet on a regular basis too. He either had a weak bladder or was powdering his nose. Probably the latter as I couldn't get a word in edgeways and he couldn't sit still. I don't think he asked me anything about my life all night. I could have told him about the time I bumped into Sinbad from *Brookside* in Soho Square.

Later on, they cranked up the music in the pub and a dance floor suddenly appeared out of nowhere. Four songs in and Jason suddenly turned into Michael Jackson, moonwalking his way back from one of his numerous trips to the toilet.

"Come on Jo. Let's throw some shapes," he insisted, as he grabbed my hand and practically yanked me onto the dance floor. It was a good job I'd had a few drinks by this point, as the embarrassment would have been even more excruciating.

'Throwing shapes' was a pretty accurate description of Jason's dance moves, as was 'having a seizure'. I didn't know whether to laugh, cry or run. I just hoped against hope that I didn't see anyone I knew. Claire, Jane and Lucy kept popping into my head. *'Ha ha! You've really picked a winner this time Josephine!'* they laughed.

After one song I decided to feign a dodgy ankle and went to sit down. Jason joined me, dripping in sweat. His hair was now slicked back with grease and the quiff was no more. His shirt was half undone, exposing the auburn carpet on his chest. A Blues Brothers number came on and he was off again, arms flailing like he was flagging a taxi.

It was past midnight and there was no sign of the place closing, or of this spectacle coming to an end. I couldn't take much more and told Jason my ankle was throbbing and I needed to go home and lie down. It worked. He helped me outside with his sweaty arm propping me up as I pretended to limp. The stench coming from under it was truly repulsive. I told him I'd be fine at the taxi rank and to go back in and continue his evening. He'd made several friends on the dance floor and looked like he was enjoying himself. He told me that if I didn't want to sustain injury on the dance floor in future, I really should loosen up. Thank God the cab came when it did. I wouldn't have been responsible for my actions had it been much longer. I was so quick to get in I forgot about my ankle, but Jason didn't notice. He was too busy trying to lick my face.

"I'll call you tomorrow," he said, as the cab drove off.

"Don't bother," I shouted through the open window to a bewildered, sodden silhouette still standing at the cab rank.

When I got home, I jumped in the shower and scrubbed myself free of Jason's sweat. He left a message the next day asking if I wanted to do something quieter next time. I couldn't believe he thought there'd be a next time. And besides, I missed the call because I was busy practising my dance moves.

# thirteen

## *A stalker and a gentleman*

---

| From: DeputyDog | To: jo-to-go |
|---|---|
| Subject: Sweet Jo | Date: 06.09.03 |

Could this be the end of my wait?

I have read your profile and I relate well to it. Thank you for the lift in spirit. Somehow it feels good to share this feeling with you. I assure you that I am GENUINE. Let's get to know each other.

I'm a sound engineer for all sorts of TV, film and video. I work long hours and I'm away from home a lot, but the money is good and the job rewarding.

I enjoy going out to bars sometimes, but am equally happy curling up on the sofa with a DVD and a bottle of red. It would be nice to find someone to do this with and you sound lovely. The vibe feels right. Hit me back so we can square the circle.

Andy

---

'Genuine' seemed to be the most over-used word in the world of internet dating, which was ironic considering the amount of lies I'd uncovered. And 'curling up on the sofa with a DVD and a bottle of red' was the most common pastime. DeputyDog was another one without a photo and he sounded weird.

| From: | jo-to-go | To: | DeputyDog |
|---|---|---|---|
| Subject: Re: Sweet Jo | | Date: | 08.09.03 |

Thanks for your message but sadly I'm not feeling the same vibe. Plus I'm quite happy with my circle being round. Sorry.

Jo

| From: | DeputyDog | To: | jo-to-go |
|---|---|---|---|
| Subject: Re: Sweet Jo | | Date: | 08.09.03 |

It's great to hear back from you Jo. You will feel the vibe if you open yourself up to it and find the connection.

I had a late night last night. I was working on a video for a new boy band. I'm shattered today so I'll be staying at home. By the way – I live near Bath, but am often in London due to work. I have friends in Shepherd's Bush and Tooting.

If you feel like a drink or something to eat sometime, my mobile number is at the top of the page. Give me a call.

Andy

| From: | jo-to-go | To: | DeputyDog |
|---|---|---|---|
| Subject: Re: Sweet Jo | | Date: | 09.09.03 |

Thanks, but I really don't think you're my type, and besides, you don't have a photo on your profile, which unfortunately for shallow people like myself, is quite important. Good luck in your search.

Hopefully I made myself clear there. I'm not interested in conversing with you, let alone anything else. I was, however, interested in the next message, especially once I'd checked out the profile attached to it.

---

From: Nick_1976          To:   jo-to-go

Subject: Hello             Date:   09.09.03

HI Jo,

I read your profile and I must say it put a smile on my face. So if your looking for a gentleman who'll keep you entertained, then look no further.

Nick

---

A gentleman hey? That was novel. Nick's profile was enthusiastic to say the least. It was littered with exclamation marks and smiley faces, but he had a smiley face of his own and it was a rather pleasant one. He lived in Chiswick, was seven years younger then me and said he was 6ft 3. I hoped he wasn't another one who had number dyslexia and was really 3ft 6. Perhaps alarm bells should have rung when I read his 'in my own words' section. Nick described his worst nightmare as *'running out of ciggies on a night out'*. Clean cut with a short back and sides, he reminded me of a younger version of Lord Brocket.

---

From:   jo-to-go          To:   Nick_1976

Subject: Re: Hello        Date:   09.09.03

Hi Nick,

Thanks for your message. Your profile is interesting. I've been looking for a gentleman for sometime but they're not in abundance on here. What exactly can you do to keep me entertained in a gentlemanly fashion?

Jo

---

It wasn't long before Nick was charming his way into my inbox every day. He sounded full of life and lots of fun. By the end of the week we'd swapped phone numbers. When we spoke for the first time, I found out that not only did he look like Lord Brocket, he sounded like him too. Plum wedged firmly in mouth, he called me 'honey' at the end of every sentence. A bit over-familiar since we'd never even met, but it seemed to just trip off the tongue. I think he probably called everyone honey. We arranged to meet the following Thursday night in Earl's Court. There was an air of niceness and confidence about Nick that made me feel at ease. I looked forward to meeting him.

---

| From: DeputyDog | To: jo-to-go |
|---|---|
| Subject: Re: Sweet Jo | Date: 17.09.03 |

Jo,

I hope you don't think I'm pestering you, but you have stuck in my mind and I know we would get on well.

A couple of years ago I was gutted when I found out my X was cheating on me after 3 years (lying bitch). Have you been there Jo? If yes, you'll know what it's like.

Since then I have stayed away from the lair of the hurtful woman, knowing the power you all have to destroy a man. But a few days ago I decided to join Digital-Cupid. Straight away you popped up and I was compelled.

I've enjoyed the few words we've exchanged, and that feeling of excitement, looking forward to getting another message from you. If only you knew how seeing your photo has restored a fantasy of mine, then you'd understand. I also wanted you to know that I'm throwing a big party this Saturday and it would be great if you would come. A massive barby for about 30 people at my place. As much as you can eat and drink. Please come Jo?

Andy

---

I admired his optimism but I certainly didn't share it. He hadn't taken the hint at all. How could he possibly think there was a hope in hell of me going to Bath on my own, to attend a party full of strangers (emphasis on the strange)? I didn't reply. I didn't want to fuel his fantasy.

———— ❤ ————

I'd arranged to meet Nick outside Earl's Court station at eight o'clock. I was ten minutes late due to confusion about which exit to take, but I still couldn't see him anywhere. I hoped that was because he wasn't there yet and not because it was another case of mistaken identity. Please let Nick be the one to break the mould.

A couple of minutes later I spotted him walking through the crowd and was quietly jubilant to see that he looked *exactly* like his picture – and he was tall. He was slim and his ill-fitting trousers would have fallen off him had they not been held up with a tight black belt. A tatty beige V-neck and some knackered old deck shoes completed the scruffy-aristo look nicely. The distinct smell of eau de mothballs wafted my way as he greeted me with a peck on each cheek.

"Hi honey," he said excitedly.

"Hi," I smiled and I actually meant it for once.

Having mentally ripped the poor bloke to pieces simply for his choice of clothes, we made for the nearest pub. On closer inspection, I noticed that the mothballs had been at his jumper. I jokingly asked if he'd bought it complete with holes, and he told me that his Mum bought all his clothes and he really wasn't interested in fashion. Talk about stating the obvious. To be honest they looked more like his dad's cast offs, but he seemed like too much of a nice bloke for it to matter.

Nick still lived at home with his parents which was a bit of a worry, but his excuse was *"It's free honey. And I've got the whole top floor. Why move out?"* I could see his point, but living at home with Mummy and Daddy at almost 30? Hardly a turn-on. In the next breath he told me that his salary was £10,000 a year, plus commission at ridiculously difficult targets. That explained his living arrangements a bit more clearly.

We had a nice evening, despite the age gap being more apparent than it probably should have been. When I suggested going for something to eat, he told me he'd already had his tea. Mummy had cooked a lasagne. Alright for some. So I ordered some bar snacks and Nick amused me with his anecdotes, which were mostly about sport, spliffs and his friends. Although he was very boyish, he was a gentleman in many ways too. He held doors open and helped me with my coat. I suppose I noticed because it was so unusual.

"Great to meet you, honey. Lovely evening. I'll give you a call and we can do something over the weekend if you fancy it?" he said, in one long exhalation of a Marlboro Light.

"Yeah, OK. Do that." I agreed.

We kissed briefly before going our separate ways. It was a weird one. There were a lot of things about Nick I normally wouldn't go for, but it was impossible not to like him. He was funny but oblivious. Attractive but immature. I wasn't sure I liked him in a romantic way, but there was no harm in seeing him again. I hadn't been bored to tears at any point which was a breakthrough. The romance might grow on me.

---❤---

| From: | DeputyDog | To: | jo-to-go |
|-------|-----------|-----|----------|
| Subject: Re: Sweet Jo | | Date: | 18.09.03 |

OK, so you're not replying now, but I still believe we would get on, and who knows what else? But like Stevie Wonder, love is blind (LOL)!!

As I said before, I've only just got back into things since my X decided to cheat and lie to me after three 3 long years together. Have you ever had the feeling after someone has hurt you that you'd like to love again Jo?

By the way, the party was fab (apart from someone

crashing my quad bike). I had all my friends round but there was nobody there who I'd choose to start a loving relationship with. I could have had sex with someone easily (yes, it was there if I wanted it), but it would have just been sex. I wish you'd been there. I wish you weren't on my mind, but you are.

I've had a few glasses of wine and I feel melancholy, so will love you and leave you before I waffle on all night about how much I think about you.

Andy

What goes on in people's heads? This was getting scary. I had my very own internet stalker. I felt a strange mixture of dread and pity. I knew what it was like to have virtual feelings, but at least I'd conversed slightly more with the object of my affections. I decided I'd better put Andy out of his misery once and for all.

| From: jo-to-go | To: DeputyDog |
|---|---|
| Subject: Re: Sweet Jo | Date: 19.09.03 |

How can I dress this up?

I'm sorry to hear you feel like this, and I don't want to hurt your feelings, but I find it difficult to comprehend how you can feel this way from the few words I've exchanged with you. Just to let you know, I've met someone now anyway, so your continued correspondence really would be a waste of time.

There's plenty of other great girls on this site. I hope you find happiness with someone suitable.

Jo.

'Met someone' was a bit of an exaggeration, I know. I'd been out with him once and the jury was still well and truly out as to what was going to happen there, but at least it wasn't a downright lie.

———— ❤ ————

Nick phoned on Saturday afternoon to see what I was up to. As if I didn't have plans already.

"Whaddaya doing this evening, honey?" he asked.

"I'm out tonight. Got a friend's party." I fibbed slightly. I was going out with a friend, but not to a party. I wasn't really in the mood for baby-sitting.

"No worries honey. I'll probably stay in tonight, watch the footie and get really stoned. How you fixed tomorrow?"

"You smoke spliffs in your parents' house?" I asked, surprised. It reminded me of being a student. Ripped matchboxes and clever use of joss sticks.

"Like I said, honey. I have a whole floor. They don't bother me up here. I do what I like. Anyway. Tomorrow?"

"Erm... yeah. OK. What do you want to do?"

"Playing golf with the old man in the morning. How about Putney in the afternoon? Little stroll by the river. Bidda pub-grub."

"OK, why not?" I was indifferent, but I guess it beat the *EastEnders* omnibus.

This time Nick was sporting a crumpled extra-large T-shirt with a marijuana leaf and the words 'please keep off the grass' on the front. But despite this, his smiley face and bounding enthusiasm won through.

"Hey!" He greeted me with a bear hug, before sparking up a cigarette. He even smoked like a posh person. Taking a big drag, inhaling deeply, looking up sideways and blowing the smoke through the corner of his mouth whilst pulling a pained expression. The odd smoke ring thrown in now and then for good measure.

We wandered along the river for a while before finding somewhere to eat. Yet another generic pub with wooden floors, rustic tables and a menu containing lots of pine nuts and caramelised red onions. It was packed with equally generic south-west Londoners with their three-wheeler pushchairs lined up in a row outside.

We got a bottle of red wine and studied the menu. It wasn't a difficult choice and two roast dinners arrived ten minutes later. Anaemic beef and too many peas, but it gave us something to talk about. Well it did me. Nick didn't notice as he was watching the football and by all accounts it was important. Every few minutes he'd go "Oooooooohh. Sorry, honey – what was that?" And then "Aaaaaarrrgghh NO!!!!!! – what an absolute bloody arrrrrse! Sorry, honey – you were saying...?"

Not wishing to come between a bloke and football, I managed to amuse myself with the *News of the World*. I knew my place, and while Nick watched the game, I read about the players' sex lives. But once the match was over, I got his undivided attention, some more wine and a pen to do the crossword in the magazine. Something we could do together, I thought.

"Nationality of one born in Indiana?" I read.

"Indian!" coughed Nick through his fag smoke. I wasn't sure if he was joking and I sensed he was bored. He was twitchy and tapping his cigarette packet on the table. He was like a puppy that needed walking.

"Fancy going back to yours for a bidduvva smoke honey?" he said after a while. We were stuck on a question about an archbishop's headgear. I looked at my watch.

"Bloody hell is that the time?"

We'd been there hours. I'd had more than enough to drink and I certainly didn't fancy a bidduvva smoke at 9.30 on a Sunday night, so I declined.

"No problem, honey!" enthused Nick. "Maybe next time eh? What say we catch up one night next week?"

"Yeah. OK."

I still wasn't sure. I liked him, but we were very different.

———— ❤ ————

When he called to arrange to go out again, I cautiously agreed. I'm not sure if I was being charitable, or desperately craving male attention, no matter where it came from.

He picked me up in his L-reg BMW and we went for a drive around Richmond Park, where Nick showed me how loud his stereo could go. The baseline was in danger of bursting the speakers and I was in danger of bursting a blood vessel as I yelled "TURN IT DOWN".

"Wassup honey?" he shouted back, as he nodded his head up and down, one hand on the wheel and one waving his cigarette in the air like he just didn't care.

"Got any Duran Duran?" I yelled.

"Whaddaya say babe?"

Babe? I thought I was honey. We had a couple of drinks in Richmond and Nick told me he wanted to be a football coach when he grew up. Or at least something to do with football. Or if not football, sport in general. I had a feeling that somehow he'd land on his feet. He was one of those people whose glass would always be half full. A lovely, genuine, enthusiastic bounding puppy of a bloke. But I doubted I'd ever get past the mothballs and Marlboro Lights.

As we walked back to the car the smell from the chippy was too inviting to ignore.

"Sorry hon – seem to have spent all my beer tokens. Wouldn't mind shouting my chips would you?" he said after we'd ordered. I handed over the £2 and we ate the chips outside the car. Nick didn't want grease on his leather seats.

He drove me home to the sound of yet another accelerated eighties power ballad being murdered by a drum machine, and I knew that as charming as Nick was, we were never going to get to that elusive fourth date. He wasn't for me. I decided he'd probably be more at home with a BMX than a BMW. Bless.

———— ❤ ————

Back to the digital drawing board...

| From: DeputyDog | To: jo-to-go |
|---|---|
| Subject: Re: Sweet Jo | Date: 29.09.03 |

I don't want to look at other girls on the site. I've looked before and they don't measure up. Call me insane, or call me drunk! Yep – I'm staring at the bottom of a bottle of gin and its empty Jo. Empty. Hope you sleep well at night!

I would have taken you on holidays, called you 24/7, bought flowers every day, trusted you with my life, had kids with you. But you'd have just run off with someone else anyway so I guess it's better this way.

Life is a constant struggle to find that special someone to love, trust and share happy times with. I am the nicest, warmest, funniest, most sincere person I know. We'd be good together because I know that underneath, you are loving and caring. We could have a good life, and I would give you security so that we could raise our kids without putting a strain on our relationship.

I watched Ghost on DVD last weekend and guess what? I cried a good few tears. Do you think love could ever be so amazing and strong?

Well it's 2.30 in the morning. I've laid my heart on the line more than ever. It's the way I am. I am in town tomorrow near Covent Garden. Lets meet for lunch? You've got the number. Call me.

Big Hugs and kisses to you. Sleep well

Andy xxx

---

The man needed help. I wasn't sure which part of *'your continued correspondence really would be a waste of time'* he didn't understand and I didn't like to ask.

# fourteen

## *Can a computer find you love?*

"You could write a book," said Claire. "All these freaks you keep meeting."

Not a bad idea, I thought, still holding out a hope that someone great could land in my inbox one day and it would all be worth it. I knew a lot more people who admitted to internet dating now and there was definitely less of a stigma. I even saw a bloke from work on Digital-Cupid. He was described as three inches taller than he is in real life and wearing a T-shirt saying 'Jesus Loves You'.

OK, it was a long shot that answering a few questions about the colour of my eyes and which paper I read was going to find me my perfect match, and I was fast finding out that playing with matches was just getting me burned. So I went out with a total mismatch, just for the hell of it.

———— ❤ ————

Johnny-B-Good was from Birmingham, but working in London for the foreseeable future. He was a builder working on a new hotel in the West End. He described himself as 5ft 10 and muscular, with brown hair, brown eyes and a 'wicked' sense of humour. There was a fuzzy picture of him on his profile. Pretty ambiguous really, but I took a chance. He didn't know anyone in London, apart from the blokes he worked with, so his social life was his computer.

I wasn't convinced he was quite on my wavelength, but he was funny and he'd been further afield than Lanzarote.

On my suggestion, we met in a wine bar off the Strand. I'd made no effort whatsoever and we hadn't even swapped numbers, so I hoped I'd recognise him. The bar was pretty empty and as I walked in, someone sitting on a bar stool gestured me over, patting the stool next to him. He was wearing a double-denim combo, a Burberry baseball cap and a moustache. This would be fun.

"Oroight bab. 'Ow's it goin?'"

"Hi. Fine thanks. How are you?"

"You've shed-a-load-a-timber since yer pictures ent ya?" A bit overfamiliar, I thought, but the sentiment was there. Somewhere.

"Errrm... yeah thanks. I bought a bike. Started cycling to work–" I started to explain. The Northern Line had finally got the better of me and it was either move house, or find a way of getting to work that was fit for humans.

"Top banana," said Johnny. "Anyway. What you avin? They don't do pints in ere. Just these southern poof bottles," he said, lighting an Embassy No. 1.

"I'll have a G&T please."

I caught the barman's eye and we exchanged a smile, with which I tried to emphasise that Johnny was NOT my boyfriend. At this point, Johnny informed me that he'd knocked off work at 3 o'clock and had been drinking ever since. He said he was sick of work and only doing it to save enough money to go back to Thailand. He'd been 'backpacking' there last year with five of his mates and fallen in love with the place. They'd never left Bangkok.

"No need bab! Everything was there!"

Picture the scene. Beautiful 'girls' for less than a fiver. Cheap beer, live sex shows and as much fake Burberry as you could cram into your fake Burberry rucksack.

"So, you're 34 bab. Knockin' on a bit ent ya. It's about time you had some kids innit, while you still can?"

He had a twinkle in his eye and a lopsided grin. If anyone

else had made a comment like that, I'd have probably swung for them. But the broad Brummy accent, coupled with the dodgy fashion made it comical. Once I'd finished laughing, I found myself admitting "Chance would be a fine thing but I can't find anyone suitable to father them."

"Look no further babydoll! Johnny Supersperm is here!" He smiled with a chink of his bottle and no hint of irony.

I imagined mixing my DNA with Johnny's and the results weren't pretty. He could hardly string a cohesive sentence together and I wasn't sure it was down to the booze. However, I managed to deduce that 'Johnny Supersperm' already had two children by two different women. His eldest was seventeen, which meant he was a father at eighteen. He didn't see his children very often, but he did contribute towards their upkeep. He had absolutely no ambition, no mortgage and not much to show for his thirty-five years, but I found him endearing. He was happy with his lot. As I sat there contemplating the different worlds we were from, I wondered if life was easier with no passion or drive. If you have nothing to aim for, you have nothing to lose. Perhaps ignorance really is bliss...

"Just going to water me 'orse," said Johnny.

... I was back in the room.

———————❤———————

I thought things were looking up when Mike got in touch. His photo stared out of his message and begged me to respond. He described himself as 'very good looking' and as I clicked through his numerous pictures I decided that if they were anything to go by, he was right. In his own words he said he was metrosexual which was a bit dubious. Isn't that just heterosexual with moisturiser?

He sounded like a decent bloke though. He was a PE teacher and he also played semi-professional cricket. When he suggested meeting for a drink after only a couple of emails, I jumped at the chance. But trying to fix a date with

Mike was like trying to crack the Enigma code – nigh on impossible. He had after school soccer club on Monday evenings, tae kwon do on a Tuesday, cricket practice on Wednesdays and Fridays, matches at the weekend and any other spare minute was seemingly spent practising his bowling. We eventually managed to arrange something for a Thursday night three weeks in advance. Once this was established we hardly conversed again until the evening of the date.

I wasn't sure what to expect with the sporting hero. His life revolved around cricket, and mine? Well, it didn't. Would we have anything to talk about? I decided not to worry about it unnecessarily on the grounds that if the conversation wasn't flowing, I'd just stare at him all night and learn about googlies.

I needn't have worried. Within minutes of us meeting, I discovered that Mike's conversation skills did extend beyond sport. His other two favourite subjects were travelling (mainly to sporting events in the southern hemisphere) and himself. We managed to have a relatively pleasant evening despite his arrogance and the fact we had absolutely nothing in common, and when he decided to end the evening with a snog, I felt it only right to oblige. He was a good-looking bloke after all. But it soon became clear that Mike wanted more than a snog and I'm willing to bet that what Mike wants, he usually gets. But not this time.

However, he seemed to think that emailing me a picture of his genitals the next day would be enough to secure some hot action on the second date, which he obviously didn't realise was never going to happen. When that didn't provoke the desired response, he passed on my phone number to some of his friends, who promptly bombarded me with scary text messages of a pornographic nature, describing what they wanted to do with me.

Call me old-fashioned, but I decided against an orgy with Mike and his revolting chums, and phoned him immediately to make it stop. He galanty denied all knowledge and told me that if I didn't stop stalking him he'd report me to the police. I said I'd happily help them with their enquiries by handing over the evidence I'd gathered on my mobile, but I never heard from him again.

———————❤———————

The computer had got it wrong again, but then I guess I couldn't blame it for not picking up that Mike was a depraved, psychotic mentalist from his carefully worded profile. I had a sneaking feeling I should leave internet dating well alone after that experience. He was as close as I'd got to meeting someone dangerous like Claire had predicted, but why should I let him put me off? The chances of anyone else being quite like him were slim.

Maybe-Baby (AKA Danny) seemed nice, despite the naff handle. He was a cameraman, lived in Islington and played football for a local team. We started corresponding and he sounded like a sociable person who was never short of something to do. We messaged back and forth for a couple weeks – mainly small talk – until eventually it seemed like we were running out of things to say. So feeling brave one day, I took the bull by the horns and asked if he wanted to meet me for a drink. Gosh how I'd come a long way. Then it suddenly dawned on me that he might not want to. That's why he hadn't asked me. But why else was a single bloke investing so much time conversing with someone on a dating website? Luckily he jumped at the idea.

"How about tonight?" he suggested.

He couldn't be that busy then. And besides, I wasn't free. I was also wary of investing a whole evening in someone for fear of them turning out to be a numbnut like Mike, but I didn't tell him that. We settled for Friday lunchtime.

I didn't have particularly high expectations, but I was pleasantly surprised when I saw Danny.

"Hi. How are you?" he said quietly. "Drink?"

I was glad to see he looked like his photo and was the

height he'd claimed to be. That was a good start. He got the drinks and even insisted on getting the second round. We got on well and the time went a bit *too* fast. When I got back to work, I felt a definite sense of potential. Or was I just immensely relieved to have met someone normal?

| From: | Maybe-Baby | To: | jo-to-go |
|---|---|---|---|
| Subject: Hi... | | Date: | 28.11.03 |

It was good to meet you at lunchtime. We'll have to do it again sometime.

Dannyx

| From: | jo-to-go | To: | Maybe-Baby |
|---|---|---|---|
| Subject: Re: Hi... | | Date: | 28.11.03 |

Definitely. It was really nice to meet you too. Have a good weekend. Speak to you next week.

Jo x

Well that was promising. We both felt the same. And there was another message waiting from Danny on Monday morning when I got in to work.

| From: | Maybe-Baby | To: | jo-to-go |
|---|---|---|---|
| Subject: Morning | | Date: | 01.12.03 |

Hi Jo.
Good weekend? Did you do anything exciting? I had a few beers on Friday, played football on Saturday and chilled on Sunday. What did you do?

I avoided the obvious Craig David joke and we seemed to quickly revert back to small talk. Neither of us mentioned going out again, and it was as if our meeting had never happened. Perhaps he'd found someone else at the weekend. Still the messages kept coming, but I got bored after a couple of weeks in limbo, and his lack of enthusiasm started to bug me. Eventually I had to say something.

| From: jo-to-go | To: Maybe-Baby |
|---|---|
| Subject: ? | Date: 10.12.03 |

This idle chit-chat is all very well, but unfortunately I'm not looking for a pen-pal. Do you want to go out again or not?

I prepared myself for the worst. He obviously didn't want to go out again. He didn't fancy me. There was no spark for him. That was fair enough. I just wanted to know one way or the other and not be kept dangling like this.

| From: Maybe-Baby | To: jo-to-go |
|---|---|
| Subject: Re: ? | Date: 13.12.03 |

Sorry it's taken a while to get back to you. I didn't know how to put things into words really. I really liked you and I meant what I said after we met, but I haven't been entirely straight with you.

I didn't mention in my profile that I'm divorced with three kids. I don't know why I didn't say, but I just thought it would put people off. Then I got chatting to you and we got on, and there never seemed to be a right time to tell you. I was scared you'd run a mile I suppose.

I got divorced last year after my ex admitted to an affair. I then found out that the youngest child isn't mine. She has been trying to get back with me but I am honestly not interested. She's gone completely mad, to the point where the kids might have to come and live with me in the next couple of weeks because she can't cope (I love the youngest as my own, even though he isn't mine).

The fact that I live in a one bed flat doesn't help things, so I'll probably have to give it up and move in with my parents in Oxford for a while until I sort something out.

I know this is all a bit unexpected, but I guess you needed to know. I hope you don't think too bad of me and I understand if you're not interested.

Danny.

---

All the conversations we'd had over the last month and no mention of his real life. I didn't know him at all. Was anyone actually what they seemed? Once it had sunk in, a few things began to dawn on me. The small talk. The reluctance to discuss anything personal. The fact that it was me who'd instigated the date. He'd done the right thing by coming clean, but was it was too little to late? I sent him a few lines back, wished him good luck with his plight, and filed him in a folder marked 'Excess Baggage'.

———————❤———————

I gave up internet dating for Christmas. But New Year – new list of ideal matches. There was one prospective date amongst them. A man of few words.

---

| From: Crazyfool | To: jo-to-go |
|---|---|
| Subject: Happy new year. | Date: 07.01.04 |

You look nice.

D x

---

Hardly Shakespeare, but I must admit, he looked nice too. When I clicked on his profile I was greeted with a photo of a tanned, blonde hunk standing under a waterfall. It was a full body shot, taken from a few feet away, but I could see enough to know that he looked like my type.

| From: jo-to-go | To: Crazyfool |
|---|---|
| Subject: Re: Happy new year. | Date: 08.01.04 |

Thanks very much. So do you. How are you?

Was my equally substantial response.

| From: Crazyfool | To: jo-to-go |
|---|---|
| Subject: Re: Happy new year. | Date: 08.01.04 |

I'm very well thanks. How's things with you?

| From: jo-to-go | To: Crazyfool |
|---|---|
| Subject: Re: Happy new year. | Date: 09.01.04 |

Things are good thank you. I'm looking forward to the weekend. What are you doing?

| From: Crazyfool | To: jo-to-go |
|---|---|
| Subject: Re: Happy new year. | Date: 09.11.03 |

I'm not sure yet. Do you fancy going for a drink sometime?

I contemplated the premature offer, and decided that we could either exchange these painful one-liners for ever, or just go for it. I decided on the latter because he seemed nice and I really was off those long online build-ups.

We arranged to meet the following Tuesday in Covent Garden, which I somehow managed to convince him was convenient for both of us. Me because I work there, and him – I had no idea why it was convenient for him because he worked in Canary Wharf, but he didn't seem to mind.

I studied his profile again. He lived in Surrey, was 33,

and into music in a big way. He'd also travelled a lot by the sound of things. He seemed like a regular kind of guy. So regular, that I began to feel a long forgotten twinge of excitement about Crazyfool. There was a downside. His name was Derek.

*Dez mob: Am in pub. Halfway up, brown cords, blue fleece.*

He sounded like he was going camping, but I was nervous as I walked into the pub. It was almost empty apart from a few intimate couples and too many staff. I walked up and down the length of the bar, but I couldn't see Derek anywhere.

"Oright Jo," said a short, plumpish bloke with mousy receding hair.

"Hi," I answered, hoping there'd been a dreadful mistake but knowing damn well there hadn't. To say that he didn't resemble his photograph in any way, shape or form would be an understatement. There was absolutely no resemblance to the blonde adonis with the suntan. And I mean *none*. OK, he may have been on holiday when the photo was taken. I could understand if his skin was whiter and his hair was darker now, but he'd morphed into a whole new body and aged about 15 years. I was here under false pretenses. Again.

"Good to meet you. Whadda you wanna drink?"

"Gin and tonic please," I faltered. I was in shock. It was another case of you can run, but you can't hide. We sat down. Two drinks and I was out of there.

It soon became obvious that not only did Derek look nothing like his picture, but he'd also left his personality in cyberspace. He told me how he'd grown up in Kent, then moved to Middlesex, but now lived with his Dad in Surrey. Judging by his sparsity with the truth in other areas, I wondered if backpacking around the Home Counties is what he meant when he said he'd travelled. My eyes glazed over.

"I nearly had an argument with this bloke on the tube

s'mornin'" he said. "The train just stopped for no reason. Sat there for about half an hour. Tell ya what, I was fackin' fumin' when I got off, d'ya know what I mean?"

I ordered more drinks and listened to another riveting tale about when he'd almost missed a flight to Alicante due to the Stansted Express breaking down just outside Tottenham Hale. I was losing the will to live by now, but still trying my best to pretend otherwise. It was 6.45.

The waitress came over with not two, but *four* drinks, and told us it was 2-for-1 happy hour. I could have throttled the silly cow. It really was my lucky day.

"I'm not sure I can drink all that," I told Derek.

"Go on, be a devil," he replied, in his monotone voice.

I zoned out and fantasised about what to have for tea. Baked potato with beans and cheese. Or maybe tuna pasta... Derek was now telling me about his friend's extensive record collection. Apparently he had more vinyl than anyone he'd ever met. I thought about reading him my horoscope or telling him about the dream I'd had the night before. The thought of food was making my stomach churn. I didn't think I could wait until I got home.

"Do you want to get something to eat?" I asked.

"Eatin's cheatin'!" he advised me with a grin.

Yes, I thought. It is when you're a student, but you're 33. I ordered some potato wedges anyway. They would pass the time and probably have more charisma than Derek.

We did manage to while away a few minutes talking about Australia. He'd apparently been backpacking there at the same time as me, but if I'd bumped into him then, I doubted I'd remember.

"Can I ask you summink?" he said all of a sudden.

"Errrm. Yeah, of course," I said cautiously, wondering what was coming next.

"Am I what you expected? Do I look like my photo?"

I nearly spat my drink out. Was he for real? What could I say to that? Well actually I had an impression of you in my mind that couldn't be further from the truth, because it turns

181

out your picture was fake, plus you've just talked about train journeys and your friend's vinyl collection for an hour and a half...? I managed to compose myself.

"No. You're not really what I expected actually. You look nothing like your photo."

"Don't you think so? Is that good or bad?"

HELLO. Was he thick-skinned, or just thick?

"Come off it!" I said. "Putting a false picture on a dating site and claiming it's you is lying! I don't think that's very fair do you?"

"It is me. Honestly!" he insisted. "It's one of me shots from Australia. Taken in Cape Trib–"

"What, In 1993!"

"Well yeah. But it's one of me best pictures. I ain't gunna put a crap one on there d'ya know what I mean?"

Was I stupid, or was he stupid? I couldn't work it out, but at least I had a get-out clause.

———————❤———————

A few days later, I gasped in admiration when Pat landed in my inbox. It was a cold, January morning but his pictures were the hottest I'd ever seen of all the people I'd conversed with on Digital-Cupid. He was tall and slim with a mass of wavy sun-lightened hair, and I soon found out, hilarious with it. The only trouble was, he was finishing a contract in Sri Lanka for the next three months. But I could wait, and wait I did.

He'd been working there for almost three years and had just joined Digital-Cupid in preparation for coming home and finding himself single, while all his friends were suddenly married with children. He was putting out some feelers so to speak, and good on him.

We bonded immediately and started exchanging long, amusing monologues via email on a daily basis. The way he wrote was brilliant and I could see myself falling for him in a big way. I had palpitations at the mere thought of Pat and

I couldn't wait to meet him. We seemed to have a lot in common, not least an unhealthy appetite for crap culture and all things chavtastic. For our first date, he'd promised to take me to Angus Steak House to celebrate our union.

But sadly it never happened. After two and a half months, we fell at the last hurdle. He's the one that got away. The week before we were due to meet he sent me a long, apologetic message explaining that he'd recently met someone by more traditional means and he felt he should give it a go. He did say he'd still like to take me to Angus Steak House when he got home, but it didn't seem appropriate anymore. Who wants a bittersweet Knickerbocker Glory?

# fifteen

## *Romancing the Travelodge*

I would have ignored the uninspiring instant message that popped up on Digital-Cupid one Friday afternoon. Not least because it was from someone named after a motorbike. Something I found a bit tragic. Well, it was more cars really. Did Porsche_Guy, Mercedes_Man and the odd Ferrari_Driver honestly believe they became a better catch with a performance car attached to their moniker? The message from Ducati_Bloke was just another boring one-liner.

*Hi. How are you?*

How am I? How long have you got? It was quiet at work and I'd only logged on to read my messages while I waited for the clock to hit 5.30. But then I'd become deeply engrossed in a conversation about package holidays with someone called Darren. I was practically one yawn short of a coma, so I clicked on the link to Ducati_Bloke's profile and nearly choked on my afternoon Kit-Kat. He was gorgeous. Well, the picture on his profile was. It didn't look fake. Why would anyone trying to impress pose in front of pastel painted woodchip with a floral border?

*Very well thanks. How are you?*

While I was waiting for a response I read his credentials.

The good-looking ones usually tended to be short, married or mentally imbalanced, but Adam was allegedly 6ft 2 with dark blonde hair, a dry sense of humour and a penchant for Metallica. He worked as an IT manager and was also into banger racing. I'd never met anyone who was into banger racing. I didn't know much about it, but in my head it was in the same place as fairgrounds. I don't know what that said about Adam. He had his own banger racing car, but thankfully there was no picture of him posing with it.

*Damn. Sorry. Got to go. Talk to you Monday I hope.*

Is that it? No sooner had this vision appeared, had it vanished back into cyberspace leaving only a couple of sentences and a very nice impression. I was already thinking about the logistics. He lived in Leeds, so we were never going to meet. I shut my computer down, went to the pub and forgot all about it. So I was pleasantly surprised on Monday morning to find a new message from him.

| From: Ducati_Bloke | To: jo-to-go |
|---|---|
| Subject: Happy Monday | Date: 08.03.04 |

Sorry I had to dash the other day. Emergency at work.
Just what you need at 5.30 on a friday afternoon. How about you – good weekend?
Adam

| From: jo-to-go | To: Ducati_Bloke |
|---|---|
| Subject: Re: Happy Monday | Date: 08.03.04 |

No problem. I was counting the minutes on Friday anyway.
My weekend was good thanks. I went to Brighton for a friends party. Great party, shame about the weather.
It was grim. Bit like oop north! What did you do?
Jo.

| From: | Ducati_Bloke | To: | jo-to-go |
|---|---|---|---|
| Subject: Re: Happy Monday | | Date: | 08.03.04 |

Ah. The usual really. Took the whippet out on the moors.
Smoked a couple of pipes. Played with my pigeons.
Drank some ale. Ate some pies...
And now its Monday again and I'm back down the pits.
You're right. It's grim oop north!

Adam

And so began another long-distance online relationship that
made me look forward to switching on my computer in the
morning and reluctant to switch it off at night.

Adam made me laugh. He certainly did have a dry sense
of humour, but he was reflective with it, and a bit unsure of
himself. The one thing he was sure of was his need for
speed. Apart from the banger racing car, he had the Ducati
motorbike and a Fiat Punto (just a runaround for work
apparently). He hadn't had a girlfriend for at least a year.
The last one had cheated on him and he was understandably
cynical. I got the impression he was going through the
motions of trying to meet someone but he really couldn't be
bothered. He'd been on one internet date with a girl in
Norwich. They'd chatted for months before he went down
to see her on his Ducati. He said he enjoyed the journey
more than the actual date and never saw her again.

The more I corresponded with Adam, the more intrigued
I became. And the more I felt we were on the same
wavelength. Then he asked for my phone number. He
thought it would be nice to inject some humanity into
things. Typing messages was too anonymous and we'd been
doing that for three weeks now. I knew he was right, but I
was comfortable with our virtual relationship. Reality had a
tendency to ruin things. But I couldn't justify that without
sounding ridiculous. I knew I'd have to talk to him sooner
or later if things ever had a chance of progressing.

He arranged to call one night. I wondered what his voice would be like. Barry White or Joe Pasquale? Hopefully somewhere in between. Would he have a strong northern accent? I kind of hoped so. I waited in anticipation for the phone to ring, and when it did I leapt out of my chair and put on my best casual phone voice, only to find it was some idiot on a recorded message telling me I'd won a trip to Barbados. I could have thrown the thing out of the window if it hadn't been for the prospect of Adam calling.

But ten o'clock came and I still hadn't heard from him. I doubted he'd ring now and I was half disappointed and half glad. Saved by the non-existent bell. Then it rang.

"Hi Jo," said a deep, quiet voice.

"What time do you call this?" I joked.

"Ten past ten."

His soft voice and mild northern accent didn't fit with the leather-clad motorbiking head banger I had in my mind. Conversation was easy. Adam was passionate about three things. Fast vehicles, Leeds United and his house. He'd recently bought a place in the country and was doing it up. Apparently it had views across the moors as far as the eye could see. Sounded bleak to me, but by the time I put the phone down two hours later I was living there with him, two kids, a dog and an Aga.

———————❤———————

After that first phone call, we spoke for at least a couple of hours a night. He was a creature of habit, leaving work around six to go to the gym, home about eight to cook his dinner (usually steak) and eat it in front of the Kerrang Channel. Once that was all out of the way around ten, he was free to call me.

After about two weeks of these long conversations about life, love and the universe, he brought up the issue of meeting. In the flesh. A proper date. Of course, by now I wanted to meet him more than anything. I was falling for him without ever having met him. Hadn't I been here before? Yes, but I couldn't let that put me off.

He invited me up to Leeds, but knowing how these things can turn out I daren't take the risk. So I asked him down to London but he was worried his bike would get nicked. Off to a good start. After much deliberation, we decided that the fairest and easiest thing would be to meet in the middle. It was still quite a way to go for someone you'd never met, but the intimate phone calls, the constant banter and the virtual attraction made it a must. I had no doubt we'd get on. Meeting was simply a formality, so we may as well get on with it. So after much to-ing and fro-ing, emailing, phoning and studying of maps, we agreed on a date. Two weeks on Saturday in sunny Birmingham. We booked two rooms at the Travelodge just off the M6. Heaven.

———————❤———————

I'd kind of forgotten (or rather chosen not to remember) that I'd arranged to go on a date with someone called Jonathon. He'd been lurking in my inbox for weeks and if it hadn't been for Adam taking up so much space in my head, I might have been more enthusiastic. But rather than completely ignore Jonathon, I'd humoured him with the required responses to his questions and it had just snowballed. He emailed me informing me he lived 'just down the road' from me. I replied acknowledging the sheer coincidence that someone else lived in the London Borough of Wandsworth, and before I knew it, I was agreeing to meet him for a drink. He didn't strike me as being my type, but then neither would a banger racing heavy metal fan in theory.

In another bid not to put all my eggs in one basket, I met Jonathon at The Sun pub in Clapham. A great place for warm evenings like this one, and plenty of background noise. When I walked into the garden to meet him, I saw him straight away. Sitting on his own wearing a beige linen suit, he stuck out like a sore thumb. Once again, it was a classic case of someone looking nothing like their photo, but this time I didn't care. How irrational was that? At least Jonathon was a real person sitting here in front of me. Adam wasn't. He was a voice at the end of a phone, a message on a computer and a few choice photographs.

We ordered some wine and chatted amiably about how lovely the weather was. Later on we got some food and I listened as, between mouthfulls of Thai green curry, Jonathon waxed lyrical about his family's villa on the Costa Del Sol, his father's fruit import business and the fact that one day it would all be his. My mind drifted to Birmingham.

I snapped out of my daydream when I felt my phone vibrate in my bag. I wondered if it was Adam. It was about 10 o'clock. Time for the routine phone call. And time for me to go home. I pretended to look for my purse and had a quick look at my phone.

*Adam mob: Where R U?*

My heart did that somersault thing it hadn't done for ages. What was I doing here? I couldn't really reply in front of Jonathon. I don't think he'd noticed my eyes glazing over while he discussed the quality of Spanish tomatoes, but blatantly texting someone was a bit much.

I finished my drink, casually looked at my watch, assumed shock at the time and made my excuses. I told him it had been a lovely evening but I had an early start in the morning. He shook my hand and picked up his briefcase.

"Nice to meet you Jo. Hope to do so again sometime."

I felt like I'd just closed a deal with the man from Del Monté. He say yes. But I say no. Poor bloke never stood a chance. My mind was totally preoccupied. I mumbled the appropriate pleasantries and flagged down a passing cab. Jonathon looked confused. We were going the same way. Should he get in the cab too?

"See you then," I waved and shut the door.

I phoned Adam on the way home. He asked where I'd been and I lied. I didn't want to tell him I'd been on a date.

It felt like I was betraying him. How utterly ridiculous. He wasn't my boyfriend. Yet.

———————❤———————

At last. The day of the big date arrived and I was nervous. It wasn't like I could flag down a cab and be home in twenty minutes if this one went wrong. But it was full of promise and I so wanted it to work out. All this build-up and it was to culminate at a Travelodge just off the M6 at three o'clock this afternoon.

I took so long getting ready I was half an hour late leaving. I'd tried on all the clothes I owned at least twice and discarded all of them. Adam had insisted he had no idea about clothes, he couldn't care less, and for that reason he'd decided I probably wouldn't be attracted to him. Me being the fashion conscious clothes-a-holic that I am of course. I told him as long as he didn't wear slip-on shoes with tassles or decorative gold bits on the front he'd be fine.

The weather was atrocious. In fact it couldn't have been worse. It was raining so hard I could hardly see the car in front of me. It was like being in a movie. Nothing could come between me and the enigmatic biker. Not even the torrential rain was going to stop me getting up the M1 for our romantic rendezvous. Adam would be there before me. He'd check into his room. Maybe use the trouser press. Then he'd look at his watch. Look out of the window. Wonder where I'd got to, or if I'd ever arrive. Then just as he was about to give up hope of us ever being united, he'd see me pull up in my Clio. He'd come rushing out into the car park in his leathers and we'd throw our arms around each other, ecstatic to finally be together. Either that or I'd die in a fatal car crash, just as my struggle to find true love was about to end.

All sorts of things were going through my mind. I hadn't told anyone where I was going, or even that Adam existed. It hadn't entered my head that it would go anything other than well. But the old axe-wielding murderer cliché flashed through my mind briefly as I passed Northampton.

I phoned Claire. Someone else in the world should know where I was. And if someone was going to be the last person ever to talk to me it may as well be her. She was practically family after all. She thought I was crazy. Mainly for taking my car outside the M25, but I promised to text her every hour, on the hour, to let her know I was OK.

Adam phoned me at 3.15 to say he was there. Oh God. He really was there. I arrived about half an hour later to find that the car park was overlooked by all the rooms. Adam was no doubt going to see me walk across the car park in this hurricane. He had the upper hand. He would see me before I saw him. It would give him time to leg it if he didn't like what he saw. I put my hood up and pretended to receive a phone call as I made a dash for reception.

"Vehicle registration?" said the girl.

"I don't know," I replied. I'd only had my car six years.

I made it up, found my room, breathed a sign of relief and thanked God for hair straighteners. Then I phoned Adam to announce my arrival.

"About bloody time!" he said. "What time do you call this?"

"Half past four," I replied.

If he'd seen me from his window, he wasn't letting on. We discussed our room numbers and the terrible drive for about five minutes, then decided not to procrastinate a minute longer and meet in the bar at 5 o'clock.

The moment of truth was almost upon us. I got changed a couple of times and then put my jeans back on. It was now or never. I made my way down the corridor and tried not to think about it. Tried to look at it as 'just another date', but it was more than that. We'd built up a relationship over the last couple of months and there was no denying that we were close already.

I didn't want to be the first to arrive, but when I got to the bar I couldn't see Adam anywhere. It was empty aside from a miserable-looking couple and the barman. Should I turn round and walk out again and come back in a minute? I needed some Dutch courage.

"Double gin and tonic please," I said to the barman.

"And a bottle of Rolling Rock," said a deep, northern voice behind me.

I turned round and there was Adam. All 6ft 2 of him. An unfamiliar feeling engulfed me with the realisation that he looked even *better* in the flesh. And for someone that had gone on about his lack of fashion sense so much, he looked perfectly presentable to me. Casually dressed in jeans and a black T-shirt, even his footwear was perfect. Blundstone boots. Very nice.

I felt a rush of blood to the face as I was overcome with shyness. Like a schoolgirl who'd come face to face with her 6th form crush at the tuck shop, I was lost for words for once.

An excitable "hi" was all I could muster as we engaged in a strange clinch reserved only for people who knew everything about each other but had never met. Half handshake, half bear hug type thing. We sat down with the drinks. I wanted to say something but nothing seemed to be appropriate. Adam was staring at me with an intense look on his face. I tried to stare him out but I couldn't even do that, so I laughed nervously and turned away.

"You've got wonky eyes," he said eventually.

Oh. I wasn't sure what to say to that, so I thanked him and made a mental note to look in the mirror on my next visit to the toilet. Nobody had ever told me I had 'wonky eyes' before. And if we were going to split hairs, he had a big nose but I wasn't going to bring it up.

Adam was reserved, controlled and very dry. I'd expected him to be more animated than he was, but that was OK. Maybe he was nervous too. The first half hour was awkward to say the least. I didn't know why, but conversation just didn't flow as easily as I'd expected. I thought the transition from virtual to reality would be a breeze in this case, but I was wrong.

It was like there was an invisible wall around Adam. Or a field of negative energy or something. He exuded strange vibes that I couldn't quite make out. I still wanted to be there. I had no idea what his first impressions of me were, but I fancied the pants off him.

After a few more drinks in the exclusive residents-only Travelodge bar, we got a cab and made our way into town. It was a long time since I'd been to Birmingham and I was pleasantly surprised. It was positively buzzing. We found a table in the corner of a bar on Broad Street. Despite my casual banter abilities having returned by now, Adam was still controlled and intense. At least the music was loud.

Slowly it began to dawn on me. The clues were all there. He didn't like me! Well, not in that way. I wasn't what he'd expected and he was suffering from an overdose of disappointment. I knew all to well what that was like, but the poor bloke was miles away from home. We'd talked about everything before we met. Adam had said he'd never been able to talk to anyone like he could talk to me. He'd told me his deepest, darkest secrets and his hopes and fears. It crossed my mind that it shouldn't be hard to tell each other what we thought now we'd actually met. But face to face, it was easier said than done.

I ignored this thought as best I could. There was nothing I could do about it but be myself and get on with it. I'd have a top night out in Birmingham to remember if nothing else. We went to a few different bars and he eventually seemed to loosen up, to the point where we began to have a good laugh. We started to interact more and he was almost the Adam I'd expected. Almost, but not quite.

We made our way back to the hotel around midnight. The bar was open and still pretty busy.

"Do you fancy a night cap?" I said.

"Yeah. OK. Let's get a bottle and take it to my room," he replied. "It's a bit packed in here."

I was surprised he'd invited me into his 'space'. He hadn't done that all night. This would be interesting.

When we got there I wasn't sure what to do with myself, so I switched on the TV. I just wanted some background noise to ward off any awkward silences. Adam glanced at the mirror before opening the wine.

I looked around the room. It was then that I realised he was a control freak. His toiletries were arranged in a neat row, each item equidistant apart, going from tallest to the smallest. His leathers were folded in a way I didn't realise was possible and placed neatly on a shelf. His motorbike helmet was next to them, front on with the visor down. His bag was stowed under the bed and there was a pristine, folded T-shirt on the pillow. Apart from this evidence, you'd never know anyone had been in the room. I'd only been in mine 20 minutes and it looked like there'd been an explosion.

He poured the wine. I sat on the edge of the bed wondering where this was going. We made small talk about whatever was on the TV and then Adam looked at me meaningfully.

"What?" I said, embarrassed at his stare.

"Nothing," he replied, taking my glass and putting it on the bedside table.

Still staring, he took my arms, pinned me down and his lips descended onto mine. At last, we have lift-off, I thought, before realising I couldn't move. It was a good kiss, but the fact that I was shackled made it totally disconcerting and a bit scary. I couldn't move an inch. He was so strong.

I thought I'd better assume a more comfortable position before the blood supply to my wrists was cut off, so I waved my hands in a bid for him to release me. He let go of one of my arms, which moved inadvertently towards his head. I've never seen anyone move so fast.

"Not the hair!" he exclaimed as if his life depended on it.

"Hey?" I said, confused about what was going on here. Was this a romantic interlude or not?

"I don't like anyone touching my hair, OK?"

Was he joking? What was so unique about his hair? I reached over and picked up my wine glass. Adam wiped away the ring it had left on the Gideon Bible with a tissue.

I was more confused than ever now. Just as I'd resigned myself to the fact that my feelings for Adam weren't reciprocated, he'd invited me back to his room and kissed me. Just as I'd changed my mind, he'd leapt up and told me his hair was out of bounds.

I suddenly felt uncomfortable. I liked Adam, but I had no idea what was going on in his head and I was tired of trying to work it out. It had been a long, strange day and it was now nearly two o'clock in the morning.

"I think I'll head back to mine now actually," I said. "I really need some sleep."

"Oh. You don't have to," he replied. "You can sleep in here if you want." I don't think I'd ever had such a tempting offer or felt so wanted. But it was no good. The moment had gone. And besides, I was worried I'd crease the pillow.

"No, thanks. I need my stuff..."

"OK then. If you're sure," he said. "I'll see you in the morning for breakfast."

He smoothed the quilt where I'd been lying, saw me to the door and kissed me goodbye. I kept my hands in my pockets, wary of the clearance zone around his head.

"See you tomorrow. Call me when you wake up," he said with a warm smile.

I made my way back to my room which was at the other end of the hotel. All the clubbers were coming in now and looking at me like I was doing the walk of shame. If only they knew. I could have been, had I not made the terrible faux pas of touching Adam's hair. Never had I been so glad to close the door behind me and climb in to bed in a Travelodge. As I switched the light off, a text came through.

*Adam mob: Thanks for a good night. Sorry about before. I just have some strange ways. Sleep well. x*

Strange ways? Too right you do! I thought about him lying in his bed and wondered how he organised his head on the pillow so as not to affect the perfect coiffing. I fell asleep and dreamt about hairspray.

I woke up at seven o'clock the next morning. My head was pounding and my stomach was rumbling. I wondered if Adam was awake. It was a bit early for breakfast, so I ate the Bourbons by the kettle and tried to go back to sleep. But I couldn't. The events of the night before were playing over and over in my head. I felt so fuzzy that I didn't know what I felt about Adam any more. And I was certainly none the wiser as to what he felt about me. Had his attempts at seduction actually meant something, or was it just the easy option? What was going to happen now?

Adam phoned at 9.30. If we hurried up we'd just make breakfast. He told me he'd been up a while but hadn't wanted to wake me. He was all showered and ready to go. I caught a glimpse of myself in the mirror. The words 'polish' and 'turd' came to mind, but I did the best I could in the time I had and made my way to breakfast.

There were a couple of croissants left, the odd over-ripe banana, or cereal. Adam looked fresh as a daisy. I fancied him all over again, and temporarily forgot about his strange ways and my hunger. He was chatting away like a new person. What a difference a day makes. I just opted for a cup of tea before we got our bags and checked out.

Adam was fully leathered up when we made our way out to the car park. I'd like to say it was a good look, but I'd be lying. He walked me to my car.

"Well..." I said. "It was good to meet you at last." I had no idea what else to say.

"Yeah. And you," he agreed. "So what happens now?" he asked with a grin. He was asking me?

"I'm not sure," I smiled. All I knew was that if I steered clear of the hair, I should be OK.

"Do I have to kiss you on both cheeks or something?" he asked dryly. I almost bent over and said yes. Instead I said "You don't have to do anything."

"But I want to," he insisted. He stepped towards me and we did the bear hug/handshake/clinch thing again, but with some kind of kiss on the lips thrown in. Most peculiar.

"I'll see you soon," he assured me. "Maybe I'll come to London next."

"Yeah. That would be good."

With that we were off in opposite directions, back to where we came from. The journey home was a lot quicker than the journey there had been. It was a glorious sunny day, and as I looked through my rose-tinted sunglasses, I felt excited at the prospect of seeing Adam again.

———————— ♥ ————————

But by Tuesday afternoon I had that sinking feeling. I hadn't heard from him since we'd left Birmingham and I was beginning to wonder why. I'd texted him to say I'd got home OK and that I hoped he had too, but he hadn't responded. My brain had obviously decided not to process certain things about our meeting and concentrate on others, thus tricking me into thinking I'd fallen for him completely.

Wednesday came and still no word. He wasn't even online, which was unusual. But right on cue, at ten o'clock that night the phone rang. My heart jumped. It must be him. He was the only one who rang at that time. I picked it up but nobody spoke.

"Hello. Hello. Who is it...?" I asked. The line went dead. I dialled 1471, but the number was withheld. It must have been a wrong number.

The next day and still no sign of Adam in my inbox or anywhere else. What was going on? I decided to email him and find out. Apart from anything else, I just wanted to know he was alive.

| From: Jo | To: Adam |
|---|---|
| Subject: Earth calling Adam | Date: 22.04.04 |

How are you? Did you get home OK on Sunday?
I haven't heard from you since and I just wanted to know you'd got back in one piece.

To my relief, he replied almost instantly.

| From: | Adam | To: | Jo |
|-------|------|-----|-----|
| Subject: Re: Earth calling Adam | | Date: 22.04.04 | |

Hiya,

Really sorry. Been meaning to ring you but my phone died, I lost my charger and works gone mad. Server went down over the weekend and I've been trying to sort it. Bloody nightmare.

I got home fine by the way! I'll ring you tonight.

---

Thank God for that. A simple explanation after all. Normal service would hopefully resume tonight. But what was normal service? I didn't know any more, but I suspected that we were in danger of reverting back to a virtual long distance relationship. One where invisible walls and negative energy couldn't get in the way. Where we understood the parameters and knew where we stood.

The phone didn't ring that night. But it did ring at seven o'clock the next morning. It woke me up. The only person it could be was Fiona in New Zealand. I got there just in time.

"Hello stranger," I said, taking the phone back to bed. This was usually a long conversation, but no one answered.

"Hello?" I said again. There was a bit of heavy breathing before the line went dead.

I was wide awake now, so I got up and went into work early. I called in to see Mario. Something I didn't do much since I'd been cycling to work. I was shocked when they told me he'd gone back to Italy for six months. The place was wrong without him. I got a coffee anyway. Not a patch on Mario's but I didn't want to leave empty handed.

I got to my desk and checked my messages. There was an email from Digital-Cupid telling me my subscription was about to expire, a feedback request from Birmingham Travelodge, and a message from Adam.

| From: Adam | To: Jo |
|---|---|
| Subject: Morning | Date: 23.04.04 |

Sorry I didn't ring last night. Had to work late (again).

I'm going through a bit of heavy family shit at the moment as well. On a bit of a downer. I do think you're great though, and I'll see you soon. I promise.

I wondered what 'heavy family shit' was to someone who claimed he never saw his family. He'd talked about them quite a lot in our late night phone calls. They weren't close. In fact he seemed to pretty much hate them. Perhaps they'd had the audacity to re-arrange his toiletries. Or touch his hair. I'd heard these kind of excuses before. The ones that suddenly appear from nowhere after weeks of everything seeming rosy. This smacked of Tom Evans.

The phone calls where the line went dead increased over the next few days, but I didn't think much of it. I assumed it was a wrong number or an automated message that wasn't kicking in properly and reminded myself to call BT. I still didn't know what was going on with Adam until he logged onto MSN one day and started conversing straight away with a sense of urgency.

*Adam says:* Hi

*Jo says:* Hi

*Adam says:* You OK?

*Jo says:* Fine thanks. You?

*Adam says:* Been having a few problems. Sorry I haven't been in touch.

*Jo says:* What kind of problems. You OK?

*Adam says:* Not really. Going through shit. Have you been getting any funny phone calls lately.

*Jo says:* Errmm... Yes. Now you come to mention it.

*Adam says:* Oh god. What did they say?

Jo says: Nothing. Just put it down. You sound concerned. What do you know about it?

Adam says: Fuck. I don't know where to start.

Jo says: The beginning would be good...

Adam says: I miss our chats Jo. I could talk to you about anything.

Jo says: I'm flattered. Where is this leading?

Adam says: I've never had that before with anyone.

Jo says: What do you know about the phone calls?

Adam says: Don't got mad. It's my ex...

Jo says: Right...

Adam says: She found my phone bill and saw your number all over it...

Jo says: And...

Adam says: She knows I don't know anyone in London. She started asking questions

Jo says: Sorry. I'm not with you.

Adam says: Well, she went mad.

Jo says: Sorry for being thick, but you split up with your last girlfriend over a year ago right?

Adam says: Well yeah kind of...

Jo says: Kind of?

Adam says: We got back together but split up again properly about 4 months ago

Jo says: Hold on. Let me get this straight. You had only just split up with your girlfriend when we started talking.

Adam says: Please Jo... don't be mad.

Jo says: We talked for hours and hours, for weeks and weeks about everything under the sun, and you forgot to mention that fact?

*Adam says:* Jo. Honestly. I meant every word...

*Jo says:* You let me meet you in Birmingham under false pretences.

*Adam says:* I knew this would happen...

*Jo says:* You let her take my phone number and plague me with pathetic calls...

*Adam says:* I didn't know she took your number. Honest. I'm really sorry.

*Jo says:* Who is this girl?

*Adam says:* Don't be angry. I'm so confused.

*Jo says:* Ha ha! You're confused!?

*Adam says:* Yes. I'm having a rough time at the moment. She's threatening all sorts of shit.

*Jo says:* Poor you. What's her number?

*Adam says:* She won't bother you again. I've sorted it out. I promise.

*Jo says:* Sounds like it! Your word is good enough for me Adam!

*Adam says:* I'm really sorry. I didn't know she was calling you til she told me today.

*Jo says:* What sort of woman does that? She didn't even say hello. How old is she – about 12?

*Adam says:* No. Course not. 19.

*Jo says:* 19!!!!! Things are starting to fall into place!

*Adam says:* What do you mean?

*Jo says:* You're 37 years old and scared of a teenager! That explains a lot...

*Adam says:* Look. She's had a few problems and stuff.

*Jo says:* So tell her to call the Samaritans – not me.

*Adam says:* I don't know what to do. I feel kind of responsible for her...

| | |
|---|---|
| *Jo says:* | *What... like a parent or guardian!?* |
| *Adam says:* | *No! She hasn't got anywhere else to go* |
| *Jo says:* | *Sounds like you make a lovely couple.* |
| *Adam says:* | *We're not a couple.* |
| *Jo says:* | *Whatever. Take my advice and get back together. You're more suited to someone with a similar mental age to yourself.* |
| *Adam says:* | *Come on Jo. There's no need for that.* |
| *Jo says:* | *Yeah, you're right. You are the weakest link. Goodbye.* |

# sixteen

## *Seventy sheets to the wind*

They say hell hath no fury like a woman scorned. I say honesty is the best policy. If there were a lot more honest men, there'd be a lot less women scorned. Simple.

I let my subscription to Digital-Cupid expire. I was through with those losers, but I still received a daily email with details of my 'perfect matches'. Was it my imagination or had they got better looking now I wasn't paying?

"Guess what?" Claire said when she phoned me one morning. "I'm going speed-dating on Thursday night."

"How come?" I asked, slightly bemused. "You live with your boyfriend." Claire was the last person I thought would be indulging in a singles event.

"Yeah, I know. I've told him. I'm only going for a laugh," she said unconvincingly. "You know Mad Janet at work?"

"The infamous Mad Janet."

"Yeah. Well she's desperate to go but she doesn't want to go on her own, so I said I'd go with her."

"Blimey. What did Tony say?"

"Well. Not much really."

"I'm not surprised! You should have phoned me when you booked it. I'd have gone with you. I've never tried speed dating. It has to be better than internet dating."

"Come with us! I'll email you the web address. We only booked yesterday and there were a few places left."

"Where is it?" I asked.

"Some bar on the Kings Road."

Kings Road? I wasn't sure about that. Wouldn't it be full of Sloane Rangers with pink shirts and rah accents? I was more at home with Soho media types and... well, anyone else but them. Perhaps I was out of date. I still had Lady Di and the neckscarf era in mind. And Tim-awfully-nice-but-dim. But maybe I should try it – they say opposites attract. I logged on to the website and there were still female places available. I paid my £20 and booked one. All the male places had gone. It would be difficult to keep a straight face with Claire there.

I'd read a bit about speed-dating and I'd been meaning to try it for a while. I figured that three minutes with someone unsuitable was better than a whole evening. It was also better than building up a virtual relationship with someone over several weeks, only for one or both of you to be let down when you finally met. Like reading a book and thoroughly enjoying it, then going to see the film.

At four o'clock on the afternoon of said speed-dating event, my phone rang. It was Claire telling me she couldn't go now as Tony had gone into one about it. Apparently after saying it was fine, he'd decided it now wasn't fine. I can't say I blamed him. Pretty normal for someone to object to their live-in girlfriend being chatted up by 20 different blokes and paying for the privilege. Was there trouble in paradise?

Now it was just me and Mad Janet. I'd never met Janet, but I'd heard a lot about her. And by all accounts she was, well... mad. Claire reckoned she was a drug and alcohol addicted nymphomaniac. Someone's perfect woman no doubt. Despite these issues, she managed to cling on to a job as a PA in Holland Park because of Daddy's contacts. In retrospect, the thought of going speed-dating with her on the Kings Road didn't exactly fill me with glee. But I'd bought my ticket and I was all geared up for it. Luckily Lucy saved the day. I phoned her and asked if she wanted to take

Claire's place, and ever the optimist and game for a laugh, she said yes. If I was going to go through this I'd rather do it with a kindred spirit and Lucy was certainly that.

The venue was Cactus Blue and we arranged to meet there at seven o'clock. The speed-dating was in the upstairs bar at eight. Dutch courage was needed and Claire was coming with Mad Janet to introduce us. The place was a bitch to get to from the West End, without the added joy of a signal failure on the District Line. Lucy and I arrived half an hour late.

"Mwuah... mwuah... mwauh. Hi girls," said an over-familiar Janet.

I was confused with the air kissing thing and nearly headbutted the poor girl. It was one on each cheek where I came from. Or just one and be done with it.

Janet was wearing what at first glance appeared to be a pair of curtains. Thank God Lucy was here. I felt like I was in a farce already. From our position in the downstairs bar, we could see the participants making their way up the spiral staircase into the speed-dating arena. Like a gaggle of witches we checked them out one by one. Quite an eclectic mix by the look of things.

"Oh my God. Have you seen him?" mused Lucy, as a man with floppy hair, a long leather coat and a piss-pot under his arm climbed the stairs.

"Not sure I want to do this," I muttered. "Shall we just stay here till it's finished?"

"Oh come on dahlings! It'll be a *scream*!" shrieked Janet, as she emptied the last remaining dregs of a bottle of Chardonnay into her glass.

We reluctantly said goodbye to Claire and began the ascent into the unknown. It would have been nice to make a discreet entrance and sit in a corner until it started, but that wasn't to be with Janet in the lead. She stumbled into the room, spilling half her drink in the process. All eyes were upon us. Not the best start. I would have preferred to remain incognito until the last possible minute. We grabbed a table.

"Hmmmm. I've spotted a few potentials already," Janet

announced. She was casing the joint like she meant business.

"Damn. Think I left my beer goggles at home," I whispered to Lucy.

A woman who looked remarkably like Mildred from *George & Mildred* came round and gave us all a badge with our names and a number on it. She also handed us a score card, on which we had to tick any potential suitors. If they ticked you as well, then bingo! You had a match. The organisers would take the cards at the end of the night and email you the details of any matches.

Mildred made her way to the front and started talking into a microphone that didn't work. Presumably she was explaining the rules but no-one could hear a word she said.

We managed to gather by word of mouth that we'd start at the table corresponding to the number on our badge. We'd chat to the person there for three minutes, then a bell would ring and it was the girls, not the boys, who'd move on to the next table. I'd wrongly assumed I'd be able to sit in my chair all night and wait for the endless stream of eligible bachelors to grace me with their presence. No such luck.

I found my table. I was number 19. There was a slightly built Asian man in a smart suit sitting there already. He was male number 19 and his name was Asif. We said hello and I sat down. Had we started?

Suddenly the bell rang and Mildred yelled "off we go!"

Asif was quiet and obviously nervous. Poor bloke. I asked him what he liked to do. He said he liked activity holidays and cricket.

"Do you like cricket?" he asked, suddenly becoming more animated.

"I love it." I said, in the words of the song.

"My god. A girl who likes cricket. That's so unusual."

I didn't have the heart to explain. I pretended my knowledge of cricket extended beyond drinking beer once with the barmy army and cleaning the MCG. It's a good job we only had three minutes. The bell rang and we said a polite "nice to meet you" and I moved on to number 20.

He was the man with the floppy hair and long leather coat we'd seen going up the stairs earlier. He'd taken his coat off and was wearing a pink shirt tucked into his dark blue high-waisted jeans. He had a gold ring on his little finger. Presumably it was an heirloom with the family crest on it, rather than an Elizabeth Duke piece. His name was Douglas.

"Let me guess what you do," he asked in a cut-glass English accent.

"Go on then." I was happy to let him do the talking.

"I think you work in fashion," he offered.

"Nope." I was quite flattered though.

"Oh that's strange. Are you sure? I'm usually pretty good at this."

Am I sure? What kind of a stupid question was that?

"Errr. Yes. I'm sure I don't work in fashion," I confirmed.

"Right. What do you think I do?" he said.

Was that it? I hadn't told him what I did yet. Obviously that wasn't really important. We were cutting to the chase. It was all about Douglas.

"Estate agent?" I answered.

Expectant silence ensued. I felt like I was on Who Wants To Be A Millionaire? waiting to see if I'd got the million-pound question right.

"No. Not exactly. Anyway. Do you know what I like about this speed-dating?" he asked, moving on again before we'd actually established anything.

"No. Tell me. It's the first time I've tried it."

"It's great!" he insisted. "You spend twenty sheets and you get to meet twenty chicks! On a normal date, you might spend seventy sheets on a girl. Take her to dinner, buy a few drinks, and usually get nothing at the end of it."

"Yeah," I said. Although I could see his logic, I was bemused that he was letting me in on his theory.

"Here, you spend twenty sheets, don't have to buy a drink and usually get something at the end of it. Bloody genius!" He rubbed his hands together as if he'd just discovered oil in Fulham.

"Right. Yeah. Sheets," was all that came out of my mouth.

I wasn't sure where to take the conversation from there, so I was pleased when Mildred frantically started ringing her bell. Hurray. It was time to move on.

"Nice to meet you Douglas," I stood up. "By the way – what do you do for a living?"

"Buy and sell property," he said, as if he'd really got me on that one. I couldn't wait to compare notes with Lucy.

At the next table was man number 1. His name was AJ. I'm not sure what it was short for, but I'm guessing the A stood for Arse.

"Hi Jo. Nice to meet you. I have a few questions for you if that's OK," he announced before I'd even sat down.

"Errm. Yes fine. Go ahead," I told him as he picked up a card from the table, put on his reading glasses and started to read from it.

"Firstly, what was the name of your first pet?" he asked.

"Ahhh! Are you trying to find out my porn star name?" I laughed. "Because I know it already. It's Tinker Thomas." I added proudly. I'd always thought it was a particularly good one.

"Errrrm. No." He looked at me as if I was mad. "What do you mean porn star name? These are my ice-breaker questions. There's nothing pornographic about them."

Oh dear. I'd got the wrong game. I decided it was best to humour AJ. He'd obviously spent time carefully compiling his ice-breaker questions and there was I, making light of his hard work.

"Oh sorry about that," I explained. "I misunderstood. It's a different game..."

"It's not a game," he looked bewildered.

"Yes. Sorry – I know. What's the next question anyway?"

He looked unsure. "Right. Well. OK then. What's your favourite holiday destination?"

"Mmmm. Difficult one. Maybe Thailand. Maybe the south of France. There's so many places I –"

"Mine's the Galapagos. Have you been?"

"No. I haven't actu–"

"Marvellous place. I try to get out there at least twice a year," he interrupted. "In fact I was only there three weeks ago, hence the tan."

I hadn't noticed a tan. Perhaps because my eye had gone straight to the Fat Willy's Surf Shack T-shirt circa 1987. Where was Mildred when I needed her? Thankfully she wasn't far away. This was great. We didn't even get to the third question because it was time to move on. I was beginning to enjoy this. Three down, seventeen to go.

Next up was number 2. Jeremy. He was well built and wearing an ill-fitting suit and a comb-over. He grinned at me and took a sip of his beer as I sat down. I asked him what he did for a living. He said he worked for the NHS, but was also an astrologer.

"What star sign are you?" he asked.

I was astonished. I'd never heard a man ask that question before.

"I bet you're a Pisces," he said before I could answer.

"No. I'm not actually."

"Really. Hmmmm. That's strange. I'm getting a real Pisces vibe about you. Definitely a water sign. Scorpio?"

"No. I'm not Scorpio either." God he was good.

"That's really odd. What are you then?"

"I'm a Virgo." I put him out of his misery.

"Thought so," he said.

He then promptly offered to do me a birth chart for sixty quid. (Or should I say sixty sheets?) Quite clever really. I bet a lot of lonely women would gladly pay £60 to see how their life was going to map out. When, or if, they were going to meet their husbands. This place was positively bursting at the seams with women looking for love. Twenty ideal candidates for Jeremy to flog his charts to. Well, nineteen.

Number 3 was Cliff. He looked thoroughly bored and couldn't be bothered to pretend otherwise. Was he playing hard to get? Apparently his friend had dragged him along under duress.

I glanced back at Lucy. She was two people behind me, which meant she was with 'seventy sheets'. I wondered if he'd guessed what she did for a living. She had a big grin on her face but looked deeply engrossed in what he was saying. I knew exactly what was going through her head. He really was everything Lucy would not want in a man and she was remembering every detail so we could dissect it later.

Mad Janet was one behind me. She was looking into Astrology man's eyes with a big lopsided grin on her face. She was hammered. He was licking his lips. No doubt his first sale.

After Cliff had practically bored me to death, I was glad to move on to number 4. Damian, the diminutive Aussie with the very white teeth. He was camp as a row of tents and had a big smile and highlighted spiky hair. He seemed out of place here. I could have sworn he was a Qantas steward but he said he worked for a bank. We talked about Sydney for three minutes and I moved on.

Number 5 was Lee, a journalist. He was nice. Tall, dark and I wouldn't say handsome, but quite attractive. He was a bit embarrassed about the whole thing. Said he was there to do a report on speed-dating for a magazine. He was a nice guy and for the first time that evening, I wasn't looking out for Mildred and her bell. But it wasn't far away. We said we'd catch up at the end. Lee was my first tick.

Chris was waiting at the next table. Date number six.

"Hi Jo. Sit down," he gestured. He had a strong Scottish accent and was wearing a tight polo neck jumper. In June.

"Hi. Nice to meet you Chris."

"So. What brings you here then?" he asked.

"Good question," I laughed. "I just fancied giving it a go. I think it's a good idea. What about you?"

"Basically I just want to find a girlfriend who isn't mad."

Not the best opening line and I wasn't quite sure where to take it. He went on to tell me the last four girls he'd been out with were very attractive and highly intelligent, but after a few months they'd turned out to be mad. It sounded like there was a pattern emerging to me. Nothing to do with him, of course. He was obviously perfectly sane. I nodded my head and said "right" every now and again until the bell rang. Quite what either of us got out of that three minutes I don't know.

This was like musical chairs and it was getting quite tiring. It's difficult keeping a smile on your face, introducing yourself and trying to sound interested over and over again. Still, only two more to go until the half time break. As I sat down with number 7, the waitress brought me a drink. Apparently Janet had ordered them. Woe betide anyone who let her glass get empty. It was a large glass of Chardonnay. I can't drink white wine. It makes me turn into Janet. Without wanting to appear ungrateful, I tried to signal to her I'd got the wrong drink but the look in her eyes told me to get it down me or else.

James was quite good-looking. I'd spotted him earlier and was eager to get nearer. He stood up to greet me, which is when I discovered he only came up to my shoulders. And I had flat shoes on. Why did fate always deal such cruel blows? He shook my hand and I hoped he hadn't noticed my face drop.

"Evening Jo. Lovely to meet you."

"Yes. You too James," we sat down.

James looked at me seriously and clasped his hands together as is if about to say something very poignant.

"So..." he began slowly. "If you could be anyone famous – alive or dead – who would it be?"

Was this another ice-breaker question he'd prepared earlier? It caught me unawares. After my misdemeanour with AJ I thought I better be careful to answer the question properly, but I wasn't sure what to say. I didn't really aspire to be anyone famous. I thought about saying Dr Who so I could travel in time to the next table, but I guessed he was expecting me to say someone female and glamorous. Like an actress or a singer.

"Errmmm... Debbie Harry," I offered.

I had pretended to be Debbie for several years as a teenager. Hairbrush for a microphone. I knew every lyric to every song. *Heart of Glass* was my karaoke number. If he wanted me to elaborate, I could. He didn't.

"I'd be Ché Guevara," he announced triumphantly, as if he'd come up with someone far more worthy than some measly pop star. "Do you know who that is?"

I wondered if he meant to be quite so patronising, and thought about saying no for my own amusement, but we didn't have time for a history lesson in Latin American politics.

"I had a poster of him on my bedroom wall once like every other student." I said dryly.

"I know. That's why I'd be him if I could be anyone. Such a classic picture. It must be great to be immortalised like that. You know. In a picture that everyone recognises. I went to Cuba last year. It was everywhere. You should have seen what I brought back. T-shirts, posters, books, a mug. Even the beret. You name it, I got it!"

Please hurry, Mildred.

There was only one more to go before the half time break, which by now couldn't come quick enough. Kieron. He was OK. Quiet. Unassuming. No charisma whatsoever. He was a lawyer and liked trekking. It was an average three minutes. I *really* needed a break now.

Mildred finally rang her bell with even more gusto than usual and mouthed half time into her redundant mike. I was fast learning to lip read. I breathed a sigh of relief and gestured Lucy and Janet towards the toilets. I'd been dying to go since Cliff.

"Oh my God, I absolutely adore Douglas. He's fantastic," gushed Janet. "Just my type."

That said it all really. I looked at Lucy and she gave me a knowing look and mouthed 'seventy sheets'. We went down to the bar to order some drinks. The white wine had gone straight to my head, as I knew it would. I needed some water if I was to get through the second act.

"Shall we get a bottle," slurred Janet. I was surprised she

was still standing let alone drinking. Where was she putting it all. She wasn't very big.

"I don't drink white wine," I said. "I'm having water." Mad Janet went mad on me.

"Oh come on Jo. For fuck's sake. Why do you have to be different. Why can't you just go with the flow and drink white wine like the rest of us. You have to be bloody difficult, don't you. Look at you. Bloody Jo. You make me want to hit you."

Well if I had to have that effect on anyone, I was glad it was Janet. She was rocking all over the place and in danger of losing that plum she had firmly wedged in her mouth, despite the fact she came from Belfast. Poor Janet. She still had ten men to impress yet. If it hadn't have been for Lucy I'd have made a hasty exit at this point, but I decided to soldier on. I drank a pint of water and started to feel better. I didn't want to be totally stone cold sober if the next ten men were anything like the last. A happy medium was what I was after. As well as getting away from Janet.

We went back upstairs and I looked around the room. Some people were comparing notes. Others were still talking to their last date. Some looked like they were bonding, but there were a couple of people sitting on their own. Lucy and I went to chat with a girl who looked like a wallflower in the corner. Janet went looking for Douglas.

I noticed Mildred looking flustered. She was trying to announce something but no-one was listening. Did she not realise the microphone was dead? Eventually she rang the bell and people started to filter back to their tables. By this point most of them were somewhat worse for wear and there was a delay in starting the second half as Mildred tried to herd everyone to the correct table.

My number nine was Andreas. He billed himself as a property developer and said he worked for the 'big boys'. I didn't ask who they were. He wore his shirt unbuttoned further than respectable. His chest was hairy and he had a gold chain with a cross on it round his neck. He sat back

213

confidently on his chair and talked about himself for three long minutes. He liked St Barts, salsa dancing and playing tennis. Apparently he could have been a pro if it hadn't been for injury. His parents owned a villa in Majorca (the nice part) and he drove an Audi TT. Wow. He wasn't my type and I don't think I was his.

Next was Alan. It's funny. I'd have guessed his name was Alan even without the name badge. He had chubby red cheeks and a goatee beard. He smiled and his eyes were warm and friendly. As I sat down I noticed his leg sticking out from under the table. On the end of it was the worst fashion crime of all time. A loafer with a gold chain on the front and novelty socks. Apparently this was his fourteenth time speed-dating, but he'd never ticked anyone. I asked him why that was. Surely there must have been someone he was attracted to out of approximately 280 women. He said not. He was thinking of setting up his own speed-dating event and was here for research. I didn't feel so bad then for finding him extremely unattractive. I doubt I'd have been his first tick either. Just as well really as I'd have found it hard to get past the footwear under any circumstances.

Mildred's bell ringing seemed to be getting more and more irregular. I'm sure it was about ten minutes until she signalled the next move. Was she drunk too? Number 11 was Keith. A strange looking bloke. His hair was cropped at the sides and the top was gelled upwards into a small point on his head. He was wearing big round glasses that overtook his features.

"Hi," he said.

"Hi. How are you?" I replied.

"Fine thanks," he nodded his head.

"That's good. So how are you finding this? Met anyone you like?"

"Not really," he mumbled. "I'm bored. Should've left in the break. Don't know why I didn't." Was he trying to make me feel special?

"Well you never know. There still might be someone

you like." I had to get through the next three minutes somehow. Apparently time flies when you're having fun. It certainly does, and I wasn't.

"I doubt it," he said with an air of superiority. "Everyone is intoxicated and I don't drink. It astounds me that these people think they're likely to meet someone when they haven't even got all their faculties. Look at them."

I took a gulp of my G&T. "Well I think most people are nervous at something like this. Dutch courage and all that," I suggested.

"Well there's Dutch courage and there's annihilation," he informed me. "Most people in this room don't seem to know the difference."

RING RING RING. Sermon over. I love you Mildred. I would have been over the moon with happiness even if number 12 was Quasimodo. At least I would be past Keith. He wasn't though. On the contrary. He was Andy. Attractive, tall with a nice disposition and a decent set of social skills.

"Hi Jo."

"Hi. How are you?"

"I'm fine thanks. Bit tired of the sound of my own voice repeating itself but apart from that, fine," he laughed.

"I know what you mean. Not your voice, I mean..." Bloody hell. One whiff of attraction and I had dork seizure.

"Have you ever done this before?" he asked.

"No. First time. I've always fancied it though. Have you been before?"

"No. My first time too. What do you think?"

"It's quite hard work. Well some are," I told him.

"Have you ticked anyone?"

"Just one." I had a feeling it was about to become two. "Have you?"

"No. Not yet."

Andy was an ex-stockbroker who was taking a break while he decided on his next career move. What a great position to be in. I would have thought he'd have girls

215

throwing themselves at his feet. He was going to Dubai the next week to see friends and discuss possible job opportunities. Suddenly I was dining at the Burj Al Arab and sunning myself on Jumeirah Beach. Mildred soon put a stop to that though with her bloody bell.

"Nice to meet you, Andy. See you afterwards hopefully."

"Yeah sure. See you later on," he replied unconvincingly.

I felt extremely sorry for number 13. Unlucky for some, and it certainly was being after Andy. He couldn't have been in a worse position. It was like going from one extreme to the other. If I had to describe Edward in one word it would be bland. I kept looking at Andy through the corner of my eye to see how he was getting on with the lovely Janet. Better than me by the looks of things. Another forgettable three minutes.

Oscar was less forgettable but for all the wrong reasons. He was stocky with a mass of black spiky hair and a perfectly coiffed triangle of fluff stuck between his chin and his mouth.

"What's that?" I asked, ever the diplomat.

"It's a soul beard," he told me in all seriousness.

"A what?" I thought I'd heard wrong.

"A soul beard."

"Soul beard? S.O.U.L?" I queried.

"Yeah. S.O.U.L. Soul beard," he confirmed.

"What's one of those then?" I was intrigued to hear the explanation. It sounded vaguely poetic, but it looked bloody ridiculous.

"I read it in a magazine. Someone in a band had one the same. He called it a soul beard. Loads of people have got them. They're cool," he told me.

I wanted to reach out and rip it off. The entire three minutes was taken up discussing the curious phenomenon that was Oscar's facial hair. I think he was flattered.

God I was tired. I moved round the corner to number 15. Someone called Phil. He was sitting at the table next to Mildred and her helper. As I sat down, he was deep in conversation with them and showed no signs of stopping. He hadn't even bothered to take his coat off and was rocking back and forth on his chair chewing on a matchstick. About a minute into the allotted three I started to get annoyed.

"Errrr... Hi Phil. Are you just here to make up the numbers or something?" I asked.

"Hey?" he replied.

"Well I've been sitting here for nearly two minutes and you've been chatting to the organisers like you're old mates. Just a guess."

"Yeah. Sorry. Just had a bit of business to discuss. I am single. She just calls us if all the spaces aren't filled and we come along to help out."

"*We,*" I questioned. "There's more of you?"

"Well just me and the next one you'll meet. I am single though. Split up with someone a few weeks ago. Honestly."

I didn't really care whether Phil was single or not, but I thought he could have at least pretended to show an interest. After all, I'd wasted a whole sheet on him. He told me he was an actor, which was apt. Said he'd had bit parts in *The Bill, Casualty* and *Holby City*. He was between jobs at the moment and currently playing Abbey the Clown at a kids club in Abbey Road. Wow! Next stop Hollywood.

I decided to give the next one a miss seeing as he was another one of Mildred's fillers. Janet hollow-legs had been signalling to me that it was my round and her glass was empty. I couldn't see the waitress anywhere. The last time I'd seen her was when she'd dropped a tray of drinks and the room went silent. I took this as a good opportunity for a breather and went to the bar, but it was packed and I was never going to get served in three minutes so I panicked and went back empty handed. I tried not to look at Janet. I was terrified. Would she survive the next ten minutes?

Mildred looked like she was going to combust. Several people were so drunk they were forgetting to move on. That, coupled with me missing out number 16 had totally messed things up. She was desperately trying to correct things with the help of her silent microphone, but it had degenerated into chaos. By the time calm was restored, I seemed to have missed out number 17 as well, and was straight on to my last one. Fred Elliot from *Coronation Street* (I say *Coronation Street*).

I thought about bypassing him as well, but it seemed Mildred read my mind because she was over like a shot, ushering me into my seat. I did as I was told as I'm not very good with people in authority. They make me revert back to childhood and this scenario reminded me of when I cocked up the maypole dancing at primary school. The whole thing had to be unwound because I'd gone under instead of over. Mildred had the same look in her eyes as Mrs Penn had that fateful day.

Nice chap, but there was absolutely zero potential. The age limit was supposedly 40 and he didn't look a day under 50. He said he worked in TV which at first I thought was a coincidence with him being Fred Elliot's doppelgänger. Turned out he drove lorries for the BBC. Cliff was his mate and apparently a great bloke and a top laugh. I wasn't sure if he was being ironic, and I never found out because we were interrupted by Mad Janet telling me to hurry up with the drinks. She'd paid almost five pounds for the glass of wine I didn't want earlier and demanded I get her one back. By now, the cut-glass accent had been replaced with a full-on northern Irish lilt. Bejesus! The girl was crazy. Fred Elliot found the whole thing highly amusing and told me he'd ticked her on his score card. I wished him luck.

Mildred declared time was up by going even more berserk than ever on her bell and shouting for everyone to hand their cards in. She'd abandoned the microphone at last. I'd only ticked Lee and Andy. I handed my card in and made my way over to Lucy. We watched as Janet stumbled straight over to 'seventy sheets', grabbed his arm and dragged him off to the the bar. One sheet well spent. But who for, was the question.

I was exhausted and I'd had too much to drink. I looked around the room. There were a few tête-à-têtes going on. I wondered if any real matches had been made, or whether it was all alcohol related. Andy was nowhere to be seen.

"How d'you get on?" Lee asked, as he came and sat down with us.

"It was interesting," I told him.

"That's one way of putting it. Would you do it again?" Was he interviewing me for his article?

"Yeah. I think I would," I admitted.

Lee said that most of the girls had been pleasant enough. I was intrigued about the Gothic with the long black hair and ghostly white face. Apparently she was very nice but he couldn't picture himself down the local with an Elvira lookalike on his arm. We admitted ticking each other. But he and Lucy had ticked each other too. Guess that was the danger of going speed-dating with friends. He'd also ticked one more. Three wasn't bad seeing as he'd only gone along for work.

I looked downstairs and saw 'seventy sheets' with his long leather coat on looking rather sheepish as he made his way outside. I watched him as he ran down the road. Janet was slumped over the bar, glass of wine in hand, looking absolutely slaughtered. I still couldn't see Andy. Lucy hadn't ticked him. Said he was too corporate.

It was 11.30 and time to go home. We went downstairs to tell Janet we were leaving and offered to get her a cab but she wouldn't tell us where she lived.

"I'm not fock'n going anywhere," she slurred. "I'm having another fock'n drink. Come on. Don't be so fock'n boring. Have another fock'n drink with me."

"I don't want another *fock'n* drink!" I pointed out. She was really starting to piss me off now. "And I can't believe you need any more. We're getting the last tube. Are you sure you don't want me to get you a cab?"

"I'm not going in a fock'n cab. Get me a fock'n drink."

It was clear I wasn't getting anywhere with Fulham's

answer to Nancy Spungen and quite frankly, why did I care? Lee got a cab in the opposite direction and Lucy and I walked to the station.

———— ❤ ————

Speed-dating definitely has its advantages and I'd certainly do it again. The concept is great. Three minutes with the biggest loser in town is bearable by anyone's standards. Out of the twenty, I'd ticked two. That's ten per cent. Not bad. Douglas was on to something with his seventy sheets theory, although the poor bloke was probably scarred for life now.

Lee emailed a couple of times and asked if I wanted to go out. I kind of did. But I think the whole thing had exhausted me and the thought of spending another night making polite conversation with someone I barely knew didn't appeal at the time. We never arranged it and it fizzled out.

I liked Andy, but sadly the feeling wasn't mutual. I never received him as a match and I never heard from him again.

Mad Janet left her job working with Claire and was last heard of in fock'n rehab. I hope it worked out.

# seventeen

## *A flash in the pan*

---

*Digital-Cupid♥*

Hi jo-to-go! Several messages are waiting for you at *Digital-Cupid♥*. You'll also be pleased to know that you appear high on the match list of 63 guys keen to meet someone just like you!
Did you know – just by logging on to *Digital-Cupid♥* twice a week, you'll significantly increase the level of interest from guys? Be seen – keep 'em keen!
***Special offer! Buy 1 month, get 1 free! <u>Click here!</u>***

---

Yeah right! Sixty-three guys just like all the others. Sixty-three guys with magic mirrors, a charisma bypass or trying to recapture their youth.

More and more people were turning to the internet to find love these days. I read it in a magazine. And apparently the typical user is male aged 35–40. Perfect, you'd think. It also said that men out-numbered women 3-to-2. Could that mean new blood at Digital-Cupid? There were several messages waiting for me. And two months for the price of one. I was clicking the link before I knew it. My card details were held on their system, my profile was still there. All I had to do was click *continue* and I was up and running with access to thousands of blokes. Again.

| From: | bradford_ smiler | To: | jo-to-go |
|---|---|---|---|
| Subject: | Other half | Date: | 01.07.04 |

Hi Jo,

My name is Dave and I'm 43 and from Bradford. I'm kinda cuddly but have started doing weight training to get a few pounds off and get some muscle.

I love to make people feel special, loved and happy – that's my aim in life. I also love to laugh. My nickname at work is smiler, LOL. I recently split from my wife and I have a son who is 5. I see him one day a week and then every other weekend he stays at mine. I work a 3 day week in a food factory.

I'm looking for a partner for romance and a steady relationship. I've just read your profile and I see we have a lot in common. Will you be my other half?

Dave.

Sorry Dave. I'm afraid I can't be anyone's other half because I'm already whole.

| From: | talk2me | To: | jo-to-go |
|---|---|---|---|
| Subject: | Mademoiselle | Date: | 10.07.04 |

How are you?

I am french. I like simple things and I only like shopping at supermarkets for the minimum like soap, shampoo and washing powder. I prefer to go to farmers market, charcuterie, boulangerie, and patisserie. But do not worry, I am not fat.

I like cocktail bar, country pub and funky night club but no drugs or too much alcohol. Woman is the one thing that makes me soft and happy. The countryside in south England is fantastic, are you ready for a walk?
I feel lonely. I am not depressed but imbalanced.

Pierre

---

From: Victor_XXX To: jo-to-go

Subject: Are you the one? Date: 12.07.04

---

Good morning.

I have just ended a relationship with a Danish woman after 12 years together. I am a one man woman and once I have my partner I never look at others. I am 55 years old, feeling young but with the experience of age. The combination is rare.

I am looking for a sexy, attractive, slim, trustworthy woman. You will need to share the same interests as me, which are hunting, fishing, hang-gliding and sailing. I believe sharing interests is a fantastic glue.

Please give me your phone number, date of birth, and a time when I can call you and we can discuss further.

Victor.

---

Damn! I just sold my hang-glider on eBay.

---

From: Troy_Boy To: jo-to-go

Subject: Hi there Date: 14.07.04

---

I'm troy. 6ft 2" mxd race. I work 4 myself buying & selling property. I live a nice life but always remember I come from a council estate hee hee. Luv meeting people. Dont drink or smoke. Just changed my pic on this site coz the old one was of me & my car but everybody was interested in my car & not me haa haa.

People say im good looking & I look like a footballer when I drive my sports car. People are always taking pictures of me hee hee. Am very dwn 2earth not looking 4sex on this site just people 2hav a laugh with.

Hopefully spk soon.xx

---

Spoilt for choice again. And then there was Marcus...

---

| From: Marcus_35 | To: jo-to-go |
|---|---|
| Subject: Hi! | Date: 14.07.04 |

Hi jo-to-go,

Are you still here or have you gone? I just joined this thing on a 3 day trial. Saw your page. Not sure what to do next! Hello!

Marcus

---

Unenthusiastically, I clicked on his name, which led me to his profile. Was he going to be posing on the beach in a pair of Speedos? Up a mountain disguised in ski-gear? Leaning proudly on the bonnet of his newly polished car? I was surprised and rather happy to find none of the above.

There were two pictures. Both quite clearly showed a good-looking man with dark hair and a lovely smile. All good so far. My shallow self kicked in and I started to get excited before I'd even read his profile. Calm down, I told myself. He could still be a 5ft, chain-smoking, married man with ten children, living in the Outer Hebrides yet.

He wasn't. He was apparently a 6ft 2, recently divorced, childless solicitor. Perhaps with my previous experience of the too-good-to-be-true internet profile, warning bells should have rung. But if they did, I couldn't hear them.

---

| From: Marcus_35 | To: Marcus |
|---|---|
| Subject: Re: Hi! | Date: 15.07.04 |

Hi Marcus_35

Yes – I'm still here I'm afraid. Well done for getting this far anyway. Now we need to exchange polite messages for a while, before deciding whether we have enough in common to warrant meeting in real life.

Sell yourself Marcus!

Jo

---

| From: Marcus_35 | To: jo-to-go |
|---|---|
| Subject: Re: Hi! | Date: 15.07.04 |

Sell myself! Bloody hell! Everything's on my profile isn't it? Have you read it? Took me ages to fill the bloody thing in. Especially the last bit.

Anything else you need to know, just ask!

Marcus

---

So ask I did. Marcus was 35, worked in the city and lived with a friend in Wanstead. We had a lot in common. More so than anyone else I'd met on the site, because he was also from Northamptonshire. About as far away in the county as you could get from where I grew up, but with Northampton town in the middle, we were convinced our paths must have crossed. We were both members of Northants Roller Disco when we were twelve and we both signed a petition when the council knocked it down to make way for a car park. Our early socialising years had followed the same route – Welly Road, Forty Bridge Street, Camilla's and Cinderella's, and we vaguely knew some of the same people. We had to meet.

We arranged a date for a week on Thursday and swapped phone numbers. I had the same worries in my mind that I always had when the potential was so exciting. What if he sounded like he'd swallowed helium? – that kind of thing. But I was relieved to find that he didn't, as we chatted away on the phone for the first time.

He'd been with his wife for ten years (married for two). According to him, the relationship was over before the wedding but they went through the motions to please everyone else. She eventually left him for another woman, and after a lengthy rebound period, he was now ready for something more meaningful. He was surprised when I told him I'd never been close to being engaged, married or any commitment much bigger than 'will you go out with me?'

| From: | Marcus_35 | | To: | jo-to-go |
|---|---|---|---|---|
| Subject: Re: Hi! | | | Date: 19.07.04 | |

Are you winding me up? Not only are you funny, attractive, bright, down to earth, successful, and enjoy a drink, but you have absolutely no baggage? And you're meeting me on a blind date next Thursday?

Sounds too good to be true. How come you're single? You're lying. I bet you're really a 3ft dwarf with B.O, halitosis and warts. Am I right?

| From: | jo-to-go | | To: | Marcus_35 |
|---|---|---|---|---|
| Subject: Re: Hi! | | | Date: 19.07.04 | |

Oh no! I've been rumbled. Do you still want to meet?

| From: | Marcus_35 | | To: | jo-to-go |
|---|---|---|---|---|
| Subject: Re: Hi! | | | Date: 20.07.04 | |

Ermm... yes if your the first one. No if you're the dwarf.

Oh go on then! Let's throw caution to the wind. Personality goes a long way. You sound OK either way!

| From: | jo-to-go | | To: | Marcus_35 |
|---|---|---|---|---|
| Subject: Re: Hi! | | | Date: 20.07.04 | |

Cool. I'll be the short one with the beard & the fishing rod.

Thursday came and I had butterflies. I hadn't felt like this for a while. What should I wear? Should I dress up and look like I'd made a real effort, or dress down like I really hadn't thought about it? I met myself halfway and wore jeans and a decent top.

I went for a stiff drink or two with my work mates first.

We were meeting at 7.30 in the Punch & Judy. It was the first place that had sprung to mind. The first place that springs to everyone's mind when they can't think of anywhere else to meet in central London. Loud and busy. I wasn't sure if that was a good thing or a bad thing under the circumstances. I guess it was good for potential disaster and awkward silences.

We were meeting in the downstairs bar by the fruit machine. I loitered in the shops until 7.35, then texted Marcus to ask if he was there. He was, so it was safe to enter. I glanced at myself in a shop window. A bit windswept but nothing too drastic. As I walked through the door at the Punch & Judy, I couldn't see him straight away. I hate it when that happens. Feeling conspicuous, I looked around nervously until I spotted him in a corner, nowhere near the fruit machine. He was laughing at me looking for him. I felt relief that I'd found him, and embarrassment that he'd been watching my plight. He stood up to greet me.

"Hi. Good to meet you at last," he said.

We did that strange greeting again. Half old friends, half 'never met you in my life' type thing.

"You too," I replied. "Thanks for hiding round the corner so I couldn't see you. I thought you weren't here!"

"I wanted to check you out. If you were minging I was going to leg it," he laughed. "Anyway. What do you fancy?"

"You!" I felt like saying but thought it was a bit early. "Gin and tonic would be good. Thanks."

He was very attractive. He looked just like his picture, if not better. While he was at the bar I began to wonder what the catch was. Did he have a dark secret? Or perhaps some kind of impediment not yet obvious. Or worse still – a hairy back? I'd checked out the shoes. They were fine.

"Well thank God you look like your photo," he announced when he arrived back with the drinks. "I did wonder what to expect. You never know with these things do you? Anyway – cheers."

"Cheers," I raised my glass. So far so good.

A few more drinks and we were getting on famously. Marcus was confident, with a good mix of funny and serious. He made me laugh with his dry humour and I listened when he was being serious. It sounded like he'd been through the mill with his marriage, but he was glad to be out the other side. He wasn't bitter, but he carried a few scars. There were no awkward silences. Our personalities bounced off each other naturally and the time flew. About 10 o'clock we decided to go for something to eat. As we stood up to put our coats on a group of people approached the table.

"Heeeeyyyy! Marcus. How's it going my son?"

"Yo Marcus. What you up to?"

"Marcus dahling... great to see you! mwah... mwah..."

"What are you doing here guys?" he asked with surprise. "Great to see you. This is Jo. Jo, this is Gav, Robin, Darren and Jemima." He introduced me.

Gav and Robin were his friends from university. Jemima was Robin's girlfriend. I'm not sure where Darren fitted in. What were they doing here? Was it a coincidence? Had he called them when I was in the toilet to rescue him from the nightmare internet date he was on? They wouldn't have got there that quickly. They were all a bit worse for wear. Turns out they'd been in the upstairs bar all afternoon. They were now going for something to eat.

"Why don't you join us," trilled Jemima. "It'll be fun!"

Who for? I thought.

"What do you think, Jo? Fancy it?" asked Marcus.

I wasn't averse to it, but I hadn't expected to meet his friends quite so soon. It was bad enough meeting him. Friends could be influential. What if they didn't like me? I could already see that myself and Jemima weren't cut out to be bosom buddies.

"Come on! Come for supper!" she shrieked, as if to read my mind. I hadn't heard the word supper since I last watched a period drama.

"Yeah. OK. That would be great..." the words spilled from my lips.

As we made our way to China Town, I wondered again if this was a set-up. Had he told them we'd be there and asked them to be on stand by? Maybe they'd been in view all the time with a secret signalling system in place. One wink for *'get me the hell out of here she's boring the pants off me'*, two winks for *'get lost it's going well'*, three winks for *'it's OK but I could do with some help'*. I decided against that theory. It would be too hard to wink three times without looking like you had a serious affliction.

We ended up in Le Ho Fuk, otherwise known as Ho Le Fuk. Quite fitting really. Someone ordered a sharing platter of everything, which seemed to take forever to arrive. In the meantime, Marcus and his friends drank Tiger beer and I drank cheap wine and talked to Jemima about shoes. Come midnight, I was feeling decidedly worse for wear and realised I really ought to go home. I managed to say the obligatory pleasantries and get out of the restaurant without disgracing myself. Thankfully Marcus, who was keen to carry on, hailed me a cab.

"It's been a great night," he said. "Great to meet you. And not a disappointment in any way, shape or form."

"Well thanks, Marcus. And whatever you just said but the other way round," I slurred.

"Shall I get in the cab with you?" he grinned cheekily. It was tempting.

"No! I'm knackered. I'll speak to you tomorrow."

"You sure?"

"Pozzzutive."

We kissed before I got in the cab. It was a romantic fusion of Chinese food and beer. My head was spinning and I thought it best to quit before something untoward happened.

"See you soon." I said.

"Absolutely."

———————— ❤ ————————

I called into the café on my way to work. It was definitely a coffee and bacon sarnie day, despite the disappearance of

Mario and his refried bacon. My head was vague but there was a spring in my step. If only Mario was here to share my joy. I got into work and checked my email, and my headache miraculously disappeared.

| From: Marcus | To: Jo |
|---|---|
| Subject: Hi again! | Date: 23.07.04 |

Morning Jo

How's the head? I'm feeling pretty vacant. We went to another bar after you left. Huge mistake. Sorry about the invasion – I hope you don't think I planned it! They all thought you were great. What are you doing later?

Mx

What am I doing later?

| From: Jo | To: Marcus |
|---|---|
| Subject: Re: Hi again! | Date: 23.07.04 |

Morning. Head's not too bad considering. Just drinking my 3rd cup of coffee. I can't believe you carried on. You're hardcore! No worries about your friends turning up. They were really nice. Not up to much later. Why?

Jo x

I'd planned to go straight home after work. I was so tired and hungover.

| From: Marcus | To: Jo |
|---|---|
| Subject: Re: Hi again! | Date: 23.07.04 |

A friend of mine's having a birthday do tonight. He's got a guest list at one of those poncey Soho members clubs. Fancy coming with me?

I think one is supposed to play harder to get in these situations. I haven't read any of those books that tell you how to conduct a relationship. When to be available and when not to be. When to phone and when not to phone. The strategic rules you need to put in place in order to snare your man. And quite honestly I couldn't care less. This was Marcus with the nice smile and he wanted to go out again tonight.

| From: Jo | To: Marcus |
|---|---|
| Subject: Re: Hi again! | Date: 23.07.04 |
| Yeah OK. Why not. Where is it and at what time? | |

Marcus said he'd put my name on the door and he'd meet me inside at eight. I looked in the mirror. An emergency trip to Topshop was called for after work, via the hairdressers.

———— ❤ ————

"Jo Elliott," I announced like Hyacinth Bucket.

I was about an hour late arriving at the venue and it looked like it might be a problem. The door-bitch was orange and sporting a skin-tight lycra catsuit and a Croydon facelift. She looked me up and down, checked her clipboard and tapped her pen on her ultra white veneers.

"You shoulda bin 'ere at eight," she informed me.

"I know. Sorry. I got stuck at work," I lied. More like stuck in the hairdressers trying to scrub up.

She shook her head and tutted, before reluctantly unclipping the rope and letting me through. And people paid to be a member of this classy joint?

The place was full of gorgeous people, and people who thought they were gorgeous. Marcus came to meet me and introduced me to his friends. No sign of Jemima and co. tonight. These were his work mates. A nice bunch of people who worked in the city. Without further ado I had a glass of champagne in one hand and Marcus's hand in the other.

I still felt jaded, but the champagne took the edge off for a while. We both started yawning about eleven o'clock. The party thinned out a bit then too, as a lot of people left to catch the vomit-comet home to Essex. I told Marcus I wasn't sure how much longer I could keep my eyes open and that I was going to get a cab home fairly soon. He gave me that cheeky grin again and said "can I come with you?"

I'd only really known him a day, but because of our virtual relationship, it was kind of longer. I knew everything about him. I knew where he came from, which school he went to, his mother's maiden name (Etheridge), the first record he'd ever bought (*12 Gold Bars* by Status Quo) and his innermost emotional feelings on his marriage and divorce. I knew he was a nice bloke too, and I knew that I was attracted to him. So I did what any self-respecting singleton experiencing a drought would do. I said yes and prayed for rain.

———— ❤ ————

It poured down that night. Marcus left early the next morning as he had to go to Ikea. He'd just moved house and had no furniture. He asked me to go with him and I told him I liked him, but not that much. We hadn't made any other plans to see each other. He'd just left saying he'd call. I hoped he would and that I wasn't going to be just another stage in his rebound therapy.

*Marcus: R u watching the game today*

The text came through on Sunday morning. England were playing Australia at rugby. I'd arranged to watch it in a pub in Wandsworth with friends, so I texted him back with this information and said that him and his friends were welcome to join us.

*Marcus: Great. C u around 4.*

I jumped out of bed and literally skipped to the kitchen.

He must be keen. Three meetings in four days. Could this be a mutual match? I really wasn't playing by the so-called rules and I spent longer getting ready than I usually would to watch a rugby match in a pub.

When we got there it was already so busy you could hardly move. There was a good balance of Aussie and England fans and the good-natured banter was going on long before kick-off. Luckily someone had got there early enough to save us some kind of area. I texted Marcus and directed him and his friends over.

"Hi," I shouted. "Good to see you."

"You too," he yelled above the noise. These are my friends. I'll introduce you later. Drink?"

"No – it's OK. They're getting me one." I pointed at Jane and Lucy frantically trying to shove their way to the bar. It was mayhem. Everyone wanted to get as many drinks in as possible before the game started. You either had to endure the crush or leave. Marcus had been in a pub most of the afternoon and was already slurring his words. I was getting shoved in every direction and hadn't had anything to drink.

We got separated when the game started. Everyone focused on the big screen. It was fast and furious and I couldn't move an inch. I was glad when the first half was over. People started to disperse a bit and I turned to find Marcus so we could say hello properly and do the introductions. He was doing shots of tequila at the bar.

"Have one Jo. Come on," he pleaded. So not wanting to be a killjoy, I did a shot of tequila and nearly threw up. Marcus looked wasted. He grabbed my arm and said "stay here," as the second half kicked off. The place was raucous by now. Hardly an ideal setting for romance and I was only pretending to watch the rugby. England were in the lead I think. Just.

Pints of beer kept appearing on the bar and disappearing just as quickly. Marcus was whispering indecent proposals in my ear. My friends were winking at me. I was pretty much sober and wished we were somewhere else.

Australia won. The whole pub erupted and *Men At Work* started blaring from the speakers. It thinned out a bit after that, and at last I could breathe. Marcus ordered another round of tequilas. He was kind of swaying on the spot with his eyes half closed and an inane grin on his face.

When they rang the bell for last orders, Marcus suddenly announced he was going to show us his elephant impression. I noticed the look of terror on one of his friend's faces as he proceeded to turn the pockets of his jeans inside out and undo his flies.

"NO!" I yelled.

"Don't be boring, Jo!" he laughed. "Look! I'm Jumbo."

"Put it away for Gods sake," said the sensible friend.

Lucy started laughing. I wasn't sure whether it was with him or at him. Claire and Jane looked at me with the same pitiful look on both of their faces that suggested 'rather you than me'. I just stood there. If it was anyone else it would have been funny. But it was Marcus with the nice smile. He was standing in a packed pub exposing himself in front of my friends. The bouncer didn't take too kindly to the cabaret either and forcibly removed him.

"Don't worry about him," said the sensible friend. "He gets like this when he drinks Stella. I haven't seen him like it for years."

I thanked him for trying and we all filed out. Marcus was nowhere to be seen. We looked in the kebab shop, we looked at the bus stop, the taxi rank, in the corner shop, everywhere. But he was nowhere to be seen.

"He'll have got a cab," said another of his sober-ish friends. "He does this. He's like a homing pigeon. Always finds his way home, no matter how battered. He won't remember a thing in the morning."

I took his word for it.

"Nice to meet you anyway Jo. We're getting a cab north. Do you want dropping anywhere?"

"No, I'm fine thanks. I only live up the road."

They got in a taxi and disappeared. My friends were

heading off one by one, so I decided to join everyone else in the kebab shop. As I waited for my chips to fry, I thought about Marcus and Stella. I hoped he did get home OK. He was absolutely wrecked.

"Sorry about earlier," mumbled a voice in my ear. "I really shouldn't drink Stella. I get a bit excited."

I turned round to see a dishevelled looking Marcus. He looked like he'd been in a fight. His shirt was all open and he was soaking wet.

"You're friends thought you'd got a cab home. Where've you been? Are you OK?"

"Sorry," he slurred. "I'm fine. Where we going, Jo?"

"I'm going home," I said.

"Can I come with you?"

I looked at the tramp standing before me and I couldn't decide whether he looked handsome or pathetic. It was a different scenario to the last time he'd asked that question, but it was apparent that I didn't have much choice. Where else was he going at this time on a Sunday night, in this state, on his own?

We made it back to my place. He only fell over twice, one time taking my chips with him. Now that did upset me. When we got in he stumbled straight into the bedroom, collapsed on the bed, closed his eyes and muttered "cheers Jo. You're a good girl".

By the time I'd cleaned my teeth he was fast asleep. I got in next to him and dozed off pretty quickly too. I was awoken some time later by an unfamiliar noise. At first I thought there was a pneumatic drill in bed with me. I'd forgotten Marcus was there and it took a while to register. I think he'd lost track of all his senses because not only was there noise, there was smells and motion too.

"Stop snoring!" I pleaded, as I shook the big lump lying next to me. It mumbled and lashed out with an arm, catching me with a right hook to the side of the head. Ouch. That hurt. Keep calm. He didn't mean it.

"STOP BLOODY SNORING," I repeated.

He took heed this time, and normal sleep resumed. For a while anyway. About an hour later I was awoken again, this time with strange mumblings and the sense that someone was getting out of the bed and walking around the room. I pretended to be asleep. He's obviously going to the toilet, I decided. And lo and behold he was! Right there, in the corner of my bedroom. On my brand new carpet.

"OH GOD. WHAT THE HELL ARE YOU DOING?" I cried with horror, leaping from the bed and trying in vain to stop him. No response. He simply finished his wee and casually went back to bed. At this point I began to think the relationship was probably doomed. I'd known him four days.

I spent the rest of the night on the sofa in a bid to get some sleep. It was Monday morning and God how I wished it wasn't. I woke up to find Marcus still in his beer-stained clothes, kneeling on the floor beside me with an angelic look on his face saying "what are you doing in here, Jo?"

Butter wouldn't melt that lovely smile. I couldn't believe it was the same person that a few hours earlier was flashing in a packed pub and pissing on my bedroom floor. I told him what had happened from start to finish and he was mortified. He couldn't remember a thing. Said it was all down to the Stella and that he really shouldn't drink it. I told him I'd already established that. He couldn't apologise enough. I accepted his apology somewhat dubiously and told him not to worry about it. These things happen. Especially when you mix copious amounts of Stella with several shots of tequila. I wasn't keen on being punched in the middle of the night, but I decided to give him the benefit of the doubt on the grounds of diminished responsibility.

———— ❤ ————

To add insult to injury, I got the tube to work. Marcus came with me and neither of us said much. I wasn't sure whether that was down to sheer embarrassment on his part, but you could practically smell the tension. Either that or it was his breath. He still looked like a vagrant.

What was going to happen now? We'd only met three times and it felt like we'd lived through a whole relationship already. As I sat at my desk pondering the thought, an email came through.

| From: Marcus | To: Jo |
|---|---|
| Subject: Oh dear... | Date: 26.07.04 |

Hi Jo.

How are you? Better than me I hope. I'm not feeling good either physically or mentally today. I feel terrible about my behaviour yesterday. I'm not sure how to take this forward, or indeed whether we should. What are you expecting from us having met? Please be honest.

Mx

| From: Jo | To: Marcus |
|---|---|
| Subject: Re: Oh dear... | Date: 26.07.04 |

Hi. I'm not feeling too bad. A bit tired for some reason.

I don't know what I'm expecting from us meeting, but as you know, I didn't join the website to find a drunken fling, and as far as I thought, neither did you. I can't predict what's going to happen after one weekend, which let's face it – didn't go according to plan. But I'm not looking to marry you just yet, don't worry. Why? What do you expect from us having met?

| From: Marcus | To: Jo |
|---|---|
| Subject: Re: Oh dear... | Date: 26.07.04 |

I don't want a drunken fling either, but if I did it would be with someone like you – attractive, outgoing, good laugh etc. In fact it'd be fantastic if you were up for that! I think you're great. But I don't want to string you along and I think we have too much in common to have a relationship.

And rightly or wrongly, I think subconsciously I was trying to test you yesterday. I used to do the same with my wife. I think the theory was that if I was bad and she forgave me, then she must really love me. It's so destructive. I don't want that again. I think I would have preferred it if you'd kicked me out for my behaviour last night. I need discipline. I need someone to keep me on a tighter leash. What do you think?

What did I think? I was stunned. If I'd wanted a dog I'd have joined a different website. Credit where credit's due though. Telling someone you had too much in common was a novel way to dump them.

| From: Jo | To: Marcus |
|---|---|
| Subject: Re: Oh dear... | Date: 26.07.04 |

Unfortunately I'm not into screaming matches and throwing people into the street in the middle of the night. I prefer to leave that to the people with ASBOs.

Having said that, I didn't enjoy having a sleepless night, getting a slap, or mopping up your urine, but I didn't really have much choice. I'm flattered that after all that, you'd like to have a fling with me but not a relationship. That makes me feel fantastic.

Thanks!

| From: Marcus | To: Jo |
|---|---|
| Subject: Re: Oh dear... | Date: 26.07.04 |

I'm confused. I don't want to hurt you. We could be good mates. I'm glad I met you but I don't think it could be a long term romantic thing. I still feel awful about Sunday. I don't think its funny to wee on someone's floor and give them a slap. It really scared me I assure you.

I can't pretend I wasn't upset because despite everything, I liked Marcus a lot. But perhaps he was right. He was still reeling from the demise of a ten-year relationship. Our five-day one meant nothing. I could have gone along with his idea of a fling. We had all the right ingredients. But there'd be a 100% destruction guarantee with the knowledge that he was waiting for something better to come along.

| From: Jo | To: Marcus |
|---|---|
| Subject: Re: Oh dear... | Date: 26.07.04 |

You're confused. I'm confused. If you think having too much in common is not a good basis for a relationship, then we haven't got much in common!

So I guess that's it then.

| From: Marcus | To: Jo |
|---|---|
| Subject: Re: Oh dear... | Date: 26.07.04 |

I really am very sorry. I genuinely like you a lot. I had a great time on Thursday, Friday and Sunday. My mates had a great time with yours too. Maybe when the dust has settled we can all go out again.

I promise I won't get my cock out next time...

# eighteen

## *My bloody valentine*

"Seen Jumbo lately?" said Claire.

"Yeah – how's the flasher?" Lucy asked.

After a little white lie which saw me dumping Marcus because of his performance at the rugby, the subject was thankfully changed.

"I read something the other day about internet dating," announced the safely married Jane. "It said that men are four times more likely to want sex from it than women."

"Tell me something I don't know!" I exclaimed.

But however soul-destroying it can be, there's no getting away from the fact that the internet gives you access to hundreds of people you wouldn't normally meet. And every time I swore I was through with Digital-Cupid, like falling off a horse, I'd get straight back on.

| From: PlayStation | To: jo-to-go |
|---|---|
| Subject: Hi | Date: 14.08.04 |

Wow bab,

You look great. A bit older than you say in your spec, but the rest aint bad. I'm half viking half brummy, look young, act younger, divorced.

Yum yum
Kevin

Wow yourself, Kev! I pictured a cross between Hagar the Horrible and Noddy Holder and decided against a reply.

| From: GS_Biker | To: jo-to-go |
|---|---|
| Subject: Hello | Date: 22.08.04 |

How are you? I'm Greg, 32 from Newcastle. I'm an M.O.T tester and mechanic. I'm single and like motorbikes, sex, playstation, sex and fishing. I'm happy with a can of tennents super in my hand and a packet of B&H.

I'm 5' 6" and of medium build and very hairy. I'm not very good at flirting. Can you teach me? If interested please email me with pictures of you. Do you wanna trade your pictures for mine? I have naughty ones if you like.

Greg.

Well that certainly conjured up a vision of absolute beauty.

| From: Cuckold_Desire | To: jo-to-go |
|---|---|
| Subject: Want to be a cuckold | Date: 25.08.04 |

I imagine you have lots of messages as you look stunning, but please consider mine. I am a 39 year old reliable, responsible and caring guy, from East London.

My name is Malcolm and I would like to get to know you. As my name suggests, I want to be a cuckold.

I am happy to undertake all household chores and anything else you require. I am very good at cleaning, cooking and ironing (which I love). If we got together, you could have complete freedom with real men while I would stay at home and remain totally faithful to you.

Malcolm xxx

Errm... not quite what I'm after Malcolm, but I might be interested in a cleaner.

| From: DJ-Wicked | To: jo-to-go |
|---|---|
| Subject: feelin irie??? | Date: 27.08.04 |

hi huni. i liked ur profile & ur pic & wana get to know u...
so sexi... can u answer the following questions???

ru u single???

wer bout u 4rom???

im indian does that bother u??

wood u come to 1 of me giggs??

cheers

DJ Wicked.

---

Very tempting. If only we spoke the same language.

So much talent, so little time! It was clear I was still attracting the wrong kind of man. Where did these people come from? Were they for real, or did I just not get the joke? I'd been nothing but truthful in my profile. Did anyone actually read it? Probably not. Vital statistics and decent photos is where it's at, let's face it.

In a fit of irksomeness, I decided that honesty was no longer the best policy and went to my profile and hit edit. At that precise moment in time, I couldn't care less if I never went on another internet date again. I clicked all the buttons with total abandon. Now I could speak French, German, Italian, Spanish, Dutch, Finnish, Norwegian, Swedish, Japanese, Mandarin, Cantonese, Arabic, Greek, Turkish, Korean, Urdu and Russian. I left out Afrikaans. I didn't want to appear *too* intelligent. My essay now read:

---

### In my own words

As you can see, I'm positively stunning. Added to which, I'm academically brilliant, very witty and absolutely bloody loaded.

I used to work in advertising. I liked it so much I bought the company. Now I just sit in the board

room (bored being the operative word) and bark
orders at my subordinates. In my ample spare time
I like to travel. Five star hotels are OK, but I prefer to
get down with the kids and rough it. After all, money
shouldn't mean losing touch with reality.

I enjoy eating out. I'm happy dining at the Ivy, but
equally happy at home with a Budgens ready meal
and a glass of Blue Nun.

Inconceivable as it is, I'm still single. I know – I can't
believe it either! Fancy a life in the lap of luxury?
Drop me a line and I might get back to you.

( Save edited profile )

What would they make of that? Nothing I suspected, but it
made me laugh for a few seconds. Then it crossed my mind
I might have gone mad.

| From: Cool_Breeze | To: jo-to-go |
|---|---|
| Subject: True connection? | Date: 31.08.04 |

Hi Jo,

I enjoyed reading your profile. It was very lively. I bet
you're quite good fun to be around. I guess that running
your own business and the problems that come with it
gives you that drive and confidence which come across
in your words. I like people around me to have the drive,
determination and enthusiasm that I picked up from your
profile. That would be my ideal woman.

It says on your profile that you don't have any kids but
would like to in the future. I have 2 kids and am divorced,
but don't let that put you off. I'm sure that if you thought
someone had the potential to become what you were
looking for (right age, skin colour, hair, eyes, etc), the fact
that they'd been married before would not stop you

considering them as your partner. You might be reading this thinking 'what does this guy think we have in common?' Is he after my money? But who knows how we will get on unless we meet?

Running your own company you must have taken chances on things and had to make decisions. So why not take a chance on this tall, dark, handsome, sincere, confident and loyal guy from Wolverhampton?

Glenn.

---

## Words fail me, Glenn.

| From: | DrewPeacock | To: | jo-to-go |
|---|---|---|---|
| Subject: Hey Jo | | Date: | 03.09.04. |

I like what I see and read about you, although I don't like blondes. I look forward to your reply.

Drew Peacock

---

## What a great name! I bet he had a brother called Chris.

| From: | Matt_1234 | To: | jo-to-go |
|---|---|---|---|
| Subject: It could be you... | | Date: | 12.09.04 |

Love your profile Jo. I can't understand why you're single either. I'm in a similar position to you (not Wandsworth). I mean I'm also extremely rich. I won the lotto a couple of years back. At first I didn't know what to do about the begging letters, but I decided to carry on writing them.

By the way – I'm impressed that you speak 12 languages. Did you study advanced linguistics at uni?

Drop me a line sometime and I'll get one of my people to write back to you.

Matt.

---

Now that was funny. I had a look at Matt's profile, which was also very witty. His picture was nice too. He definitely deserved a reply.

---

| From: jo-to-go | To: Matt_1234 |
|---|---|
| Subject: Re: It could be you | Date: 13.09.04 |

Dear Matthew (It is Matthew we assume).

Just to let you know that Jo is in receipt of your earlier message and will get back to you upon her return from the Ivy, where she has just popped to purchase a sarnie.

Jo's People.

---

| From: Matt_1234 | To: jo-to-go |
|---|---|
| Subject: Re: It could be you... | Date: 14.09.04 |

Dear Joanne (it is Joanne we assume).

Firstly, Matt wishes it to be known that his name is Matt. Not Matthew, but Matt.

Secondly, Matt thanks you for your correspondence. In fact he recalled the time he and a friend took packed lunches to the Ivy before he won the lottery. The waiter told them they weren't allowed to eat their own food, so they swapped.

Matt's People.

---

| From: jo-to-go | To: Matt_1234 |
|---|---|
| Subject: Re: It could be you | Date: 14.09.04 |

Dear Matt,

You assume wrong. My name is Josephine, not Joanne. I've just sacked all my staff and decided to correspond with you directly. They advised me against you. Said you were after my money so I gave them their P45s and sent them on their way. I would advise you to do the same.

Jo(sephine)

---

| From: | Matt_1234 | To: | jo-to-go |
|-------|-----------|-----|----------|
| Subject: Re: It could be you | | Date: | 15.09.04 |

I like the sound of you Jo. Very interesting and obviously extremely bright. I'm so glad I selected you as one of the 1,655 profiles to send a speculative mail to. I'm hot property on single street Jo. Get used to it.

Should we ever get to the stage of going on a date, I'll pay for the first and you can cover the second (if I think you're up to scratch). I thought we could go to Pizza Hut for the first and the Ivy for the second.

I like your profile by the way. Not many people make me laugh but you do, and that's just your photo.

Matt.

Matt's messages had me hooked straight away, to the point where I was checking my inbox on an hourly basis. I loved the tone of his humour. He was very witty and clever with it. Was he a comedian?

He wasn't actually, but he should have been. He worked for a big law firm and had too much time on his hands. He was wasted there. The messages kept coming and they had me cracking up over my desk. So much so that I couldn't concentrate on much else. I did my best to respond with equal hilarity, but he was probably just humouring me.

Between the jokes, I learned that he'd never been on an internet date before and found the whole thing extremely embarrassing (by now a distant memory for me). He said he'd joined the site for a laugh and enjoyed winding people up. Was he winding me up?

I began to wonder when it got to the fourth week of corresponding and there was still no talk of us meeting. Surely it was only a matter of time. I secretly hoped he'd suggest it, but still he didn't. Were we destined to be comedy pen-pals for ever? I could have brought it up, but I was frightened of the response. I even told him I was going on a date one night. He told me to stop cheating on him and make up the spare bed.

At last, after six weeks of this, he finally suggested going for a drink. I readily agreed, half expecting a punchline. It never came, so I deduced that we really were meeting outside the Nag's Head in Covent Garden on Thursday night at 7 o'clock. This would be interesting. Would he be able to keep up the repertoire in real life? Would I?

In the meantime I found out various other snippets of information about Matt. He was 40, and according to him, had absolutely no baggage. No ex-wife, no kids, no stalker ex-girlfriend and no pets. A rare find indeed. Or another con-artist. Although I was on the verge of losing faith in mankind, I decided to reserve judgement and enjoy it. I was confident that if nothing else, we were bound to have a laugh. Probably at my expense.

———— ❤ ————

As I walked in the pub ten minutes late, I spotted Matt leaning on the other side of the bar. He watched me walk through the throng of people and around the bar, and when I got there, the first thing he did was laugh. Somewhat disconcerting when you're trying to appear cool.

"What!" I said, smiling nervously.

"Ahhh nothing. You're OK actually. Seven out of ten. What do you want to drink? Cinzano is it?"

I laughed. "No. Spritzer please."

"Spritzer!" he mocked. "What the bloody hell's a spritzer? You'll have Cinzano and count yourself lucky."

I don't know why I asked for a spritzer with my white wine problem, but he got me one anyway and we sat down. He looked just like his photo, but was taller than expected and much slimmer.

Matt then told me that I was a much better prospect than his ex-girlfriend. I was flattered and asked him why. He said she was a cinema usherette and still carried a torch for him.

He was just as funny in the flesh. Everything he said was tinged with humour and delivered brilliantly, with a deadpan expression and seemingly no effort. I couldn't compete with him so I didn't bother trying. It was like being at a comedy gig but without the audience or the crap food.

I was glad when he suggested going for something to eat later. The spritzers were starting to take their toll and I was starving. We found a cheap Italian and, as I sat across the table from Matt, I saw a rare glimpse underneath the humour. He was quite shy and didn't talk about himself much. Apart from a few moments of near-seriousness, the evening was a barrel of laughs from start to finish. I was still smiling when I got home and re-played the evening in my head. I liked Matt. My heart wasn't going crazy, but it did flutter when he emailed me the next day.

| From: Matt_1234 | To: jo-to-go |
|---|---|
| Subject: Morning | Date: 29.10.04 |

Jo,

Just to let you know you scrubbed up OK last night. Well done. I intend to issue a date for you shortly as to when I intend to take you out again. Probably giro day.

Matt x.

| From: jo-to-go | To: Matt_1234 |
|---|---|
| Subject: Re: Morning | Date: 29.10.04 |

Matt,

I am humbled and over the moon. It's fantastic that such hot property is willing to date me again. Please get back to me at your earliest convenience to finalise the details.

Jo. x

We met again the following week. I have no idea why, but

we went to the Tate Modern. Probably Matt's idea of a joke as it didn't strike me as being his cup of tea at all. It made a change from meeting in a smoky pub and getting inebriated and it was hilarious wandering around listening to his special commentary. It added a whole new dimension to most of the exhibits and made it so much more entertaining. I for one will never look at modern art in the same light again. Afterwards we went for something to eat nearby and Matt told me what he really thought of modern art. It was the first time I'd heard him swear.

It was a romantic farewell at Waterloo. We went to kiss for the first time but I burst out laughing. After he reassured me twice that it wasn't a joke, it was third time lucky.

On the third date we went to the cinema. I'm no fan of the movies so I left it up to Matt to decide which film. He chose Napoleon Dynamite, the romantic fool. It was very funny though, and I recognised a few of the characters from Digital-Cupid. Before I knew it, that elusive third date had been and gone. And the fourth, fifth and sixth. Suddenly I was cooking dinner and Matt was bringing me Jacob's Creek and cheap carnations from the Seven Eleven. Were things getting serious?

We did things, me and Matt. We went to the theatre and the cinema. I think you call it dating. Christmas was coming up and I introduced him to my friends. They thought he was great. I went to Australia for the festivities. Matt wasn't into family or Christmas so he didn't do anything. I missed him, but we spoke and emailed a lot. I thought of him on New Year's even when the clock struck twelve, so I rang to wish him happy New Year. He pointed out that it wasn't New Year in the UK yet and told me to call back in twelve hours.

I met Matt the day I got back. Although it was good to see him, I didn't want to explode with excitement at the prospect. We went for a drink but I was like a zombie, so I bored him with my holiday snaps and went home early.

I was back on the planet by the weekend and Matt got tickets for a show. He said it was a surprise as to what we were going to see. I could hardly contain my excitement as I prayed for *Mamma Mia*, but it turned out to be a harrowing play that I'd never heard of about the First World War. We went back to mine afterwards. He always stayed at mine. I'd never even been to his place, but then he did live miles away in Harrow with a lodger.

'*We would like to request the pleasure of the company of Jo and guest to celebrate the marriage of our daughter...*' Matt read from the wedding invitation on the mantelpiece.

"Who are you taking?" he asked.

"Maybe you if you play your cards right," I replied.

Well who else was I supposed to take as my '*and guest*'? But apparently the the idea of going to the wedding of two people he'd never met was totally ridiculous. He'd got to the age of 40 without ever having attended a wedding or a funeral and he wasn't about to start now. Not even for free champagne and a weekend away with me.

The next Saturday it was Lucy's birthday. She was having a party at the Chinese restaurant with the Chinese Elvis on the Old Kent Road.

"Make sure you bring Matt," she insisted.

So I asked him, but he didn't sound too enthralled. He wouldn't commit one way or the other until the morning of the party when he made the commitment not to come. So it was just me, Lucy and about six couples. People were going to start talking about me and Lucy soon if we weren't careful. I was disappointed that Matt didn't come, but apart from everyone asking where he was it was a good night.

He phoned on the Sunday morning and asked if I fancied a roast dinner. I'd never sampled his cooking and I got excited for a minute, but I needn't have done. He'd seen a pub in town that did one for £5.99, and it was showing the football. He was such a flirt.

I went along anyway. I fancied a roast and I had nothing else on. I told him he'd missed a good night and he said he couldn't stand all that couply stuff. I never said I could, but these were my friends. He said he wasn't interested in spending time with my friends. My roast was tasteless.

——————— ❤ ———————

The following Monday it was Valentine's Day. I kept the night free, as Matt would no doubt be arranging something. I bought him a card but I wasn't sure of the protocol. It had been just over three months. Not long enough to warrant a present, I thought, but long enough for a card and a night out. The day came, but there was no word from Matt. I checked my email every five minutes but the only thing in there was a message from an old friend called Andrea asking if I wanted to go to a Valentine's singles night at London Bridge. She obviously wasn't up with the gossip.

Five o'clock in the afternoon and still no word from Matt. He was obviously dashing around organising a top surprise. Or was this one of his jokes? If it was, he was cutting it a bit fine.

| From: Jo | To: Matt |
|---|---|
| Subject: Happy Valentine's Day | Date: 14.02.05 |

What are you up to tonight?

| From: Matt | To: Jo |
|---|---|
| Subject: Re: Happy Valentine's Day | Date: 14.02.05 |

Wasn't planning on doing anything tonight? Why – do you want to do something?

| From: Jo | To: Matt |
|---|---|
| Subject: Re: Happy Valentine's Day | Date: 14.02.05 |

Well I thought I might see you at least. What with it being Valentine's Day...

| From: Matt | To: Jo |
|---|---|
| Subject: Re: Happy Valentine's Day | Date: 14.02.05 |

C'mon Jo!

You don't believe in all that nonsense do you? We're going out Friday aren't we? We don't have to go out tonight just because the card shops tell us to. We can be romantic any time.

Get a grip girl!

---

*'Get a grip.'* Not quite the response I was after. *'We can be romantic any time.'* I remembered the Seven Eleven carnations and my heart sank as I realised I was clutching at straws.

Everyone around me seemed to be receiving flowers or planning their evening, and me and Matt were staying in. At separate addresses. Well bugger that for a laugh. I phoned Andrea and told her I'd be there for seven. Ironic really. The first time in ages I was with someone on Valentine's Day and I was spending the evening at a singles night.

When I got off the train at London Bridge there was a voicemail from Matt. Oh no! What if he had been winding me up? What if he'd turned up at work and I'd missed him? Too late now, but I called him back. He told me he couldn't believe I was bothered about Valentine's Day, it hadn't even entered his head to do anything tonight, but if it meant that much to me we could go to the cinema or something. Well that was an aphrodisiac if ever I'd heard one. I told him I'd made other plans and he said not to worry – he'd see me Friday.

I met Andrea and her friends and it turned out to be a good night. There's a certain solidarity amongst singles and I like it. Just as well because it looked as if I'd be re-joining them very soon. It occurred to me that not being half of a couple in a bar on Valentine's night wasn't such a bad thing. It was packed with opportunity.

———— ❤ ————

It was now gleamingly obvious that myself and Matt didn't want the same things. Was it unreasonable to want him to be my 'and guest' at a wedding? Was it wrong to ask him to a friend's dinner party? And he could have just humoured me on the Valentine's issue. After all, I'm a girl.

But you can't change someone and there's no point even trying. A friend of mine put that in perspective when he told me "*my wife spent ten years trying to change me and then left me saying 'you're not the man I married'*".

Friday came and I met Matt. We went to a restaurant and made small talk over the menu. It was obvious he had something on his mind and I was glad when he asked me where I thought the relationship was going.

"Nowhere," I admitted.

"I'm glad you said that," he agreed.

Underneath the humour there was nothing. We didn't have that spark. We'd tried to, but something was missing. It wasn't uncomfortable. Five minutes later the food arrived and Matt was back to his comedic best. Relief all round I think. We said we'd stay friends and he promised he wouldn't be a stranger to my inbox.

# nineteen

## *Once more into the quagmire*

**VIRGO**

*Your stars for week commencing 10th April 2005*

*Venus is in your romance zone today so watch out for Cupid's arrows. The past is in the past. Make today the beginning of a new future. A future where you refuse to take life's leftovers. It's time to take on the world. Go for it, Virgo!*

Is that Digital-Cupid with its virtual arrows, I wondered, or the fat little cherub with wings? Either way, it was exciting to know that a new future was waiting in which I'd no longer be taking life's leftovers. I hadn't been on an internet date since Matt, but I was still receiving ridiculous propositions and my subscription continued to quietly debit my bank account each month. The nice Indian man in my local shop said he'd seen me on Digital-Cupid and asked me for a date. I'd only popped in for a pint of milk. It was time to call it a day and resign my love life to the hands of fate. Make this the beginning of a new future, I said to myself. It's in the stars. It's over, Digital-Cupid. We're through. Finished. Kaputt.

But I soon discovered that although it was easy to join the site, it was far from easy to 'unjoin'. Nowhere could I see anything about terminating my membership completely and deleting my profile. Instant messages were popping up all over the place and apparently lots of men were checking me out.

As I tried in vain to navigate myself to the cancellation page, someone called Prince_Charming was staring at me, telling me he'd sent me a message. I swear he was winking at me. I was loath to click on his smiling face, but as had happened so many times before, curiosity got the better of me and the next thing I knew, Prince_Charming was 6ft 2, 37 years old and lived in Camberwell. He had blonde hair, and from his small photo, appeared to have two eyes, a nose and a mouth that were quite pleasantly arranged. He described his job as 'managerial', but didn't say much else and his message was unfortunately inviting.

| From: Prince_Charming | To: jo-to-go |
| --- | --- |
| Subject: Nice profile | Date: 12.04.05 |

Jo,

Just saw your profile and for some reason it stood out. Your photo's not bad either. I'm off to Greece on holiday soon and could do with a translator. I notice you speak loads of languages! Fancy it? Or maybe a drink first?

Andy.

P.S. I'm not into firing messages back and forth for weeks on end. I'd rather just get on with things.

The P.S. was a bit presumptuous, but I knew what he meant and I was tempted. But I was in the process of trying to cancel my membership and knock internet dating firmly on the head. But what if this was fate, and just as I'd been about to kiss goodbye to Digital-Cupid for ever, I was being rescued in the nick of time by Prince_Charming? What if instead of an Audi TT, a pilot's licence or a fast motorbike, Andy came riding a white horse?

It got me every time. What the hell, I thought, and against my better judgement agreed to meet him for a drink the next day in Covent Garden. It was pretty hasty. I didn't know anything about him, but I didn't particularly care. He looked nice, his profile was in order, but I'd come to learn that you never really know much until you meet.

Nerves were a thing of the past and I arrived at the pub five minutes late, feeling happily pessimistic. Andy was sitting round the corner from the bar with his head buried in the *Evening Standard*. I knew it was him straight away. It must have been intuition because, yet again, he didn't resemble his photo.

"Hi," I announced.

"Oh hi," he looked up. I wasn't sure if he was trying to act cool, or was genuinely miffed that I'd disturbed him from his paper. My heart sank, almost as much as his eyes had sunk into his head. He looked like he hadn't slept for weeks. Eventually, he stood up, looked me up and down for a few seconds and said in a strong south London accent "what d'ya wanna drink?"

You're not 6ft 2, was my first thought, followed closely by the realisation that he was wearing Arthur Daley's coat.

"Gin and tonic please." I fixed my now legendary false grin and tried to sound vaguely enthusiastic.

"Read the paper while I go to the bar," he muttered as he more or less threw it at me.

Thanks, I thought, discomfort setting in straight away. I knew I should have trusted my instincts and searched for that cancellation page a bit harder. I picked up his paper and went straight to the TV listings. A couple of drinks with Prince_Uncharming and I could be home in time for *Bergerac* on UK Gold. He came back with the drinks, put them on the table and sat down without saying a word. I folded up the paper and passed it back to him. Starter for ten...

"So what do you do in your job?" I began.

"Not a lot for much longer I 'ope. They're makin' people redundant at the moment. I've been there nine years so I should get a wicked payout innit."

Oh great. He had the dreaded 'innit' affliction on top of everything else.

"Oh right," I said, pretending to care. "What would you do? I think I'd do more travelling if I came into money."

"Nah! I'd spend it all on drugs," he said, with a bizzare laugh reminiscent of an excited pig. This was going well.

"Have you had much luck with internet dating so far?" I tried a new angle.

"Whadda you fink?" he replied. "I'll tell you what really gets on my tits. I've been on about 40 dates wiv women off the internet, and most of 'em seem alright online, but you meet em in real life and they're so fackin boring."

Black pots and kettles sprang to mind.

"I don't fink nuffin' of doing a runner if they ain't up to scratch. You've gotta be roofless innit?" he went on.

There'd been several occasions where I'd like to have done just that – this being one of them – but I didn't have the heart.

"I legged it after ten minutes once coz the bird was mingin'," he carried on. "She was about ten years older than she said and had fack all to say." He didn't look at me while he delivered his rant. He looked at his beer bottle and peeled off the label. I looked at my watch. It was only 6.20, but at least my glass was empty.

"Same again?" I offered.

"Oright. Nice one. Ta."

As I stood up to go to the bar, I realised I still had my coat on. A thought flashed through my head. Should I take a leaf out of his book? I couldn't, could I?

I walked round the corner with every intention of stopping at the bar but my legs just kept going. They carried on walking right out of the pub and down the street. Quicker and quicker, they carried me all the way to Leicester Square station, down the stairs and onto the platform. As if by magic, a train was there. It wasn't going where I was going, but I didn't care. I was high on adrenaline at what I'd just done and it felt great. Of all the dates I'd been on, and all the evenings I'd endured when I'd rather be watching paint dry, I'd never considered doing a runner. But there's a first time for everything and there was no-one more deserving than Andy. And as he said himself, "You've gotta be roofless innit".

— ❤ —

What happened next was somewhat unexpected. It was like a sign. As if to reiterate what my week-ahead horoscope had told me about leftovers and leaving the past behind. I went to check my emails, half expecting something from Andy and half wondering if I should deliver him an explanation. But instead, blatantly sitting in my inbox like the proverbial bad penny, was a reminder of what (or whom) had got me into all this in the first place.

| From: Tom Evans | To: Jo Elliott |
| --- | --- |
| Subject: Blast from the past | Date: 14.04.05 |

Hey Jo. How's things? I was going through all my old contacts the other day and I saw your name. I was curious as to what had become of you. Are you well?

Tom

Oh my God. I was shocked at the very sight of his name. What the hell did he want? The last time we'd had any contact he'd told me he was married. Presumably to the girl he'd dumped me for. And now, here he was after all this time asking about my welfare? They must have split up. I should have left it. But that would be dignified.

| From: Jo Elliott | To: Tom Evans |
| --- | --- |
| Subject: Re: Blast from the past | Date: 14.04.05 |

What a surprise. I'm fine thanks. And you?

| From: Tom Evans | To: Jo Elliott |
|---|---|
| Subject: Re: Blast from the past | Date: 14.04.05 |

I'm very well thank you. I just got back from vacation.
What's new with you these days?

**What's new with me? Errrrrmmmm... Let me have a think about that. Nothing.**

| From: Jo Elliott | To: Tom Evans |
|---|---|
| Subject: Re: Blast from the past | Date: 14.04.05 |

Gosh where do I start!

I met a handsome millionaire a while back and we fell head over heels in love. He's just sold a couple of oil fields in Russia and we now live in Monaco.

We've got four kids. Two natural and two adopted (one Chinese, one Romanian – going for an African next).

Have you not seen me in Hello! magazine looking decidedly orange in my faux-tudor mansion?

| From: Tom Evans | To: Jo Elliott |
|---|---|
| Subject: Re: Blast from the past | Date: 14.04.05 |

Ha ha! I see you still have your fantastic sense of humour. That's what I always liked about you.

| From: Jo Elliott | To: Tom Evans |
|---|---|
| Subject: Re: Blast from the past | Date: 14.04.05 |

Thanks. It's good to know you don't think it's possible that such things could happen to me.

But you're right. Not much is new. Same job, same home, still single. You?

Was he really going to say he'd split up with his wife, or would he just rub my nose in his happiness now that they probably had kids and a big house in the country.

| From: | Tom Evans | To: | Jo Elliott |
|---|---|---|---|
| Subject: Re: Blast from the past | | Date: 14.04.05 | |

Really? Sounds like both of us are in exactly the same place as we were when we last saw each other. Do you think we're destined to be single for the rest of our lives? Are you familiar with the term 'friends with benefits'?

In the same place? Single? Where was the wife in this? Or was she a figment of my imagination? Or his? I couldn't believe it. But I could see where we were going now. I certainly was familiar with the term 'friends with benefits' and I was shocked by his nerve. For a start we weren't friends. And secondly I couldn't see the benefit of being associated with him in any way, shape or form. But I was interested to find out more, so I played along.

| From: | Jo Elliott | To: | Tom Evans |
|---|---|---|---|
| Subject: Re: Blast from the past | | Date: 14.04.05 | |

I seem to recall that the last time we corresponded, you told me you'd just got married. Perhaps I dreamt it?
And yes – I'm familiar with the term friends with benefits. It's the same as fuck buddies I believe.

| From: | Tom Evans | To: | Jo Elliott |
|---|---|---|---|
| Subject: Re: Blast from the past | | Date: 14.04.05 | |

Well, the last time we spoke I was engaged but that didn't work out. It was a bitter split and I went a bit off the rails for a while. Drank too much, but I'm over it now. Yes. Fuck buddies.

| From: | Jo Elliott | To: | Tom Evans |
|---|---|---|---|
| Subject: Re: Blast from the past | | Date: 14.04.05 | |

I'm sorry to hear that. I wonder what made me think you were married?

Reading between the lines, am I to assume you contacted me because you want a fuck buddy and you think I have the credentials for the role?

| From: | Tom Evans | To: | Jo Elliott |
|---|---|---|---|
| Subject: Re: Blast from the past | | Date: 14.04.05 | |

Are you offering? Lets talk on MSN.

This would be fun. Did he really think I was interested in his selfish games? I logged on to MSN and added him to my contact list once again. He was ready and waiting, the deluded fool.

*Tom says:*    *So. Friends with benefits? Interested?*

*Jo says:*    *Possibly. How would it work?*

*Tom says:*    *I guess we'd just meet up every now and then for no strings attached sex.*

*Jo says:*    *As simple as that?*

*Tom says:*    *Well we couldn't get emotionally involved. I don't want a girlfriend. I just want sex.*

*Jo says:*    *Ideal! So that's the benefits taken care of. What about the friends?*

*Tom says:*    *We're friends already aren't we?*

*Jo says:*    *Course! You got a photo? I've forgotten what you look like and I lost the ones I had...*

... when I used them as a dartboard before dousing them in petrol and throwing them on the fire.

---

From: Tom Evans    To: Jo Elliott

Subject: Re: Blast from the past    Date: 14.04.05

---

Picture attached. So when are you free to meet up?
I think it's best to meet somewhere neutral. I could book
a hotel. How does tomorrow suit?

---

---

From: Jo Elliott    To: Tom Evans

Subject: Re: Blast from the past    Date: 14.04.05

---

Actually it's a bit short notice. I'm shagging someone else
tomorrow. How about sometime next week?

---

He looked weird in his picture. Not like I remembered. More
like the geek I'd imagined the first time he'd ever emailed me.
The eyes that I'd once thought unusual and amazing were
now cold and creepy. I went to lunch, wondering if further
details of an illicit encounter would greet me when I got
back. It's funny how things turn out, especially when they
involve Tom Evans.

---

From: Maria Evans    To: Jo Elliott

Subject: Tom Evans    Date: 14.04.05

---

Hello. I'm Maria Evans. Tom Evans' wife.

I've just got home from work this lunchtime to find the
following message on my computer screen from you to
my husband:

"...it's a bit short notice. I'm shagging someone else
tomorrow. How about sometime next week?"

A bit of a surprise as I'm sure you can imagine. Please fill
me in on who you are and what your relationship is with
my husband.

Maria Evans

---

Shock, horror, guilt, stupid – I felt them all at once. And then I thought 'poor girl'. Someone had actually married him. What was his game? All sorts of things went through my head including the possibility that the email might be from him, pretending to be his own wife. I imagined how I'd feel finding such an email from a random stranger on my husband's computer and it wasn't very nice. I'd done nothing wrong except play along with the fantasies of a dishonest cyber-nymph for my own amusement, but I still felt bad. She deserved an honest explanation and though I doubted she'd get one from him, I was happy to oblige.

| From: Jo | To: Maria Evans |
|---|---|
| Subject: Re: Tom Evans | Date: 14.04.05 |

Hi,

I was equally surprised to read your message just now as I didn't know you existed. But you'll be pleased to know that I don't have a relationship with your husband. He's someone I met on a website a few years ago, and dated a few times until he pretended to move abroad.

He emailed me out of the blue this morning, said he was single, and offered me the enviable position of becoming his 'fuck buddy'. Although I went along with it on screen, I can assure you that I had absolutely no intention of doing so in real life as I think he's a devious fucked-up loser.

I'm truly sorry for any upset caused, and as for your husband – once a liar, always a liar. Good luck in the future. You might need it.

Jo.

# twenty

## *Hopefully ever after*

I felt like I'd come full circle. Would I ever have got into internet dating if it hadn't been for Tom? Probably. If it hadn't have been him tempting me out from behind my keyboard it would have been someone else. Contemplating my life as an internet datee, my success rate wasn't exactly breathtaking. Was it really worth the investment of £18 a month plus time and expenses? The comedy value was worth every penny but the joke was wearing thin.

I was sitting at my desk, still determined to cancel my membership, when I realised it was almost four years since I joined Digital-Cupid. FOUR YEARS! Wow – loneliness sure is a lucrative business. But am I actually lonely? I haven't really got time. And I've been on a lot more dates in the last five years than I would have done without Digital-Cupid. Admittedly I've met a lot more freaks than I would have done otherwise, but that's not the point. I'd like to say there's been never a dull moment, but I'd be lying. There's been quite a few. But amongst the smorgasbord of deluded, dysfunctional desperados I've met the odd decent bloke. It certainly hasn't all been bad.

Take Alex, for instance. He's my agony uncle. I met him on Digital-Cupid about two years ago when he messaged me saying he was there for sex and was I up for it? I replied with two words, one of which was an expletive, and we struck up an unlikely virtual friendship which endures to this day. He moved to Canada last year, so the chances of us ever meeting are remote, but I've met his friends. He kindly tried to fix me up with one of them, but unfortunately he was short, stocky and wearing loafers. Alex remains an enigma, and although that's probably best, I'd secretly love to meet him. He looks gorgeous.

———————❤———————

I'm 36 now. Still got a one-bed flat in Wandsworth, a P-reg Renault Clio, 55 pairs of jeans and a Topshop store card. I still work in advertising and I'm still a statistic in a magazine. But the statistics are different now, in an increasingly singleton society. I haven't found the man of my dreams on Digital-Cupid, but I haven't found him anywhere else either. I might meet him in a bar, but that's a gamble too. There's just as many misfits hanging out in bars as there are online. At least if I meet him on the internet I'll know in advance whether or not he likes drum 'n' bass.

Being single is a lot more fun these days. Internet dating has come of age. The stigma has gone and everybody's at it. And as I found out – you don't even have to be single. With the amount of choice available (too much choice, as my mum would say), you'd think I'd have more luck. I've tried to broaden my horizons but perhaps I'm still too fussy. I mean, how irrational is it that shoes can alter a first impression beyond repair? Why aren't I attracted to shorter men? I don't know. I'm just not. Apparently in a recent survey on internet dating, the average height of men as stated on their profiles came out at two inches taller than the national average. That says it all really.

I've decided to hang out at Digital-Cupid a bit longer. I haven't cancelled my membership, but I haven't been on a date for a while either. The suspense of walking into a bar and wondering if the person you're meeting will live up to your expectations is something I can't handle too often after four years of anti-climax.

Surely my luck has to change. After all, it's a numbers game – my number just hasn't come up yet. And until it does, I remain hopefully ever after.

There are currently over 9 million single people in the UK.

— ❤ —

The internet is now the third most popular method (along with the workplace), for getting a date.

— ❤ —

Personals websites are now attracting three million UK visitors per month.

— ❤ —

In an average month, over 1 million hours are spent by UK visitors on personals websites.

— ❤ —

A third of internet daters admitted to lying to some degree on their profile in a recent survey.

— ❤ —

74% of respondents in the same survey said the way someone looked in their photo was an important factor in deciding to contact them.

*Source: Nielsen//NetRatings*

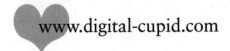www.digital-cupid.com

## Jo Elliott

Jo Elliott was born in Hertfordshire in 1969 and grew up in rural Northamptonshire. Shortly after graduating from art college she embarked on a round the world trip, before returning to London where she's lived ever since. In 2001, having not yet met the man of her dreams, she accidentally discovered the weird and wonderful world of internet dating. Her first book, *I'm celibate... Get me out of here*, is a memoir of her experiences. She works in advertising and lives in the London borough of Wandsworth.